The Children's Bill of Emotional Rights

The Children's Bill of Emotional Rights

A Guide to the Needs of Children

Eileen Johnson

JASON ARONSON
Lanham • Boulder • New York • Toronto • Plymouth, UK

Published by Jason Aronson
A wholly owned subsidiary of The Rowman & Littlefield Publishing Group, Inc.
4501 Forbes Boulevard, Suite 200, Lanham, Maryland 20706
http://www.rowmanlittlefield.com

Estover Road, Plymouth PL6 7PY, United Kingdom

British Library Cataloguing in Publication Information Available

Library of Congress Cataloging-in-Publication Data

Johnson, Eileen, 1951-
The children's bill of emotional rights : a guide to the needs of children / Eileen Johnson.
p. cm.
ISBN 978-0-7657-0850-2 (cloth : alk. paper) — ISBN 978-0-7657-0852-6 (electronic)
1. Emotions in children. 2. Child development. 3. Child psychology. 4. Child mental health. I. Title.
BF723.E6J64 2011
155.4'124—dc23 2011030443

∞™ The paper used in this publication meets the minimum requirements of American National Standard for Information Sciences—Permanence of Paper for Printed Library Materials, ANSI/NISO Z39.48-1992.

Printed in the United States of America

Contents

Introduction

> Unless the investment in children is made, all of humanity's most fundamental long-term problems will remain fundamental long-term problems.
>
> *UNICEF, "The State of the World's Children" (1995)*

In 1989 the United Nations held a Convention on the Rights of Children, based on the fact that:

> " . . . in the Universal Declaration of Human Rights, the United Nations has proclaimed that childhood is entitled to special care and assistance."

At the end of the convention, the UN issued a Charter on the Rights of the Child. This charter mainly deals with political equality; it covers very important areas such as preserving the legal rights of the child and advocating for the child's economic, social and cultural rights. However, there is a need for a more fundamental bill of rights that asserts the full emotional equality of children, a bill that would recognize the child as an equal, intelligent, and feeling being with rights that must be recognized and respected.

The need for this bill of rights is very obvious: children are vulnerable beings who are dependent on other beings—adults. Their powerlessness and dependency is similar to other kinds of powerlessness, as experienced by women and minorities in various parts of the world. Though the condition of children is similar to the condition of minorities and women in some ways, the state of children is significantly different, because children by nature must remain dependant for a certain period of time, and cannot have full rights until such point as they are able to exert them competently. Allowing full and equal rights to children in all ways would be counterproductive to their good, as well as the good of others, and so it is appropriate that children's rights in certain ways be limited. Children do not have the life experience necessary to make fully informed decisions in every respect, and so they may be open to exploitation.

Children, for instance, should *not* have the right to vote, to drive, to consume alcohol, or to carry guns. Nor should they have the right to make contracts such as marriage or joining the army. Because they are vulnerable and inexperienced, children need to be under the protection of those who can safeguard their future right to make those decisions for themselves. So childhood, in political terms, is a conditional or temporary state of submission, a kind of apprenticeship. However, the state of being a child differs from the state of being an oppressed adult in a more important way. Childhood is a state of being that is common to all humans. Childhood is a formative stage, wherein all that happens has a lifelong and often irrevocable impact in shaping the nature of the adult.

Many people underestimate the cognitive processes of the child and interpret their "errors" as lack of intelligence. Children are, in fact, more "intelligent" than adults in certain ways, but they lack the experience needed to have perspective on the data they do have. The child's brain takes a long time to develop, during which time he needs to gain organizational and management skills in order to prioritize and make good judgments. A child's logical process is impeccable, but it is applied to a limited set of experiences and so children can come to erroneous conclusions; for instance, they may believe a tall person is older than a short person.

Though they may not be politically equal to adults, children are emotionally equal and have the right to be treated as equal. *Children have the same set of feelings as adults.* We do not grow new emotions as we age, and children can experience complex and conflicting emotions just as adults do, such as anger/fear/embarrassment or regret/shame/disappointment. Our deepest hurts can be traced back to the feelings we experienced in childhood.

Children can survive deprivations such as hunger, cold, and even physical damage without suffering long-lasting consequences. Emotional damage is not so easily overcome. If a child is respected emotionally, if he is treated with respect for his rights, he will be likely to develop into a positive, creative, and socially adapted adult who can make a great difference in the world. And conversely, if a child is denied his emotional rights and treated as if he is a being of little importance, he may develop into an adult who has the potential to unleash unimaginable horror on the world. We are all too familiar with individuals whose actions have caused great suffering in the world. Many of these people were disrespected as children.

In order to develop emotionally and to fully function as members of society, children need two things: First, they need to have their emotional rights accepted by benevolent adults who care for them. Secondly, they need to have continued respect and guidance while they develop into self-supporting adults. The benevolent adult must accept the child's emotional *equality* to him and must grant him the respect this equality confers. Treating a child as if he were an inferior being who must unquestioningly comply with the adult's dictates is an abhorrence equal to that of slavery. "Because I say so" is not the kind of response a husband should give a wife, a president should give a constituency, or a parent should give a child. Sigal (2003) insists that granting a child equal rights is a moral issue:

> The basis for moral relations between adults and children requires an acceptance of the child qua child, contrary to the formation of childhood around an anticipation of its ending. The struggle to change the other cannot be the basis upon which just moral relations between two social groups are formed, provided neither of the groups violates any basic moral requirement. Moral relations between adults and children cannot justifiably be construed around a demand of the one group fundamentally to change the other. Such formulations are comparable to defining workers' rights only in light of retirement, or to conditioning women's rights on their becoming more similar to men.[1]

Coercion is not justifiable, based on the assertion that the adult knows best, or based on the assertion that the end (a well-behaved child) justifies the means (shaming, physical punishment). Parents often feel conflicted about listening to children and allowing them to be active participants in the family, for fear they will undermine their standing as authority figures. Teachers often feel the pressure of curriculum and tight schedules, and think there is simply not enough time in the day to allow for listening. Both parents and teachers may feel the best way to maintain control is to talk rather than listen. This coercive or controlling model does not work on any but the most superficial level. However counterintuitive it may seem, listening to and respecting children gives both parents and teachers more control.

Many psychologists over the years have advocated for schooling that is in tune with a child's emotions. Freud (1925) said: ". . . none of the applications of psycho-analysis has excited so much interest and aroused so many hopes, and none, consequently, has attracted so many capable workers as its use in the theory and practice of education."[2] Jersild (1971) asserts his belief that: ". . . the most important task for child psychology and for education is to find out how the educational program from nursery school through college might help the growing person to understand and accept himself."[3] Parens (1979) believes that schools can play an important role in teaching children about psychological functions such as "parenting functions . . . human development . . . and object relations, dyadic, triadic, familial and societal."[4] Anna Freud developed the Matchbox School in London and gave many lectures throughout her life on the potential of teachers to work with children on an emotional level.

At the Sara Curry Preschool in downtown New York City, I have developed a curriculum of Emotional Education. In our school we honor the child's emotional rights and respect children as individuals. Emotional Education is a practice that is woven into the daily routine. While we are working on puzzles, math games, art projects, or dance, we address children's feelings. When issues come up we do not suppress feelings or distract children from feelings in order to complete the task at hand. Instead, we put the task on hold while we work to give the children insight into their own emotions. We also conduct classes where we discuss problems—for instance a group discussion about exclusion, or a discussion about anger or death. Three-year-old children have important thoughts about important subjects. When children have conflicts we work to help them respect their differences and also to enjoy each other's sameness. In this way they can connect with the other person's humanity.

We realize that feelings are not like pajamas—a child does not take off his feelings and leave them at home when he comes to school. Feelings go on every moment of the day in every person who is alive. In preschool feelings are more visible, and we like it that way. In the upper grades, feelings have often been made to go underground. However, whether a child is three or sixteen, she still has feelings. The approach we use, I call ART. We Accept, then we Reflect, and finally we Teach. This approach is explained in the Afterword. There are many benefits to this system, which basically invites and accepts a child's feelings into the classroom, and treats a child's feelings with the respect and importance they deserve.

Academically speaking, when a teacher listens to a child he will get to know her concerns. He will find out what she wants to know more about. He will find out whether she has understood the lesson he is trying to teach. Emotionally speaking, listening to a child's worries or problems will help the teacher to know why a student is acting out or failing to participate. This knowledge and insight into the child's feelings can give him ideas on how to motivate her and help her to focus on her work. Adults are often afraid to accept that children have strong feelings, and they often try to distract them. "Oh it's not so bad," they might say when a child is hurt, trying to minimize the problem and speed up the recovery. However, allowing a few minutes for tears at the moment when a problem happens will save a lot of time later on.

Problems that go underground invariably surface at a later time. Dismissing or "redirecting," as many teachers are told to do, is a bad policy. When a child's feelings are routinely dismissed, he or she may fail to develop empathy for others. This can cause problems in school, as children are liable to act out their feelings and bully others. And it can cause problems at home also. If children don't think they will be listened to, they may keep their difficulties to themselves and turn to unhealthy ways of soothing their problems, such as by abusing alcohol, sex, or drugs. On the other hand, if children are given sympathy and allowed a few minutes of comfort and resolution, they can build their own internal "comfort center" where they find refuge when they need it.

Good teachers know children learn best when they feel involved. Making a child feel involved in the room means giving him or her a say, a voice. When a child is listened to in the classroom, he or she will be more likely to cooperate and act responsibly. Teachers spend five to six hours a day teaching, amounting to at least three hundred minutes every day. Many teachers spend around sixty thousand minutes in a year without once asking a child how he or she feels. Out of each day, twenty minutes could be allotted for children to speak, and to listen to one another, and what a difference it would make in a child's sense of belonging. Studies show that conflict resolution meetings help to decrease routine squabbles, and so teachers need to exert less effort to control children. By expressing their feelings verbally, children release tension and develop skills for managing conflicts. When asked to, children will actually come up with very good solutions to their own problems and the problems of others, and will benefit from hearing they are not alone. Heydenberk (2007) reports that children perform better academically in schools where conflict resolution meetings are regularly held:

> How does conflict resolution education impact such important educational outcomes? First, conflict resolution education empowers students to resolve their own conflicts rather than relying on the external control from administrators or teachers. Second, students who are competent in conflict resolution skills are more confident and feel a greater sense of psychological and physical safety in the school environment. This sense of safety is requisite for school attachment. Then, as the upward cycle continues, students are more likely to think in broad, integrative (win-win) ways and take the academic risks necessary to become competent critical thinkers.[5]

We all remember the teacher who understood us; we all feel connected with an adult who made us feel important and gave us the attention we needed. While teachers may be afraid to hear deep feelings, they should realize their job is not to fix everyone's problems, but to simply reflect back to children what they see. Trying to keep a lid on feelings is far more exhausting than allowing them to be shown.

Most teachers are nurturing individuals who go into the profession to help children, and with proper staff development and encouragement from school administration, they can enjoy a great sense of fulfillment in their work. As Greenwood (2002) says: "Enlightened understanding, secure management with reference to children's vulnerabilities and a (year-long) nurturing and trusting relationship with a teacher can slowly open a child's heart to a different way of being. . . . This can sound like a tall order, but developing our own capacities to be empathically available, while remaining detached enough to be able to stop momentarily and think before acting, can enhance our confidence and job satisfaction."[6]

Parents probably have an even more difficult time being objective during an emotional crisis, since they may wonder, "I'm supposed to be in charge. What if I lose control? I can't allow my child to think he is the boss." When a toddler grabs another's toy or hits a child because he won't share with him, those anxieties are aroused. Parents may feel, "I have to change him. He is bad; I have to make him into a good child." While it is absolutely true that children have urges that are not socially acceptable, it is also true that children have the capacity for great love and empathy. The adult has to teach the child how to manage those opposite feelings.

Wanting to be in charge is a very valid concern for parents. However, compliance is not the same as voluntary cooperation. Suppose you are four years old. Your mother says to you, "Go upstairs right now and clean your room." How do you feel? Do you feel like doing it, or do you feel resentful at being talked to in such a way? Suppose your mother says to you, "You did a nice job on your room last week. I need you to help me and put your toys away now. See if you can finish by the time I'm done with these dishes. Let's have a race." You probably feel motivated to help. The second approach keeps the parent in charge, assigning tasks and setting expectations, but respecting the child's rights: the right to approval, the right to play, the right to be seen as an individual. The first approach might get outward compliance, but the second approach gets inner compliance. This child will feel involved in the family since his rights are being respected. He will grow up to be a responsible and involved citizen, happy to give a helping hand and not a disgruntled teenager, resentful of authority figures in general.

All these strategies can work, and in an ideal world, they would. It must be mentioned that there are children who "act out," children who are so angry that their behavior cannot be dealt with in a calm and reasonable way. Adults do not need to compromise their values, and they should not give in to children who act this way. Adults have the right, and the duty, to take control of children who cannot control themselves, if it is in their best interest to do so. A good example of this is shown in *The Miracle Worker*. In this movie, we see a dramatization of how Helen Keller's parents felt so guilty about their child's disabilities that they allowed her to be disrespectful and destructive. They set no rules for her and allowed her to disrupt everyone's life. This lack of discipline kept her in an infantile stage of development. Her teacher, Annie Sullivan, had to gain control of the "wild child" before she could even begin to teach her sign language. She had to use tough love to do so. There is a difference between tough love and shaming or brutality. In cases where a child has built up negative patterns and defenses, adults have to use their creativity and strength to guide the child to socially acceptable behavior.

Recently I was visiting a class to do some emotional work. I was having a discussion with the children, who were sitting in a circle on the floor. Children were raising their hands to answer the question, "Have you ever felt left out?" One four-year-old boy began kicking and bunching up the rug with his feet and whining very loudly "I didn't get picked! I didn't get picked!" It was distracting and disruptive. I turned and looked right at him. "I am getting very annoyed with you doing that," I said. "I feel like you are trying to force to me pick you. You know what that does? That makes me feel like not picking you at all. I don't like people pressurizing me that way." He responded, a lot more mildly: "But I want you to pick me!" I said, "You are four years old. You need to be able to wait. Now fix that rug, and I will pick you shortly." Sure enough, he quieted down and straightened the rug. I made him wait a little, and then I listened to what he wanted to say. My response was strong, but it was done as a way of expressing a social truth: if you act that way, this is how it affects others. I did not say, "You are bad," I did not say, "You need to stop," I did not say, "Everyone else is waiting." I came from my own feelings and did not spare him the truth. I did not make it a big issue; I made the point, forgave him, and moved on. This child was not ready to have discussions or to reflect on his feelings. He needed to be given some boundaries first before he could learn to work on what is bothering him.

Parents and caregivers need to have *their* rights respected. Respecting children's feelings involves respecting one's own feelings and sharing them appropriately. If a child hits a parent, the parent should not ignore the attack. The parent can point out that she understands how angry the child is but she will not accept being treated badly. A parent might say, "I see you are upset because you are crying and yelling. I understand how angry you are. It's OK to show your feelings, but you *cannot* kick me; it hurts." When an adult shares feelings and demonstrates equality, this sets the stage for mutual respect and provides for a healthy family, no matter how the family is constructed.

Notes

1. Sigal, B. (2003). "Autonomy and Vulnerability: On Just Relations Between Adults and Children." *Journal of Philosophy of Education* 37:1, 133.

2. Freud, S. (1925). "Foreword." In Aichhorn, A. (ed.) (1935), *Wayward Youth*. New York, NY: Viking.

3. Jersild, A. (1971). *In Search of Self.* New York, NY: Teachers College Press, 3.

4. Parens, H. (1979). *The Development of Aggression in Early Childhood.* Lanham, MD: Jason Aronson, 340.

5. Heydenberk, R. and W. (2007). "The Conflict Resolution Connection: Increasing School Attachment in Cooperative Classroom Communities." *Reclaiming Children and Youth* 16:3, 18–22.

6. Greenwood, A. (2002). "The Child Who Cannot Bear to Feel." *Psychodynamic Practice* 8:3.

Chapter 1

Children Have the Right to Be Listened To

> *"We are children whose voices are not being heard: it is time we are taken into account."* (A World Fit for Us: Address to the UN by child delegates 8 May 2002)

Children have the right to be listened to when they speak and responded to when they ask questions. They are entitled to be considered seriously when they try to communicate with us in whatever way they can. We need to accept that children are in the process of learning to communicate, and we should make every effort to understand them.

In various cultures, minorities are considered to have lesser value than the majority population, and their ideas are not listened to. Women and people of minority ethnic groups have suffered from this kind of discrimination over the years. Children are the one social group whose status has little improved. There are 7 billion people in the world, and 2 billion of them are children. Children are often considered to be inferior to adults and are granted little input into what happens in their own lives, much less in the lives of others. There are very few societies where children's ideas have value. Most educational systems have the goal of setting children straight, or of giving them the facts, rather than of listening to and encouraging the interests and ideas of the children themselves.

Of all the rights of childhood, being listened to may be the most important. Communicating with other people is one of the most vital aspects of human life. Talking to others and being heard is the basis of emotional intimacy, without which human relationships cannot thrive. Communication is the foundation of friendship, marriage, and healthy family life. Development of one's ideas and thought processes, as well as consolidation of one's sense of self, are contingent on being listened to and validated by respected caregivers.

It is vital that we listen to a child's feelings, a child's questions, and a child's ideas.

Children mean everything they say with great intensity and sincerity. At times this intensity is coupled with the lack of verbal facility. The human brain develops very slowly, and though this may be a good thing for us in an evolutionary design, it makes childhood a particularly difficult time. At the very point in our lives when we need to get our feelings across and have our basic needs met, we do not have the words to express ourselves. That is why adults should make the effort to listen to young children. Unfortunately, here are the kinds of things that can happen when a child tries to communicate:

- Adults misinterpret what children are saying.
- Adults fail to understand that children are often confused.
- Adults do not take time to understand what a child is saying.
- Adults do not give importance to the thoughts of children.
- Adults react to children's words as if they are humorous, trivial, or wrong.
- Adults contradict what children are saying.
- Adults minimize what children are saying.
- Adults shy away from the expression of strong feelings.
- Adults correct the way in which children communicate to them, such as their grammar, without hearing what they are trying to say.
- Adults try to fix problems without hearing them fully.

I recently walked behind a mother and child on their way to school. The mother was focused on getting to the bus on time, and the child was walking beside her, talking about trees. "Mom, that's an acorn tree over there!" she exclaimed, delighted at herself for noticing. Without turning her head to the child, the mother instantly responded, "It's not an acorn tree; it's an oak tree."

The mother was not listening to what the child was really saying, or responding to the child's thought process. A better response would be: "Oh yes, you're right. That tree grows acorns. People call it an oak tree." This way the mother would have responded to and reinforced the thing that mattered: the child's process of observation, and her own delight in putting things together. The mother's statement that the tree is an oak came from a place of authority—she wanted to set the child straight. However, she was incorrect—these trees are not always called oak trees. The tree is also called *dair* in Gaelic, *roble* in Spanish, *quercus* in Latin, and so on—it is not universally called an oak. By correcting the child the mother is limiting her rather than expanding her ideas. What really matters though is that the mother is cutting off the child's natural drive to communicate her observations to her mother, because now the little girl may be afraid she might make a "mistake" and keep her thoughts to herself. There are valid reasons why adults do not understand the communications of children:

- Children are not as articulate as adults and their words may be difficult to decipher.
- We have been taught that children are not as intelligent as adults or that their thought process is not developed, and so we tend to think they are not able to think logically. However, the difference between the logical processes of children and those of adults is that children do not have the benefit of experience. For example, a child is told that heaven is "up there". When his pet dies, he assumes the pet is in heaven, and asks why he can't get in an airplane and fly "up there" and see the pet. This is perfectly logical, given the information the child has accumulated.
- Children think concretely. I once had the children come to the window to look at the "giant hole" the workers were digging in the road. The next day a parent approached and asked me if I had really told the children a giant was living in the street. Often children hear "word pictures" rather than concepts.
- Adults may be embarrassed by children's uncensored thoughts, which can be inappropriate in social settings: "Mommy, why does that lady look like a clown?"
- Parents often are stressed and feel compelled to live their lives on schedule. Getting your child to school on time may seem more urgent at the time than listening to your child's observation about a tree.
- Teachers are stressed; they feel the limitations of time and the pressures of curriculum. They worry that taking the time to listen to a child will slow down the learning process, causing them to fall behind in their academic goals.
- Teachers are made to feel that a child's feelings do not belong in school.
- Teachers can fail to see the value in asking children questions, and instead exhaust themselves by talking too much.
- Teachers do not realize the importance of pupil feedback to their teaching strategy.

THE IMPORTANCE OF COMMUNICATION TO A CHILD

It is a relatively short time since people believed babies were partially blind and incapable of feeling. When babies smiled, the general belief was that they were grimacing due to excess gas in their stomachs. Recent studies show the opposite to be true; small babies are able to distinguish their mothers from other people and their smiles are a response to the emotional interaction with caregivers. Gopnick (2009) says: "Very young babies already are able to recognize familiar people—newborns can quickly recognize and prefer their mother's face and voice—but at first they greet all grown-ups, familiar or strange, with the same blissful smiles and engaging coos. By the time babies are about a year old, though, they have discovered that some people treat them in a special way and that these people are the ones they should turn to for love."[1]Children communicate at first by looks, gestures, and cries. Children's communications are very important to them, since their survival and success in adapting depends on how well they understand what is going on around them and what is happening to them. Once they have learned to speak, they communicate by asking questions and by making statements. Children communicate in order to help them to make sense of the world around them, express their ideas, understand their own feelings, and connect with the feelings of others.

GATHERING THE FACTS

Children are filled with ideas, but they lack information. Their self-appointed job in the early years is to gather the information they need in order to formulate their ideas fully and make sense of the world. Some adults laugh at children when they make pronouncements that do not make sense. Though these pronouncements seem illogical, and therefore humorous, the child is putting together the limited amount of information she has and adding it to her limited experience, but the process is totally logical. Children are not less intelligent than adults. They just do not have the extent of experience that adults have.

Children apply their logical ability to the facts they have at hand. Since they do not have access to all the facts, the combination of logic and missing data can lead to misunderstanding and miscommunication, particularly when adults fail to grasp the depth of thought of which a child is capable. While the results may be comical to adults, they are not comical to the child, who is earnestly processing the new information and combining it with a limited amount of existing knowledge. When my young daughter got out of the shower and said to me, "Mom, I used your Head & Shoulders (dandruff shampoo)," I said, "Oh, that's not for children. You shouldn't use it; it might irritate your eyes." She said, "What do you mean? How could it irritate my eyes?" I said, "Well, when you put it on your hair and you rinse it off, it might run into your eyes." She said, "Oh, I didn't put it on my head; I put it on my shoulders."

Children approach the world with a sincere and passionate desire to understand. They are thoughtful and naturally adaptive creatures with inquisitive minds. They are full of joy and wonder; that is the one thing everyone agrees on. But in addition to the wonder and joy, they are often confused as to what is going on. Much of their time is spent trying to figure out the place into which they have arrived. The only way they can do this is by asking questions.

Children are born fairly helpless, and it is our job as caretaking adults to give them the tools to help themselves. However, most of their lives are spent having things *happen to* them, and having things *told to* them. Very seldom are they asked for their opinion or given a say in what happens. For instance, how many schools give children a say in the things they are going to learn about? In the home, how many children are given a choice in what they wear each day, or a say in what they will eat? How many children select their own lunches at the grocery store? How many children participate in family decisions that affect them directly? And how many adults make decisions and ask for a child's feedback?

It is only in a small number of enlightened social groups that children are taken seriously. Many people are afraid to take children seriously and allow them to have input. Their assumption is: "You can't listen to children's ideas; it would give them too much power. They would just eat sweets all the time, go to bed late, wear clothes that don't suit the weather," and so on. However, this is not true. The more say a child has in what goes on, the more he or she will feel part of the group. The more a child feels part of the group, the more likely he or she is to respect group life, respect authority, and want to cooperate in group activities. The more dictatorial the authority figures are, the more likely a child is to rebel later on when he or she has the power. When a child resents authority and feels she has no voice in the family, the more likely she is to rebel against authority and make bad decisions, such as doing drugs. And powerless children are more likely to be angry and to take their anger out on others.

Too much choice is not good for children, however. Listening to children does not mean asking open-ended questions of a young child, like "What do you want to do today?" Children cannot handle choices like that. Parents are able to prioritize in a way children cannot, and they should present limited choices. Asking a child what he wants to do without giving him guidelines or limiting his choices is not a responsible thing to do. It sets a child up for failure and frustration, since he may choose something inappropriate such as going to the beach when it's not possible. Adults can present a couple of safe and appropriate choices and then give a child a choice in what happens. Limiting choices is part of an adult's role.

ASKING QUESTIONS

Young children often ask endless questions about what is going on and why it is going on. If we think about this for a moment or two and put ourselves in their place, we will understand why. Children spend most of their lives being directed by adults. They do not have the freedom to wander about at will or make decisions regarding much of what happens to them. Picture yourself being told what to do at almost every moment of your day.

Picture yourself having little or no choice about what time you get up, what you eat, what you wear, where you go, and what you do. You are dressed and taken out into a world you don't understand. You do not know where you are going, and why, and for how long, and you do not know what is going to happen when you get there, whom you will meet, and what will be expected of you. Your only way to figure it all out is to ask questions: "Where are we going?" If the answer does not make sense, children may repeat the question: "Where are we going?" If there is an answer to their question, it may not make sense. Unfortunately many adults just repeat the same answer, thinking this will make things clearer. But then the child, still puzzled may ask, "Why?" The adult assumes the child *must* surely understand what is going on and may give a perfunctory answer such as, "I told you!" If the child still does not understand, often his only recourse is to repeat the question over and over: "But why?" "But why?"

At this stage in a child's life, many adults become frustrated—perhaps they were frustrated themselves at this stage of their lives—and they pass the frustration on to their children. When confronted by constant "Why?" questions, some adults think the answer *must* be obvious to all these questions the child is asking. They may be in a hurry, stressed, or tired and may be irritated at having to answer the child's questions. They may think the child is trying to annoy them. They can't comprehend that the child is trying to grasp things the adult takes for granted. Adults often forget what it felt like to not understand what's going on.

If an adult does not understand the constant questioning, she may snap at the child, tell him to be quiet, say, "Because that's the way it is," or just tune him out. Some parents try to answer as fully as they can and keep listening to what it is a child is really asking. Those parents can learn a lot from their children. A parent once made a wonderful observation to me about her child: "The more questions he asks, the more I learn." This is a really enlightened comment. If you answer a child's question and he asks another one, and you keep answering him until you can't answer any more, then you will realize you have come to the limit of your own knowledge. You will finally have to say, "Actually, I don't know. I'll have to find out." You may even realize you had never questioned that fact you had acquired. And if you are an open-minded and creative person you may ask, "Why does it have to be that way? It could be done differently." That point of realization can be very liberating for parents as well as for teachers. Teachers need to see themselves—and to show themselves to their pupils—as people who realize there are things they do not know and would like to learn more about. That's a far more valuable and realistic role model to present to a child than the image of someone who knows all there is to know and has stopped being curious.

Many people do not realize they need to take the time and figure out what is in the child's head, and why he is asking them so many questions. The first thing they should ask themselves is, "What does he really want to know?" The child may need reassurance, or he may be trying to find a way to relate the information to information he already has. At times children ask questions because they are filled with anxiety about what is going on and how they will be expected to fit in. Adults need to figure out what a child really needs in asking the question.

When I first went to school I was told I was going to have a teacher named Mrs. Wall. I was happy, since I assumed this was the same sweet old lady who lived around the corner from us. When I did go to school, I could not figure out where Mrs. Wall was. I kept waiting for the lady who did not look at all like Mrs. Wall to leave the room and for the real Mrs. Wall to come in. I kept asking, "Where is Mrs. Wall?"—and I can only guess at how puzzled everyone was about my questions. It was not easy for me to grasp the fact that there were two people with the same name. That realization was quite shocking to me. I can remember at age four being very disconcerted that two people could have the same name. Every adult in a young child's world assumes mythic proportions, and the discovery that a person's name is not unique was a startling revelation.

If you want to try to understand why a child asks so many questions, you might try to imagine what it feels like to be a child—it is like being an alien who has just landed on a planet you have never visited before. If you can't make yourself understood by the locals, then you need to ask questions of the other aliens like yourself in order to get their opinions about what is happening. If a child does not get information from his parents, he will look to other children, who may be ill informed.

It is a child's right to ask questions and be answered. There is an old saying: "The customer is always right." We can apply the same philosophy to children and say: "An inquisitive child is always right." He is the citizen of the future, and he is fulfilling his job of inquiring about the world. Our job is to help him out to the best of our abilities. If we don't know the answer, we need to admit it.

CHECKING INFORMATION

Children check the validity of the information they have by running it by their peers and respected adults. This is why children often make pronouncements to each other—to try to establish what is real and why things are the way they are. They rely on each other for information and interpretation. Here is a conversation that happened in a classroom of children aged three and a half to four years old:

Jack: "I like jelly beans."
Joelle: "I don't like jelly beans. My mother told me that they're made out of cows' feet."
Jack looks very puzzled, turns his head sideways, first to one side, then to the other. His nose is wrinkled in disbelief.
"Cows' feet?" he says, incredulous.
"Yes, my mom told me. It's true."
Jack pauses, thinking.
"You must have seen that in your *dream*," he says.
"No, I didn't. My mother told me that they are made out of cows' feet. Really. My mom knows all about things like that, and I believe her."
Jack pauses, thinking for a while.
"But how do they get them in there?" he says. "They would be too big."
Joelle thinks for a minute.
"Maybe they hit them with a hammer!" she says. They both laugh, probably picturing the whole absurd process in their own imagination.

These children are doing what young children do in order to make sense of the world. They take facts they have heard and run them by other people in order to make sure they are true. It is not uncommon to hear a child make a statement, which is his way of asking for confirmation like this: "We're both boys. Right, Max?"

This might seem cute and adorable, as does the story about the cows' feet and the jelly beans. However, it is serious business to a child. Children need to verify the most basic ideas. They are not totally sure of anything. For all they know, giants might lurk around corners, and alligators might live under their beds. When they go to the bathroom, they might easily get flushed down the toilet. They might have once been a girl and have turned into a boy, and that process could even revert itself. In their world those possibilities are very real, since they haven't lived long enough to see that those things, more than likely, will not happen. They question in order to construct their own theories about the world and check it with people they trust. Sometimes those people are other children.

VALUING CHILDREN'S IDEAS

There is a lot to be gained from listening to children. Children are in touch with deep wells of creativity, and they come up with wonderful ideas with ease. Children's ideas spring from their minds without being censored. They are unlimited by obstacles they have not yet encountered. Many of our own ideas have been suppressed to the point that we cannot tolerate new or different ideas. As Sigmund Freud said: "What a distressing contrast there is between the radiant intelligence of the child and the feeble mentality of the average adult." Ideas children form are also unconstricted by rules and therefore more likely to be innovative, fresh, and creative. Given a chance, children come up with wonderful solutions to problems.

If a culture is not open to new ideas then it is not capable of growth. Our culture will be strengthened and enriched by nurturing the ideas of the young. A child's idea is like a seed: If a seed is not watered and given light it will not grow. If a child's idea is not listened to or is criticized, it will wither away and die. Many lives are unfulfilled because of the lack of encouragement of ideas during childhood. Conversely, many great thinkers and inventors have had one adult who believed in them. Even when parental support is lacking, a "charismatic adult," using Robert Brooks' phrase, can give a child the encouragement she needs to overcome great obstacles. He says: "Very importantly, resilient children have in their lives the presence of adults who believe in them, who encourage them, who support them and who focus on their strengths, or 'islands of competence.'" (1998)[2]

In the early part of the twentieth century, a number of artists began to realize the value of children's artwork. They became inspired to try to recapture their own childhood freshness and many discovered how difficult it was to rediscover this wonderful fountain once it had been covered over. Artists such as Kandinsky, Klee and Miro recapture the vibrant visions of childhood in their paintings. Pablo Picasso acknowledged that it took him a lifetime to learn how to paint like a child. And yet, almost a hundred years later,

Illustration 1.1

children's art is still not respected fully. A wonderful website such as www.naturalchild.org shows a wide range of children's art. However, on this Web site, below the beautiful pictures, the children are only identified by their first name and last initial, such as Mark M. or Claire C. Imagine if adults were identified in that way; we would have a website of artists such as Pablo P., Leonardo daV., and so on. There seems to be a different standard when we acknowledge the work of children.

Children speak through their artwork, and what they have to communicate comes from a very deep source of innate creativity. Even so, they are told to draw *properly*; they are asked, "What is it?" or "Why did you paint the sky green?" Or worse, told, "That doesn't look real." The questions adults ask are often designed to elicit specific answers, and a child quickly comes to realize that a question is like a "quiz"—he has to try to figure out what answer the adult has in his head rather than reflect on what he was intending. In this way children lose trust in themselves; they learn to stop communicating in a spontaneous way and begin the work of undoing their own vision. Unfortunately, unless you are a genius like Picasso, that may be a vision impossible to recover. The artwork of children should be respected and treated as if it is of importance, since it is the communication of an original mind.

Illustration 1.1 is a children's painting, done in watercolor by a three-year-old girl, completed in a few minutes. The painting has all the elements a trained artist strives to achieve—balance, contrast, harmony, unity. It came to fruition quickly because it came from a deep source with which the child is still in touch. There are four circles placed in a square format. The circles seem to float on the page in relation to one another. Each circle is separated from the other with a pleasing sense of space. The fourth circle is colored in, creating an asymmetry in the otherwise symmetrical composition. There is progress from complete darkness below into a bright open circle on top. An interesting factor is the little girl recently experienced the birth of a baby brother. The fourth circle (or baby) is still in darkness, as the other circles have opened and become lighter.

In addition to the beauty of the composition, there is a mythic element to this drawing. Many ancient cultures feature the number four, particularly four circles, which symbolize various fundamental elements of their worldview. Mandalas, the sacred symbol used in many cultures, have, as their basic construction, four circles combined into one. Alchemists had one of their goals as the squaring of the circle; the merging of two primal shapes, the circle and the square, was believed to lead to enlightenment. This particular child seems to have tapped into ancient symbols, conveyed it beautifully on paper, and done it in minutes.

Many parents and teachers fail to take the time to look at what a child is intending to do. They ask, "What is it supposed to be?" or "What are you drawing?" Adults can make open-ended comments so the child feels supported such as, "You are working very hard on your picture," or "I notice you made circles," or "You used lots of tiny dots on the page," so the child feels her work is noticed. All she needs is to be seen and acknowledged.

EMOTIONAL RESPONSE

A child's voice is the key to his survival. His first communication is a cry to his parents, expressing his needs. If he does not get enough to eat, or does not stay warm or cool enough, he will die. If a child is not given emotional warmth, if he is left alone without hugs or smiles, he is also liable to die. When a child cries he is demanding attention for his most urgent needs. Attentiveness to these needs on the part of parents has a vital role in the child's life.

The way a parent responds to a child's voice impacts his emotional development. When a parent responds to a child's cries, she is assuring the child that he is going to be taken care of physically; he will survive since he has a protector. If a parent consistently ignores these first cries or does not understand their meaning, the child can develop anxiety, hyper-vigilance or depression. If your earliest experiences are of being ignored when you are hungry or lonely, chances are you will develop anxieties about food or feel a sense of abandonment, which will last your lifetime. On the other hand, if your cries *are* listened to, you begin to think of yourself as an individual who deserves to be cared for and who deserves to be heeded.

As the child grows, his emotional life depends on the strength of this connection between him and his caregivers. A sense of trust develops between two people when one listens to the feelings of the other and responds in an appropriate way. This emotional dialog is what helps children develop into high-functioning members of society. Lack of emotional responsiveness on the part of a caregiver can result in shyness, insecurity, anger, and anti-social or self-destructive behavior.

I know a young man who developed problems in his career. He was a singer, and his voice suddenly "dried up." He had a couple of "panic attacks" while on stage—his voice would not come out. He realized he could no longer sing and had to take a break from his career. When he went to therapy, he realized that his breakdown was connected with his childhood and his need to be heard. As a child, he longed to have a connection with his father, who was often busy. He told the story about how his father took him for a walk in the woods. For once it was just him and his dad, having time together. It was a rare event, and the boy was happy to have his father's attention. He chatted away about school and confided in his father about someone who was teasing him. The father was quiet, and the boy poured out all his thoughts. Later that evening, the boy was in his room and overheard his father talking to his mother: "Wow, he really talked my ear off. I thought he would never stop talking. From the minute we got there till the minute we left, he hardly took a breath. I'm glad to get home and get a little peace and quiet!"

The boy was crushed. He felt that all the things he was confiding in his father meant nothing to him. From that moment on he was careful to keep things to himself. The child learned that his words did not mean anything to his father; all his father heard was bothersome noise. He did not hear or relate to what his son was trying to tell him. Ironically, the child's voice developed, and he became a beautiful singer—perhaps he was expressing all his feelings through his music. But finally, at one point in his life, all the pain he had endured took over, and he lost his voice. How different his life might have been if he had overheard his father have the following conversation with his mother: "Honey, I'm worried because our son is having a hard time at school. Some boy is teasing him. What do you think we can do for him?" That response would have made the child feel supported and understood.

CHILDREN IN THE MEDIA

Children are not well represented in the media. Most media coverage concerns the dangers surrounding children and the ways in which parents need to protect them. Much of this alarmist coverage is related to marketing items to parents. Children are in fact highly exploited by the media. They are the targets of expensive marketing strategies designed to excite their curiosity and imagination, and ultimately to manipulate them to have their parents purchase merchandise for them.

Nowadays there are a lot of movies aimed at children, with themes designed to attract children. In point of fact, very few of them are in tune with the child's inner life. Their fears are played upon with exaggerated and frightening dramatic scenes. Jokes are aimed at the adults rather than the children. Films dealing with real issues affecting children are very rare, and the ones that are may be adult films. There are hardly any shows or movies that are created by children or that express a child's point of view. In addition, child actors are often misused. Many child stars have written memoirs that show they were not consulted in any decisions and were treated basically like puppets. The trauma this caused can be read about in any of the autobiographies they have written.

From time to time there have been TV shows that aim to entertain the audience by talking to children. These kinds of shows are designed along the lines of "The Funny Things Children Say," or "Aren't Children Silly?" However, it is clear upon watching them that these shows are not at all about what children are thinking and are not aimed at viewers who want to understand how a child thinks. In these shows the host asks questions that are obviously not understood by the child to the extent they are understood by the adults, and that is the premise of the show. The child's response is humorous, but it is the child who is the unwitting butt of the joke. Some of the questions border on inappropriate, such as "Do you have a girlfriend?" or "Would you like to marry this guy over here?" The children's shy or defensive answers are considered funny, and the host knowingly winks at the audience.

The innocence of the child seems to be the theme of these shows; no one seems to be interested in knowing the real thoughts the child is having. The host is interested in making himself seem in control of the situation, able to elicit funny responses, and he acts bemused by the results he cleverly evokes. The children are often puzzled as to why the audience is laughing. Recently a TV news magazine came up with the idea of taking a child to the movies and asking her what she thought of it. This seemed like a wonderful idea. However, the actual show did not live up to the promise. In the show the host took the child to see a movie, and after the movie treated her to an ice cream. While she was eating ice cream the host asked, "So, Maggie, do you think the movie was one thumb up or two thumbs up?" The child struggled to give the two thumbs up while eating the ice cream. The host laughed and told the audience, "Well that's a big two thumbs up for the movie!" The child did not speak at all, and the host showed no real interest in getting her opinion. The point was simply to show that the host was friendly towards children. The little girl was rewarded with ice cream for just agreeing to whatever the host asked her to do. What a good idea it would have been to listen to what the girl had to say, and what an opportunity was missed to hear how the film impacted a young child.

LISTENING TO CHILDREN IN THE FAMILY

As soon as they can speak, children make serious attempts to be understood, often with difficulty, and at times through frustrated emotional outbursts, often called "tantrums." This can be a time when parents feel the need to control rather than understand a child's emotional expressions. Some parents do not like outbursts and may be afraid of loud expressions of feeling. Children may be required to keep their feelings to themselves in social situations outside the home and often inside the home too. However, silencing expression does not help parents in the long run. Parents need to know what a child is feeling. When they know, then they can understand him, and if they understand him they can help him understand and control himself.

Some parents and teachers use rules, such as "Use your 'inside voice' and not your 'outside voice.'" Having children think of themselves as split into separate parts can be confusing. Many people also tell children to

"Use your walking feet and not your running feet." A child has one voice and one set of feet. It is better for the child to tolerate both his positive and his negative feelings. Instead of telling a child to use the "inside voice," a parent should be honest and say, "The noise is bothering me. I've had a rough day."

Parents and teachers can train children to use their voice as an instrument to help them communicate. If anyone is in doubt about the potential of the human voice to communicate layers of thought and feeling, he should think about the way a therapist uses his voice. A therapist can say, "Hmm," in many different ways. He can convey an incredibly varied set of responses with the way he makes one sound. Teachers know that their voice is their most valuable tool. A teacher can say, "OK," in a cutting way, a funny way, or a forgiving way, depending on the tone of her voice.

A child's voice is also a very important asset in group situations. There is great value in helping a child develop her real voice. Vocal exercises are fun. Here are some games parents and teachers can play. We play these games regularly in school as part of our Emotional Education curriculum:

- Practice yelling as loud as possible, then bring the volume down to whisper, then back up again. You can use a picture or image of what is happening with the voice, a V or X, or a diamond shape, or a ladder so children can imagine what volume they are at. Children love to be able to yell with permission. Yelling for a few minutes helps let off steam.
- Practice pitch modulation. Children can learn to use the range of their voices from teeny tiny to big and blustery. This can be fun, and children can make animal noises—they have an uncanny ability to make monkey sounds and bird sounds. Then they can proceed to use their voices to talk like various animals. Children learn that the voice has a huge potential for variation and for getting a reaction.
- Practice whining. When children realize how annoying this sounds, and get a chance to do it publicly, they tend to give it up as a communication tool.
- Practice assertiveness. They can say loud and clear, "I would like some juice, please." When they learn it is fine to be assertive, and that assertiveness is different from aggression or whining, they can feel very liberated.
- Practice projection techniques. Children need to be heard in school and other group settings, and some children's voices are stronger than others. Being heard in a group is very rewarding for children. One very quiet young girl whose father died suddenly joined a drama group and learned how to use her feelings in dramatic performances. This activity helped her get through a very difficult part of her life.

FAMILY DISCUSSIONS

Studies show that children in families who sit down to dinner together fare much better in life than those who do not. Fritz (2006) says: "I wonder how much therapy time could be reduced if families ate dinner together?"[3] The reason has very little to do with the food and everything to do with the conversation. At these gatherings a lot of problems can be solved and strategies devised. There are plenty of good ideas for dinner conversation, and children should be allowed to say what they need to say. A few simple rules can help to keep the conversation flowing in a positive direction—even if it is about negative experiences. These rules should be no interruptions, no censorships, and no pressure.

Here are some good topics for discussion:

- Have everyone talk about the best moment of the day.
- Have everyone talk about the worst moment of the day.
- Have everyone say what they are worried about for the next day—parents can share feelings here but should not burden their children unnecessarily. If they say they are worried, they should reassure the child that they will be fine; children may feel frightened if a parent worries too much.
- Have family members give feedback in the form of understanding—*not advice, unless specifically requested* (people seldom want to hear advice, and giving advice puts one person in a superior position).
- Have turns allowing each member of the family to decide the menu for the next day's dinner.
- Have turns giving each member of the family a say in what they would like to do as a group on the weekend.
- Speak about conflicts within the family, giving everyone a voice. Parents should not reprimand but come from their feelings, e.g.: "I was very worried when I saw you two fighting. I thought someone was going to get hurt," or "I felt a little sad when you didn't say goodbye to me this morning. Are you embarrassed by hugging me at school, or were you mad at me for something?" or "I felt concerned that you heard us arguing this morning. Did it bother you?" Even if children cannot immediately answer these questions, at least they will develop the habit of reflecting about what they might be feeling, and comforted to know they will be heard when they do speak.
- Children should be encouraged to speak their feelings and say, "I was angry when . . ." and be listened to.
- Children should be guided away from blaming others for their feelings, and encouraged to take responsibility for their own feelings. For instance: "You made me feel bad when you said that" is blaming, but "I felt bad

when you said that" is just stating what you feel. Parents can model this way of talking too.
- Children should be applauded for sharing their feelings, even if they are saying they are angry at you. It is very liberating for a child to hear a parent say, "Thank you for sharing your feelings. I am glad you told me you were angry at me. Now I understand what is going on, and we can work on the problem together."

A good rule to follow for dealing with emotional issues is to listen. Defending and appeasing are the two strategies people use, and neither of these works. Parents need to build healthy family interaction by simply listening, not trying to fix the problem. The child will develop his or her own strategies.

WHAT SHOULD NOT BE SAID

Parents should not censor words and feelings even if they are negative feelings. However, they should forbid bullying, teasing, and dismissal or ignoring of others. Here are some expressions that should never be allowed at the dinner table or anywhere in the home as they are attempts to stifle another person's words:

- Shut up!
- Who cares what you have to say?
- I'm not listening to you.
- Don't speak to me like that!
- Says who?
- You're ridiculous.
- Don't talk to me.
- No one wants to hear you.
- You talk too much.
- You don't know what you're talking about.
- You're not making sense.
- You're a liar.
- What do you know?

HOW TO LISTEN

It is often difficult for people to listen to children, especially young children, and it does require patience. Young children may repeat the same thing over and over, since they are not always sure they are heard. Here are some techniques parents can use:

- If a child keeps saying something over and over and doesn't seem to notice that you said "I know" three times, just repeat what the child said in a pleasant but neutral tone: "You made this necklace for your friend." This way she knows you have heard.
- Bend down close to the child. Young children often do not understand that you are speaking directly to them. At an early age they have not made the sophisticated connections adults make between eye gaze, gestures, and words, and if you are not looking at them, they may not know you are talking to them.
- Reflect back what you hear in a non-judgmental way: "Oh, I see. You are angry." Children love to know they are seen and heard, and putting something into words for them is very helpful.
- Try to stay away from the word "but." If you respond, "Yes, I know you are angry, but so is your friend," you are effectively dismissing the feeling. You can use "and" though. "Oh, you are angry. (pause) And Mary is angry too."
- Accept what you hear from the child even if it seems strange to you, and keep your mind open. "Simon, you want to have a baby when you grow up." You don't have to correct everything a child says. Who knows? Maybe someday men will have babies.
- Believe what a child says. If a child says, "I'm worried," or "I'm sad," or "I'm afraid of that guy," you must believe them and act on your belief by providing them with what they need. Don't dismiss the feeling by saying, "Don't worry" or "Don't feel sad." Those statements don't help anyone and make a child feel he is not being heard.
- Reassure a child: "I hear you." When you don't know what to do, you feel helpless, or you can't understand his words. This may be all a child needs anyway.
- Explain to young children that you can only hear one thing at a time. Strangely, young children do not understand this very basic fact. They may have to wait their turn to be listened to.
- Don't accuse a child of whining. Labels are unhelpful. If a child whines encourage him to assert himself by asking for what he needs clearly and in a strong voice.

LISTENING TO CHILDREN AT SCHOOL

Some children live in families in which they know they are not heard. Those children will feel alone; they know they have to handle scary feelings without any support. Every teacher who has worked in an early childhood classroom knows what a scared child tends to do. When someone grabs a toy, the unsupported child feels he has no choice but to protect himself physically. This kind of child thinks he is alone. He is not aware of the strong presence of a teacher as someone who will support or help him, and so he is basically in combat mode. This aggressive behavior can set a bad pattern for life. When a child is aggressive, teachers may feel frustrated. They may feel they need to impose control to fix the problem. Teachers can give themselves a huge break by realizing that they *do not have to get angry* or punish people. No one enjoys that, especially not a teacher, and it is counter-productive for the adult to be angry too.

A teacher may think it is her job to reprimand the child and impose a time out. However, punishment and shame just convince an aggressive child that he is different or bad. He will feel ashamed because he thinks he is the only one who feels anger. Since he thinks of himself as a bad boy, he may act accordingly. A teacher can help a child like this if she listens to him. If the child can tell the adult how angry, frustrated, or scared he feels, he will not feel alone. At an early age, the ability to communicate strong feelings in words is a great survival skill. If an aggressive child could be listened to by an empathetic teacher, and given the words to express those feelings, then a lot of problems could be prevented.

Teachers can find it difficult to listen to children. Since young children often think they are the center of the universe, their problems come first. Children find it hard to wait their turn and listen to others. Some topics can make children uncomfortable or so excited they can't calm down. Recently I read a story about nightmares to a group of children. When we were finished I asked them what scared them most. They all wanted to talk at the same time. They began interrupting each other and talking over each other, and it was impossible for anyone to hear anything. Even when they took turns, the others could not let them finish; everyone had something to say. I knew that even though I might have the patience to hear every one of them, they clearly could not sit and listen to ten other people while they waited their turn to talk. At that point I had to give up listening and try a creative approach. So I said, "Let's all go over to the art table and draw pictures of scary things."

When it's hard to listen, teachers can pass the listening work on to the children. If the child is given the teacher's chair, he can learn how hard it is to listen to everyone. At show and tell time, a child can sit up in front of the class and allow them to ask questions. He will have the job of making them take turns, raise their hand, and pick them to ask questions. This lets the teacher off the hook for a while and shows the children what it's like to be faced with a lot of children, all wanting to talk at the same time.

THE QUESTIONING MIND

In most schools, children are actively encouraged to follow orders without question. Sit down, stand up, get in line, be quiet, and so on, often to the ringing of a bell or the ticking of a clock. Sometimes it is the voice on a loudspeaker telling you where you need to be. Success is often measured by how well children learn to suppress their own natural curiosity and follow the routines laid down for them.

There are some enlightened schools. However, most schools do not encourage children to ask questions such as "Why do we study this subject?" or "Can we change the schedule so we have Art first thing in the morning because it helps make me feel happy, and I enjoy the rest of the day and work better?" or "Can I make a film instead of writing out my project because I hate writing and I can't spell?" or "Why can't I suggest things I want to learn about?" When asked, many students wish they could have a voice in what happens at school. Hatchman (2001) reports that children want more say in school:

> Here are the words of a powerful student voice that clearly illustrates why we have to hear what students are saying. Alissa is a 12th grader. She says, "This school's like a city; the government has too much power, and the community doesn't have enough say-so. Or, you know, when we're talking, it's just like we're talking to hear ourselves talk; there's not nobody listening. But, I mean, it could be a good city."[4]

By the time they have spent a few years in school, many children have lost interest in asking questions, coming up with suggestions, or feeling their ideas have any appeal at all to the school. Individual teachers can and do make a difference, though they often feel the stress of time pressure and stop listening to children. Questioning is one of the key aspects of human intelligence and is the basis of scientific thought. Schools, which should inculcate a healthy scientific or questioning approach, instead often encourage passive acceptance of outmoded and even incorrect ideas. Questioning can even be punished rather than nurtured. Thomas Edison, noted inventor, asked so many questions that his teachers thought something was wrong with him, and he did not last long in school. Fortunately his mother taught him at home and nurtured his questioning mind.

CHILDREN LEARN BETTER WHEN TEACHERS LISTEN

We are often told that children need to learn to listen better, particularly in school. However, it is seldom mentioned that it is important for teachers to listen to children. Teachers who listen to children are more listened to by children. If someone listens you to, you will be more likely to hear what he has to say because you are more trusting of him. If a teacher gets regular feedback from children, he can improve his teaching skills and use the feedback to be a more effective communicator.

Many studies show a high correlation between the amount of listening a teacher does and what a child learns in school. The more the child is allowed input, the greater his understanding of the material. An interesting experiment by Shochet (2006) involved interviewing schoolchildren and taping their responses to questions about what they had learned and how they felt about what they learned in science class. The tapes were played for the teachers, who were quite surprised at the results. The teachers had not understood how the students experienced their lessons, and as a result of the experiment they reflected on their performance and changed some of their techniques:

> As a result David reframed his teaching so that he became more flexible to allow students to explore their own ideas and varied his teaching practices for different students. . . . Whereas the student tapes challenged the assumptions of the other two teachers, the data confirmed many of Geoff's tentative notions about student learning. For him the 'responsibility' tape was the most salient because the data confirmed his suspicions that students need to "own" the ideas they investigated.[5]

Listening to students is often not factored into the daily classroom routine. Listening can save a lot of wasted time, particularly if a teacher thinks he is doing a great job but the children do not understand the lesson. Even the best teachers learn their craft as they go along, and input from students can help make them better teachers.

TAKING THE TIME TO LISTEN

Parents and teachers ask the obvious question: How do I make this work? If I am so stressed right now, how can I find the energy to listen to the child, as well as complete all my tasks, achieve the goals I am trying to achieve, and balance the other demands on my time? The answer is counterintuitive, and yet liberating. The more time you spend listening to children, the less effort you will spend on discipline, repetition, and reinforcement. If a child's head is full of thoughts and feelings, she simply doesn't have the capacity to listen and absorb new ideas. If she has a chance to express those feelings, she will be more receptive. Children who are able to resolve their problems verbally are in a better position to concentrate on the tasks and projects of the classroom. Here is an example of how problems can be solved without making the teacher play the role of enforcer. This is an incident that happened in our school:

MATT AND JAKE HITTING

The Background

Matt and Jake are three-year-old boys in a nursery school class. Matt's parents have recently separated, and Matt divides his time between his father's and mother's apartments. Since the separation, Matt has been easily upset and more sensitive than usual. Jake's mother is also separating from his father and has a new apartment; soon they will be living apart. Since she told Jake, he too has been moody and clingier when his mother leaves in the mornings.

The action

It is playtime. Jake and Matt are building with Legos. Things are fine, but suddenly there is a squabble, and Matt is crying. Jake is looking ashamed. I need to step in. I ask, "What's the matter?" Matt says, "Jake hit me," and he is pointing to his lip. It's not bleeding and does not look like a serious hurt, but Matt looks very offended. Jake is looking very emotional; his head is down, and he looks ashamed. Now it is decision time. I need to take action. Here are some thoughts that often present themselves to teachers as good things to do in a situation like this:

1. Tell Jake it is a very bad thing to hit Matt and he must apologize immediately.
2. Ask Jake, "Why did you do that?"
3. Ask Jake, "How would you like it if someone did that to you? Don't you see you hurt him?"
4. Comfort Matt and try to help him stop crying while glaring at Jake.
5. Tell both boys they must stop fighting.
6. Give Jake a punishment such as time out or at least a good talking to.
7. Force Jake to apologize.

All of those choices would mean that I am trying to make the feelings go away and solve the children's problems for them. I decide to do none of these things, as it is not possible to fix problems by imposing punishments. It is more important to listen to the children and have them listen to each other.

The solution

I take the time to pause and reflect while Matt cries for a little bit, my arm around his shoulders for comfort. Then I say, not in a punitive tone, to Jake: "What's going on with you lately?" Jake throws his arms around my neck and cries too. At this point I have my arms around both boys. I wait for a while, as the feelings are coming out and both boys are crying. Then I ask again, "Jake, I think you are having some problems lately. What's happening in your life?" Jake is happy to have a chance to say what he is feeling: "My dad is going away, and he's going to have his own apartment; my mom is going to have her apartment." I reflect back: "It's very hard for children when their parents are living in different places." Now I see the chance to bond the two children. I turn to Matt and say, "You are going through the same thing, Matt, right? Is it hard for you living in two apartments?" Matt nods.

Now there is a chance for real listening and connection to happen between the children. I interpret: "See, isn't it strange? You both have the same problems in your lives right now, and yet you are fighting each other . . . isn't that weird?" They look at each other and they laugh. "You can give each other a hug," I say, and they jump at the chance. "Boys should help each other if they have the same problem," I say. It is surprisingly quick how the boys forgive and understand each other. For the rest of the day the two boys are the best of friends. They are arm-in-arm at story time and not only sit beside each other at lunchtime but also share their lunches. The technique involved acceptance, reflection, and then teaching. The children could not express in words what was bothering them; the teacher needed to open the doorway to communication. This method works on the principle that acceptance must come first, then reflection, and finally teaching. The teaching in this situation just meant explaining to each child that they do have a connection.

Teachers may ask, Where do I get the time for this kind of work? In fact, the solution took about five minutes, probably even less. If apologies had been demanded or punishments doled out, the problem would not have gone away and would probably have worsened. If the problem was not attended to on a deeper level, undoubtedly it would happen again later in the day. Jake would have felt angry because he was made to feel ashamed. He would have felt misunderstood and more isolated, and the combination of those feelings would have caused more acting out. If Jake were asked why he hit Matt, he would not be aware of the underlying reason. It is the adult's task to know what the child is going through and to help him understand himself.

There is no point in asking a child, "Why did you do it?" They very often don't know. If Jake had been reprimanded, then Matt, "the victim" would feel like a victim and helpless. Instead he felt compassion for the other boy, since he saw Jake's tears and heard his life story. He also felt camaraderie—"We're both going through divorce situations; we can help each other." If the teacher tried to fix everything, she would have felt exhausted, since it is impossible to force feelings on children. In this case, the teacher felt fulfilled and happy knowing she helped the children develop a real understanding of each other and learn that people should stick together and help each other when they are having problems. She felt joy when she saw the boys spontaneously bonding. She did not feel the burden of having to be police officer, judge, and jury.

LISTENING IN THE UPPER GRADES

In middle school many of the unresolved problems of early childhood begin to re-emerge. Middle school can, in fact, be very difficult for children. At this stage many children are entering a new environment with a new set of challenges. It is vital that their school experience be a positive one, because when teenagers feel alienated in school, their well-being can be seriously endangered. Being listened to in school makes a child feel like a part of the group. If children feel involved in school, they are far less likely to get into trouble.

Shochet reports:

> Maddox and Prinz's (2003) review of school bonding focused on behavioral outcomes of school bonding, including substance use, delinquency, academic performance, antisocial behaviors, and risky behavior. They reported studies indicating that school bonding mediates the effects of parental attachment on substance use, risky behavior, and delinquency. School connectedness has also been found to reduce adolescent involvement in health-risk and deviant behavior, particularly the use of alcohol, marijuana, cigarettes, and violence.

School connectedness or lack of connectedness is probably not the *cause* but more likely a symptom of underlying problems, which lead to serious issues in later life. However, it is clear that school is an arena where emotional problems can play out. It is also clear that teachers can play a very important role in helping children during this very stressful stage in their life. A recent incident in which a high school student committed suicide because of relentless bullying sheds light on a widespread problem among teenage students—the inability to express feelings openly and be listened to and understood in school. This incident is not a rare one. According to the National Institute for Mental Health, suicide is the third leading cause of death among adolescents and teenagers. Teachers can feel overwhelmed with the pressure of exams, as well as the puzzling outbursts of emotion children at this age can display. However, if school administrators are willing to allow for programs where children are listened to, middle school can be a happy and productive experience for children.

There are a number of enlightened schools where children's input is encouraged and children's thoughts and feelings are given a time slot in the daily routine. In The Studio School on New York's Upper West Side, teachers work with the child's feelings in the classroom. While one group of children work on a science project, two children sit at a table with a teacher, discussing their recent conflict on the playground. The teacher listens and reflects back to the children what she hears. In Tompkins Square Middle School on the Lower East Side, a Social-Emotional Learning initiative is designed to help children figure out "What kind of person am I?' and "How do others see me?"

Twice a week children attend "Advisory"—a 45-minute period where they meet in small groups with their advisor. Topics such as Self-Awareness, Team-Building, Communication Skills, and Conflict Resolution are worked on throughout the year. A typical Advisory period begins with each child stating how he or she feels. Those who are not comfortable talking are encouraged to at least give a number to their feelings. A "10" would indicate happiness, while a "3" would show the child is feeling blue. One child might be comfortable saying, "My stepfather is being a real jerk. I wish my mother never married him. I miss my dad," while another child might just say, "I feel like a '5' today," with no explanation. This emotional openness can prevent bullying—children are apt to feel empathy for others when they know the real story of the other person's life. If a boy is acting grumpy during the day, the other children are less likely to think, "He's picking on me" or "He's angry at me" and more likely to realize he is angry at his stepfather.

In both these schools there is a calm yet busy atmosphere. Children work happily in groups, moving freely around the rooms engaged in "hands-on" projects. The communication between children and teachers is relaxed and warm, and discipline problems are few and far between. The amount of time spent in reflection and discussion pays off, since there is little disruption of class work due to emotional problems.

LISTENING TO CHILDREN AT SCHOOL

In the classroom a teacher needs to help children understand what is going on inside themselves and inside other people, and she needs to help them express those thoughts to others. The few minutes it takes to stay with feelings instead of pushing them away pays off greatly. It takes so much energy to hold a beach ball under the water. It takes the same energy to "manage" the feelings in the classroom—it is a relief to let feelings out in a safe way. When children are relieved of the burden of "holding the ball under the water,"they are free to work and relate to others in productive ways in the classroom and at home.

A good way to create a safe and expressive classroom is to set aside time every day where children get to speak. Morning meetings or end-of-day meetings (circle time) can present the perfect opportunity for this. Teachers need to keep in mind that some children will dominate a group while others will be reticent. Making sure children do not dominate each other is part of a teacher's day-to-day responsibility, and most teachers are expert in managing children in this way, much like a conductor manages the orchestra. So it is a fairly easy task for them to work towards having children verbalize their feelings and listen to each other. There are exercises to benefit all ages, for instance:

- Have a meeting in which children say one thing about themselves that they like. Some children will want to jump right into saying something they don't like about themselves. Stay positive and keep away from opportunities for a child to feel negative about herself.
- Have a meeting in which children say one thing they like about another person.
- Have a meeting in which children talk about something that worries them.
- Have a meeting in which children talk about their favorite experiences—sound/sight/smell/taste/sensation.
- Have a meeting in which children talk about something they like to do. Shared interests can make for great friendships.
- Have a meeting in which children talk about a disagreement with another child, encouraging them to speak about their feelings and not to throw blame, thus: "I felt disappointed when you did not give me the ball even though you promised you would," or "I felt excluded when you played with that girl and not me," or "I felt angry when you took my toy without asking."
- In the meetings, encourage children to listen to the feelings of others and not react by defending themselves. Listening to others is a good social skill.
- Have a meeting in which children talk about something fearful. Sharing anxieties is a good group exercise; children are reassured that others also feel anxiety.
- Have a meeting in which children reflect on the day and go over any incidents that were troubling to them.

The list is endless, based on the creativity of the teacher, and discussions can be tailored to what is going on in the room or playground. The teacher should keep these discussions positive. If a child is worried, the teacher should not minimize the worries but reflect the worries back to the child and mention that we all worry. Discussions can last for as little as twenty minutes, but they give children a chance to express themselves. Incorporated into the daily routine, they can help the teacher to deal with the busy day by structuring a scheduled time and an arena for feelings to be worked out. If a teacher is busy doing something else and a child is having difficulties that are not urgent, the teacher can say, "I'm very busy now; let's focus on our math problem, and we will bring this up at meeting time."

Parents and teachers need to make an effort to listen to children. Whether they are asking questions, expressing feelings, or talking about their interests or feelings, children's words and other forms of childhood expression are important and should be heard, valued, and validated. Children are on the path to developing their individuality and connecting with others. Responsive adults can clear that path and make it possible for children to progress through life as productive and happy individuals.

LISTENING TOO MUCH

Though it may be true that children are not listened to enough, it has to be said that some adults fail to draw realistic boundaries for children. There are parents and even teachers who allow children to have too much say. I have heard parents say to three-year-old children, "What do you want to do now?" They kneel down and look earnestly at the child, expecting a good response. Children cannot handle these kinds of open choices. Sometimes I can't decide where I want to go for dinner, even when the choice is only between two different restaurants. How can a young child possibly decide what to do, given the universe on a platter in this way? This parent has loaded the dice against the child. If the child picks something unsuitable, then one of two things will happen: Either an argument will ensue, or the child will have to face the consequence of picking an unsuitable activity—and this is very unfair to the child.

A teacher who says to the class, "OK, shall we go to the park today?" has to realize that she will have at least one dissenter, so she has set up a losing situation for at least one class member. She can turn this into a positive and have the class vote on the decision, as that will teach them about voting. However, though teachers can frequently consult children and make them feel involved, they don't have to let children always have a say. The reason is that children don't need to be faced with the number of decisions that adults do. They need to have time to enjoy the freedom of childhood, to dream, to imagine, and to play. This freedom should be protected by adults who have the right to make plans in the best interests of children. "Let's get ready; we're going to the park!" is a statement that relieves children of the anxiety of choice. The teacher knows that the park is a good choice, and it is her right to make that decision. Not everything has to be an agonizing decision for children. Not everything has to go to a vote. Adults can set up limited choices in such a way that everyone wins.

A parent who gets a child up in the morning and asks, "What do you want to wear?" is creating problems not only for herself, but also for the child. If the parent wants to encourage free choice, she will need to prepare a limited set of items and have the child make the decision the night before. This way, the parent is preparing the child for good decision-making. Parents have the right to limit the choices of the child. If a child picks a shoe to wear that has a hole in the bottom, the parent has the right to say, "You cannot wear it." She does not have to yield to the child who cries, "This is my favorite shoe! I want it!" Listening to a child who clearly does not appreciate the consequences of her choice would be wrong in this case.

Notes

1. Gopnick, A. (2009). *The Philosophical Baby* New York, NY: Farrar, Straus, and Giroux.

2. Brooks, R. To foster children's self-esteem and resilience, search for islands of competence. *Brown University Child and Adolescent Behavior Letter* 14:6, Cover Story.

3. Fritz, G. (2006). *The Brown University Child and Adolescent Behavior Letter.* February.

4. Hatchman, et al. (2001). Students' Voices about Schooling: What Works for then: Its Implications for School Reform *Paper presented at the Annual Meeting of the American Educational Research Association* Seattle, WA, April 10-14.

5. Shochet, I. (2006). School Connectedness Is an Underemphasized Parameter in Adolescent Mental Health: Results of a Community Prediction Study *Journal of Clinical Child and Adolescent Psychology* 35:2, 170–179 (143).

Chapter 2

Children Have the Right to the Truth

> *"The child shall have the right to freedom of expression; this right shall include freedom to seek, receive and impart information and ideas of all kinds, regardless of frontiers, either orally, in writing or in print, in the form of art, or through any other media of the child's choice."*
>
> Article 43 of the UN Convention on the Rights of the Child

The truth is not a treasure to be held by a select few—the truth is a right that belongs to all. The truth is power, and power should not be withheld by one group from another. Children have a special right to be told the truth. They have the right to be given the information necessary to gain meaningful insights in their life and to learn what they need so they can grow to their full potential. They should not be manipulated through withholding the truth or presenting a biased picture of reality. Children also have the right to speak the truth as they see it, and not to be censored unnecessarily.

As adult members of the group we have responsibility to inform children to the fullest extent so they can understand the world, assess their place in it, and grow into fully functioning members of society. Article 43 of the UN Convention on the Rights of the Child holds: "The child shall have the right to freedom of expression; this right shall include freedom to seek, receive and impart information and ideas of all kinds, regardless of frontiers, either orally, in writing or in print, in the form of art, or through any other media of the child's choice." Clearly, under the terms of this convention, children have the right to receive truthful information.

Before we begin, it's important to ask ourselves, "What is 'the truth'?" It has been said that there is no reality—each person's view of the world is so colored by preconceptions that no two people see the world in the same way.

That is true, and it's very obvious in situations of war, where both sides see things from a completely different perspective and both sides are certain, to the point of death, that they know the real truth. When it comes to children, parents will want to convey their world view to children. They will want their children to believe such things as "We must be kind to animals" or "People should help each other," and some will want to convey such unsociable beliefs as "Foreigners are to be mistrusted" or "We are the only ones who have the right religion."

In speaking the truth to children, we cannot totally put aside our beliefs and prejudices. However, we should be aware of those beliefs and not transmit them unconsciously by word or action. Whether we are right or wrong, it is possible to develop a culture of truth in the presence of children. We may not be correct in our answers; we may even have some prejudice in our responses. But we should approach children with an attitude of *truthfulness,* determined to answer as much as we can, taking care to avoid hurting the child.

Truthfulness does not have a secondary purpose. This purposelessness should be the aim of the adult who respects the child. The adult should have a purpose of having no purpose other than the good of the child. He should present information to the child even if he disagrees with it. For instance, an adult can say to a child, "Some people think this is true; I do not agree with it, but I understand they do." This kind of truthfulness allows a child to be objective and to see both sides of a situation. Children who have open minds and see both sides to a situation are less likely to engage in conflicts with others or to be argumentative or combative in school. Conflict resolution is taught in many schools now, and one of the techniques used is teaching children to tolerate different "truths" at the same time. Truthfulness and trust are intricately linked. As Cooper (2008) points out:

> A human society can only function smoothly and flourish where people are able to rely on one another, to engage in a reasonable degree of mutual trust. Among the things that must be generally relied upon are the statements people make—something that would be impossible unless it were generally assumed that people usually take some care to make statements which are warranted (Accurate), do not mislead (Sincere), and honour what I called "Transparency" and "Fidelity."[1]

When the truth is distorted or withheld, trust between individuals is broken, and if this is a pattern between parents and children, it can have lifelong consequences for children and their relationships with others. Children are self-motivated learners. They find themselves in a world they do not understand, and their mission is to get their bearings and find out how things work, why things are the way they are and how they fit in. In telling them the truth, we are sharing our inner knowledge and, more important, our feelings and thought processes. This connection is what children seek. If the connection is tainted with lying, deceit or evasion, the relationship itself is weakened, and the child must take on an added burden of caution and self-protection in his dealings with others. A child who is lied to may develop an attitude of disrespect for authority figures in general.

Children have a right to the truth in the same way citizens have the right to disclosure from elected representatives. It's their world, and they need to know what it's all about. Unless information is going to be harmful to children's well-being, parents and caregivers should entrust children with the truth. Telling the truth means sharing our knowledge of the world and being open about what we are feeling and why. We have a duty to be sensitive to the child's feelings. Telling the truth does not mean telling the child hurtful things like, "You are not as smart as your brother" or "There is no such thing as the Tooth Fairy." Children should be told the truth in an unbiased way and within a developmentally appropriate time frame.

TELLING APPROPRIATE TRUTHS

Children develop as they age and process things differently as they grow; therefore, it is not required that they be informed of everything at every stage. For instance when a child is two years old, it is not appropriate that we inform her that her parents are going to die. Unsolicited information of this kind would be disturbing. However, when the child is three years old, she will have developed to the point where she has an awareness of death, and she will often begin asking questions about whether she will die, whether her parents will die, whether everyone will die. At that point it is appropriate she be told the truth with sensitivity to her reaction. Similarly, a two-year-old child may ask where babies come from and should be told the truth, however at that point he or she may not need a lesson on sexuality, which would be appropriate at a later age. A few select facts may be enough.

WHAT A CHILD NEEDS TO KNOW

The adult must be aware of a child's feelings and ability to process the information. A child usually needs information only about what he has asked. Knowing how much to tell children and how much to withhold until they are older requires that we know exactly what they are asking. It is not always easy to know what a child wants to know. We don't need to tell more than they are asking to know at a particular point. But we must keep on answering if they keep on asking. Adults should avoid saying, "That's the way it is" or "Enough questions. I told you already." When we follow a child's endless line of questions, we usually come to a gap in our own knowledge. Being truthful about what you don't know is helpful to a child since it shows you are open to learning new things.

It is not always easy to be sure what a child is asking. However, much more harm can be done by withholding or distorting the truth than by the well-intentioned provision of an honest answer. Children often know unconsciously when people are not telling the truth. They can tell by their faces, by their body language, by the tone of their voice. Children may not know how or why something is not right, but they will in fact store up the phrase that does not ring true and remember it for long periods of time. At some point it will hit them, when they are older and have more information, and they will say, "Ahh, I *knew* that didn't sound right. So that's what was going on." Many writers have drawn on this childhood perception of reality in their work.

Children are impressionable and naturally trusting, since they have no reason to doubt what they are told by the people they trust. As a result, they can be lied to easily, brainwashed, and persuaded to do things that are counter to their own good. In many parts of the world children are talked into joining armies and killing their "enemies" or into having sex for money. In these instances children are told this is the way things are, and they must comply without question. The only way to give children power in their lives is to tell them the truth so they can make good choices.

The opposite of truth is untruth. Untruth is the intent to hide the truth from another, and untruth varies in complexity and impact. There are levels of untruth, and these levels are differentiated by the intent of the one who hides the truth. The law regards different kinds of crime as being more or less serious, depending on the intent and the premeditation behind it. For instance, first-degree murder is where the crime is planned, and there is intent to kill. Second-degree murder would have the intent, but might not be premeditated, and so on. When people tell children lies or deceive them, they may or may not plan to lie, and they may intend different things with their lies, and so the impact of their lies will vary accordingly. The intent of the person who tells a lie may be to manipulate, to protect, to distract, or to divert.

At times when a child's well-being is not considered, the lie-teller may have the intent to further his own good by telling lies. In certain countries, children are enrolled in armies. These children are told their lives have no value and the good of the group is what matters. Lies may be told to distort the truth about the enemy in order to shape the child's responses. In this case, children's rights are being completely subverted. Their bodies and minds are being manipulated. Though the people who are in charge may believe in the cause they recruit for, they are distorting facts in order to achieve results. They are not approaching the child soldiers with an attitude of truthfulness; they are presenting information purposefully in order to further their own goals. The liar is aware that his words will lead the person to certain actions. There is a film that describes this process called *Gaslight*, in which a man lies to convince his wife she is going crazy in order to facilitate his own purposes, and this film's title has become a commonly used term. People can be "gas-lighted" by others—deliberately deceived by others so as to benefit the liar.

On a less extreme level, some people tell lies to protect the good of people other than the child. These kinds of lies are told to protect the family, for example—or to bolster the image of the parent, or to safeguard other family relationships—and do not take into account the well-being of the child or the child's rights to know the truth. The adult may not be deliberately trying to manipulate the child for selfish purposes, but there is still a hidden purpose behind the lie, and therefore the adult is not operating with an attitude of truthfulness toward the child. The child is not being treated as an individual with a right to the truth. Since there is a purpose behind the lie other than the good of the child himself, then it is likely the child will suffer. Parents should think twice before deciding this kind of deception is a good idea.

One young man I know suffers still from the lie his mother told him when he was young. At age three his father disappeared, leaving his mother to raise him alone. In those days, being an "abandoned woman," in the terminology of the day, held a terrible stigma. It was generally thought the woman was somehow to blame, as she was probably unable to keep the man happy or be a good wife. When the boy started school, the mother knew that questions would come up from the teachers and other children, so she told her son that his father was killed in a car accident. Years later, when the truth surfaced, though he understood his mother's reasoning, the boy felt angry that he was lied to, and he felt robbed of the chance to know he did, in fact, have a father. At that point it was too late to reconcile, since the boy's father had died in another country. He felt a terrible sense of betrayal. He also felt a breach of trust and wondered about everything else that had been told him—what else was a lie? He felt unequal to others, since other people had been told the truth, but not him. Was something wrong with him? Was he different from everyone else? Why could he not be trusted with the truth?

His mother was concerned about not leaking painful family events to the outside world, but by keeping the truth away from outsiders, the pain stayed within the family and affected the child. Had the mother allowed the information to flow to the outside and cared less about the opinions of others, her child would not have suffered so much. Lies can be toxic since they stop the free flow of information, and they are compounded with other lies to prevent the truth from being told. Telling the truth often releases the toxicity and a feeling of relief ensues.

Another kind of untruth is when an adult decides to bolster his own self-image in order to maintain the balance of adult/child authority. This lie is often spontaneous and unpremeditated. The parent or teacher does not plan to lie to the child; he is not trying to manipulate the child for his own purposes. The adult is on the spot, blinded by fear of losing control or losing face. He wants the child to think highly of him, since he is in charge and needs to maintain his position. The basic premise behind these kinds of lies is that an adult believes that a child cannot be trusted with the truth about human weakness, particularly of the authority figure. The parent or teacher is afraid to be seen as vulnerable or mistaken, and so he or she lies to the child. The motivation is fear of losing control. A pupil might say to a teacher, "I think you made a mistake," and the teacher might cover his embarrassment by saying, "I did that deliberately; I was hoping you would notice." Or even worse: "No, you are wrong, and I am right."

Admitting you are wrong is a healthy part of being an authority figure for a child. A friend of mine remembers a beloved teacher in the second grade. The year had just started, and she was a new teacher. She had her back turned to the class, writing on the board, and the class noticed the zipper on the back of her skirt was open, revealing her underwear. There was a lot of tittering and embarrassment; the children saw a weakness in their leader, and no one knew what to do. Finally one of the children stood up and informed the teacher about her gaping error. The good-natured teacher slapped herself on the head and said, "Oh, dear, I must be losing my marbles!" The class all laughed, and so did she. And they fell in love with her.

My friend remembers her teacher fondly to this day because she could laugh at herself. Her transparent and self-accepting attitude created an atmosphere of trust in the room. The children knew that if she was accepting of her own errors, she could be accepting of theirs too. If she had covered her embarrassment with a feigned dignity and said, "Pay attention to your work," she would not have made the connection she did with the children. Accepting the truth is healing in many aspects of life, particularly in relationships involving power. Many adults think that to have power and control over children, you have to pretend to be perfect, but the opposite is the case. Probably the teacher who admitted her mistake enjoyed her work more than a teacher who had to constantly pretend to be perfect and have all the answers.

Shenk (2005) talks about Abraham Lincoln's ability to draw followers to him through his absolute honesty. Lincoln was prone to depression, but his approach to it was to be honest and open. This honesty did not drive people away, it drew him to them:

> Many of Lincoln's advisors viewed him as a man who needed to be encouraged and protected. . . . After the (Decatur) convention closed, he sat with his head in his hands and said, pathetically, "I'm not very well." There was a mystery to this man, a secret pain in his heart. To some people, this made Lincoln all the more alluring. In any case, no one discussed it as a liability.[2]

If Abraham Lincoln drew such support while showing his weakness, then parents and teachers should realize they do not have to be dishonest with children about their own weaknesses and failings.

Another kind of untruth is when an adult decides a child cannot handle the truth and must be protected. This is another "crime of passion," when a parent is on the spot and feels the need to defend the child against the world. The well-meaning adult feels it is her duty to control what the child sees and hears from the outside world. Children are exposed to a lot of information in the media; if parents read newspapers and watch the news on TV it's almost impossible to prevent young children from seeing images or reading about violence and death. Parents may not know what a child is perceiving or thinking, and often a question can come out of nowhere. Parents feel the need to protect the child, which is a natural and good instinct. Telling a lie may seem like the easiest way out of the situation when a child asks a question about something disturbing to a parent. The premise behind the lie is that, for at least a short while, the child should be able to live in an innocent state. The parent hopes that for a few years he or she should be able to believe that everyone is nice and nothing bad can happen. The protective adult thinks that children are innately good and sweet and incapable of imagining bad things. They believe it is their job to protect children from the evil in the world.

In fact, children are capable of imagining terrible things, without having seen or heard anything really violent. We are all capable of imagining and even doing terrible things depending on the circumstances in which we find ourselves. In our day-to-day life, none of us would ever imagine eating another human being. We think we are civilized and incapable of doing anything as savage as that. Nevertheless, real events have shown us that civilized human beings, faced with the possibility of starving to death, will make the choice to eat their fellow humans.

Many perfectly reasonable citizens who had never done anything wrong in their lives participated in crimes against humanity because they were swept up in a culture of fear and genocide. Soldiers at war can participate in extremely violent acts because of the circumstances in which they find themselves. Not one of us thinks we are holding down rage as we walk happily to work. However, if a bicyclist cuts right in front of us on the sidewalk, startling us out of our daydream, our physical reaction is to feel a huge rush of adrenalin, a pounding heartbeat, and an instantaneous urge to say or do something really violent to the cyclist. Most of us have this impulse under some level of control.

Young children have the same depth of rage and fantasies of violent actions that parents have learned to suppress within themselves. Parents of young children are often startled by the way a normally developing child can blithely knock down another child's tower of blocks, or react to another child's incursions by biting or scratching. Since they have left this stage far behind themselves, parents often forget that young children have their animal instincts still alive and strong and close to the surface.

When it comes to seeing images of violence on TV, parents who want to protect their children need to remember that children already are perfectly aware of their own capabilities for violence. Three-year-old boys are capable of thinking up ways of destroying monsters or killing "bad guys" that would shock even directors of horror movies. If you are not sure about this, ask any small child, "What would you like to do to a monster?" They will come up with scenarios they have never seen but can imagine.

At different ages, children process images of violence in different ways, depending on their own emotional needs and growth. I know a parent who was with his son, visiting his sister's house. The boy's older cousin, a girl, was quite distressed. The girl was talking about land mines, and how sad she felt that people could design land mines that could hurt innocent people, even children. His son immediately perked up. "Land mines?" he said. "What are they?" The father was concerned about telling his son, but he was asked a direct question on the spot, and so he explained to his son what they were. He didn't anticipate his son's response. "How do you make them, daddy?" he asked. Though the father was puzzled about the two different responses, it is clear that the boy and girl were handling these issues in their own individual and age-appropriate ways. The boy was not less concerned than the girl; he was younger and taking a mechanical view of the situation. He was not shocked at the notion that people want to kill other people, while the girl was older and coming to terms with the fact that humans do have a violent side. The young child processed the information in his own way at his own level, and perhaps the older child, being more mature, was dealing with confronting her own violent feelings.

The best way to protect a child from the outside world is to tell her the truth about it, especially when she is already aware of what is going on. When I was a young child there was a horrific murder in my native city, and it was widely covered in the newspapers. This was a crime involving an Indian medical student and a young Irish girl. The student killed the girl, who may have been pregnant, and in an effort to hide the crime, cut her body up and hid the body parts in various places. In those days there was a great deal of racism in Ireland, and sex outside marriage was taboo. Those additional factors made the crime even more sensational. My parents hid the story from me, but I was aware that something was forbidden for me to hear. I had heard things whispered in the family; my parents and older siblings were discussing the story covertly, and I knew there was something bad that happened. The mysterious event filled me with fear and anxiety. In addition, the secrecy left me feeling excluded from the secret world of others. I also felt a sense of dread that there were things too horrible for me to know about.

My older brother thought I should know the truth, and he told me the story. I remember him asking me if I knew what it was all about, and feeling my face turning suddenly red with shame, because I knew I was not supposed to know. I was also afraid of the story; it might be something truly unhearable. My brother explained it calmly and tempered the horror of it by pointing out to me that sometimes people do things they shouldn't do because they panic, and because they are afraid of facing up to what they did. Though people called him an Indian monster, a wild savage, my brother explained that he cut up the girl's body not because he was a savage, but because he was acting out of fear of being caught.

Even though I was a young child, I felt a great sense of relief hearing this story. First, I felt proud my brother trusted I could handle the truth. Secondly, I was not afraid of the story any longer since he presented it in a scientific way, explaining it in such a way so I could understand the psychology of the crime. I felt suddenly older; I felt respected, I felt strong, and I felt included. I must say that knowing the story of this crime did not have any negative effects on me, and I did not feel any less safe in the world by knowing the truth. When something is surrounded in mystery, the child's imagination makes it even worse, and in that sense the truth is a relief. My brother helped me to develop an analytical approach to human nature, rather than a rush to judgment, a self-righteous or racist reaction. He was teaching me how to face the darkest aspects of human nature and giving me techniques in understanding them.

Though parents must decide what to tell children and at what age, I think it is true that children can handle a lot more than we think, since we do all have the same feelings. Crimes are motivated by deep feelings, and children should be helped to understand that this is why people do bad things, rather than letting children think there are "good" people and "bad" people.

Sometimes people who do bad things don't look the least bit like bad people. It is very common and natural for very young children to play "good guy vs. bad guy." They are working in a symbolic way at developing control over their own violent impulses. However, as children grow older it is better for them to accept that we all are capable of doing bad things. Children will feel less shame about their impulses if they know we all have those feelings; we just don't have to act on them.

Protecting children by telling them lies or hiding the truth is not a good long-term strategy. If a child does not get a satisfactory answer, the question will not go away; a child will retain curiosity about the subject and keep on trying to find the answer. If a child is asking a question and the parent feels afraid to tell the truth, uncomfortable about telling disturbing truths, or unsure how to say things, it is probably fine to stall or play for time until the right answer is clear to the parent. Parents should not blurt out a lie to cover their misgivings; they should take the time to think out a good answer. A parent can prepare for these moments ahead of time by coming up with a few phrases that will be useful for handling awkward situations. Some of these phrases might include "I don't feel comfortable talking about it now. Can we discuss it later?" or "That's a good question. Let's make time to talk about it this evening after dinner," or "I did not know it was on your mind. Let me think about it so we can talk later."

You can even say something honest like, "Talking about land mines makes me feel upset, but we will talk about it if you want." The point to realize is that what the child will be picking up more than any other thing in the situation is the adult's response, the adult's attitude. If the adult is showing he or she is afraid to talk about something, or showing he or she thinks the child can't handle an honest answer, that impression is what will stay with the child, even more than the unpleasant aspects of the actual event. The child needs to know what the parent's view of the world is, since that is how the child creates his own worldview. What a child wants to know is: "Why is my parent uncomfortable about this?" A child might wonder, "If everyone who can read the newspaper knows about this, why does my parent think I cannot be told the truth?" The child's answer will probably be: "There must be something different about me." And of course that translates very quickly to: "Something is wrong with me."

There is yet another level of untruth telling: the "white lie." This is the area that many people feel most unsure of. Though they carry on the tradition of these lies, parents worry that they should not be telling lies to their children on any level. Children are told that there is a Santa Claus who brings gifts if you are good; there is a Tooth Fairy who gives you money when your teeth fall out; there is a Binky Fairy who takes your pacifier when you are ready to give it up and gives it to other children; there is a Boogie Man who will get you if you are naughty; there is an Easter Bunny who leaves sweets for you whether you are nice or not.

Some people wonder: Why do we tell these lies to children? At some point we have to admit we were lying. Parents are not sure how much of this deceit is right, how far to go with it, and how and when to explain it was all a lie. Some people call them "white lies." White lies abound in books—parents and teachers tell stories about witches, giants, ogres, trolls, fairies, monsters, magic potions, spells, and transformations. The reason these fictional characters abound is that a child deals with the world in a more symbolic way than an adult, and fiction is his way of coping. If a child is starting preschool, for instance, and is unable to talk about his feelings, a teacher can hold a toy dinosaur and say, "What's this dinosaur feeling?" The child will readily say, "He misses his mommy," with no realization that he is, in fact, talking about himself and his feelings.

Fairy tales have existed for centuries because they serve a function for children. Bruno Bettelheim's book *The Uses of Enchantment*[3] helps to analyze fairy tales. This book is a good way for adults to understand the issues that are hidden in old stories that have been told to children through the years. His book helps to explain why children are so involved and engrossed in stories of this kind and why they have lasted for hundreds of years. Before parents or teachers read these kinds of stories to children, they should be aware of the underlying symbolism and the reason why some children might be terribly afraid of a witch, while others are not afraid of a witch but are terrified of a giant.

In one fairy tale, "Three Billy Goats Gruff" conspire to trick and finally demolish the ogre under the bridge. Through this story, children are learning valuable lessons about how problems can be handled in different ways at different stages. The youngest goat passes the problem on to the middle brother; the middle brother passes it on to the oldest one, who attacks the troll and knocks him into the water. Problems, like ogres, can be handled differently at different stages. Problems of early childhood often have to be confronted in adolescence—you can defer problems for a while, but you always have to deal with them at some point. This is an underlying meaning in the tale. Stories like this are very meaningful to children on a symbolic level. It is perfectly fine for children to think that goats can talk, that a queen can talk to a magic mirror, and the mirror will tell her painful truths, and so on. Potions, magic spells, and transformation, are all psychological devices hidden in stories that help children to realize they have hidden power and the ability to heal and change. Children know these things instinctively and can recognize them in the stories.

Stories about monsters and witches, therefore, are beneficial for children, as long as the storyteller is in touch with how these stories are impacting a child and reads them with an eye to the child's response. If the child wants to hear the story over and over again, this is an indication she is learning something from it. If she does not want to even look at it, this is a strong indication that there is something a child does not want to face. Of course the parent or teacher should never force the child to read a scary story but should take this reaction as a signal about what exactly bothers the child.

When it comes to Santa Claus, the Easter Bunny, and the Tooth Fairy, parents are not really telling lies; they are telling stories. These characters and scripts are symbolic ways for adults to endow children with gifts and pleasure, and they all involve promise, anticipation, and surprise. They are ways of allowing the child to believe that there is a benevolent presence in the world that bestows surprises and rewards. They are, in fact, stories about the bounty of the world. In the stories, the child must often be asleep while the surprise is being prepared or bestowed. The gifts are hidden, and the child must search for them. The child must be patient, must wait, or must search. There are different ways that people tell these stories. Some tell the stories as a way of rewarding children for good behavior. Others tell the stories as a way of indicating that good things are going to happen for no reason other than that children deserve to receive presents.

The real meaning being conveyed to children with these "white lies" is that there are wonderful things in store for them. Those wonderful things may require patience—you have to sleep and keep dreaming while they are being prepared. They may require effort—you have to go out there and look for them since they are hidden all over the garden. And you may have to experience the pain of change and loss—you have to give up your baby teeth before you can get the money under the pillow. But there are definitely surprises in store for each and every child. The other meaning underlying these "white lies" is that a parent's love and devotion is what enables children to have good things happen. I do not know of any child who honestly has a lifelong grudge against a parent for pretending to be Santa Claus, the Easter Bunny, or the Tooth Fairy. Many families of grown children watch family movies together where children are opening up their surprises. And children who watch these movies most often fondly remember the toys their parents gave to them. I can't imagine any person confiding in his therapist that he felt deeply betrayed when he found out about Santa Claus or the Easter Bunny. Since young parents continue to take on this gift-giving tradition, it follows that it brings them joy to do so. To call these stories "lies" would be to ignore the purpose behind them; the purpose is to give joy to a child, so that of course cannot be a bad thing. When parents use Santa or the Easter Bunny as a reward or punishment, it can be a way of manipulating a child that takes the good out of the surprise.

The final level of untruth telling is the "prank" or "joke." Some people find the vulnerability of children amusing. They often don't realize that everything they say is being processed by a child's mind, and that a child is trying to make sense of the world, so jokes at his or her expense are unhelpful. A friend told me that when she was young, her sisters thought it funny to tell her that their mother was one hundred years old. She found this hard to believe, but they "proved" it by adding up the ages of all six children. She was deeply upset by the idea of having a very old mother, and when the topic of "How old is your mother?" came up in school, she was embarrassed and hid "the truth." When she found she had believed a distortion of the truth, she felt very vulnerable and victimized, and also cheated, as though she did not have a key that others had—the truth. Her sisters probably had a sense of power knowing they knew the truth and she did not.

Withholding the truth is the same as lying, and lying usually causes more problems than telling the truth. Even if adults have the good intention of protecting a child from the truth, when the truth comes out the child often feels resentful and may never forgive the lie. Many people retain the feeling of anger they experienced when they realized someone has died and they were not told about it, because an adult thought they couldn't handle the truth. Children can often tell the truth is being withheld, since there can be a feeling of tension in the air, and when the truth comes out, however painful, it is usually a relief to hear it. People who go to Alcoholics Anonymous meetings speak of being able to heal through hearing the truth being told by other people, even though the truth is about painful things that happened to them. Hearing the truth brings people together; when people show their vulnerability it allows others to get in touch with their own vulnerability. Pretending things are fine when they are not creates tension that children are capable of perceiving.

THE NATURAL WORLD

Children have the right to understand how the world works. Life, death, birth, illness, aging, and sexuality are natural processes, and caregivers should tell the truth to children so they will be well informed and prepared to handle the emotional aspects of these processes. Depending on the age of the child, the truth can be told in symbolic or narrative form. For instance, three-year-old children can understand the process of life and death when it's told through the story of a seed.

DEATH

At around three years of age, children begin to grapple with the subject of death. Adults often try to keep information about death away from children. They sometimes do not bring children to funerals and often do not tell them the person has died. Parents use words such as "passed on" or "gone away" or "gone to sleep" and so on. This can be very confusing to children. It is better to tell them the truth and then listen to the questions they ask and answer them honestly and gently. They may ask questions about what happens when a person dies. Parents often feel conflict on hearing this question. They may feel that death is very frightening to children and that they must protect them. They may feel they themselves don't understand death or the afterlife and don't want to show they are confused. However, the truth is a way of sharing your thoughts with your child, which is what the child really wants.

It is fine for a parent to say you are not sure or to say you don't know, as long as you make it clear to the child that you have thought about it, and you have done your best to understand. Parents can say, "Well, the truth is that no one really understands death. I have thought a lot about it and read books about it, and I am still trying to figure it out. Maybe we could look at a book for you." That kind of response allows the child to see that it's a mystery we are all working on. It is equally acceptable to share your beliefs about the afterlife if you do have them, since you are sharing your world with the child. And if parents do not have fixed beliefs there is nothing wrong with asking children, "What do you think happens when you die?"

If a child asks why people have to die, then it is a good idea to tell them about birth, aging, death, and the fact that we are all part of this process. As we move forward we take on different roles, and the people coming behind us can take the place we once held. This is comforting since it shows children that we are not alone and we can feel part of a story or process bigger than ourselves. There are books specially written for children in which stories about death are told in developmentally appropriate ways.

Very young children can blame themselves for things over which they have no control. It is almost a childhood default to think everything is your fault. If a child has had angry or resentful feelings toward someone who dies then he or she can feel somehow responsible. That is why it is better to tell the child the truth: that everyone dies, it is a natural and inevitable process, and it is no one's fault. Being mysterious about the circumstances or the process can compound that guilt. If a child discovers that he or she is the only one who has been left out of the "secret," then it may be natural to assume that he or she is somehow to blame, or at the very least different from everyone else. Children will assume the worst: that being different means they are bad in some way.

When there is an extreme circumstance that might disturb a child unnecessarily, for example if someone close to them has died under very disturbing conditions, or someone close to them has been responsible for the death, it is not necessary to tell the whole story while the child is in a vulnerable state. Telling the truth is not the same as divulging everything on your mind. Telling the truth means understanding what the child is asking and responding as openly as possible, especially about your feelings.

ILLNESS AND A CHILD'S BODY

Children need to know as much as possible about the workings of their bodies, including their bodies' vulnerabilities and strengths. From the earliest age they need to know that if they run into the street a car can hit them and hurt or even kill them. This knowledge about vulnerability can be frightening, and parents need to present the information in a balanced way. It is not right for parents to emotionally cripple their child by making him afraid to take chances, by overloading him with information about how he can be hurt. Warning a child about the dangers on every side can make him afraid to do anything. Telling the truth in a calm way is not the same as pointing out dangers at every instance. A child has the right to know the truth about dangers of injury and illness: that if a car hits him his body will be damaged. But he also has the right to know that he can learn to protect himself by taking simple precautions (wait for the traffic lights to turn green). And he needs to know his body has the resources it needs to heal itself—cuts will heal, bones will knit back together, and so on. A child needs to know that if he is hurt there are people who can help him; for instance, he may need an operation to help him function better.

Young children have a lot of curiosity about their body and how it functions. Feeding this curiosity with knowledge can help them to protect themselves. Knowing your brain is important so you need to wear a helmet when riding a bike is a good thing. Knowing where your organs are located is helpful so you don't kick your friend in an area that might cause damage. Knowing why you are bleeding and how the blood will coagulate and form a scab is helpful for a child, since it frightens them to see blood coming out of their bodies when they fall. They are not sure it will stop bleeding, and they don't know why it is happening. Young children often hear about a "broken arm" and think it means their arm can break off; similarly they hear the word "eyeballs" and often think their eyes might come out and roll away like a ball. Myths abound in a child's mind regarding the body. When an old lady next door to us died, the story spread around the children of our neighborhood that she was sewing one day when she dropped a needle on the floor. When she stepped on the needle, it traveled up into her heart, and she died. I personally believed that story for a long time until I began to figure out that it couldn't have happened that way. Probably some child who was not properly informed made up the story in order to explain the death.

Misconceptions about the body are common and should be addressed by parents, who should always tell the truth about the body and its properties. Many parents think they should tell a child that if he crosses his eyes he might stay like that forever. Other parents tell children if they watch too much TV their brain will turn to mush. These things are not true, and telling the child an untruth about the body can be frightening. The parent should be honest and say he feels disturbed when he sees his child with eyes crossed or, better yet, ignore it, and he or she will stop since it gets tiring pretty quickly, especially if no one reacts. A parent can say she wants the child to read more books instead of watching TV since you can use your imagination more by reading. Many adults are surprised to hear the things their parents told them are untrue—swallowing gum does not harm you; reading in the dark doesn't weaken your eyes; you won't die if you go swimming after eating; and so on. Parents should be careful about breaching trust and stretching the truth when it comes to pain. Telling your child you will yank her tooth out and that it won't hurt might not be a good idea, since it might indeed hurt—and the next time she won't trust you.

If a child needs to have a medical procedure—for instance, if he needs to go to the dentist to have a tooth extracted—he should be told the truth and prepared for all the things that will happen. Rather than glossing over the truth, the parent should prepare the child by giving as much information as the child asks for, even if it includes getting illustrations of teeth, pictures of a dentist's chair, reading a book, using the correct terminology, and so on, so the child will be familiar with what is going to happen. Children love to master the names of things like "stethoscope," "thermometer," and "X-ray," and knowing the names of these things in advance make the child feel part of the process. When a child asks, "Will it hurt?" you can tell the truth. You can say, "It might hurt a little, but when people are afraid and tense up, things seem to hurt even more. If you can relax and hold my hand then it will hurt less." When people are entering a situation they fear, most of the fear comes from not knowing what is going to happen. There is an old saying about fear being the thing we most have to fear. Anxiety causes a heightened experience of pain. Once a person knows what will happen, the anxiety may not disappear, but it radically diminishes. Knowledge is power. Knowing what is going to happen to you gives you some control over your own reaction.

An innovative Japanese program to help children manage their anxieties about undergoing hospital procedures has had very positive results. Children and caregivers watch a video at home, and this video documents the procedure in detail. The results of an evaluative study indicate that after watching the video with a caregiver, there is less anxiety on the part of the child, attributable to the fact that information helps assuage fear. Wakimisu (2009) reports:

> The present study showed the effects of at-home psychological preparation, using a videotape and booklet on Japanese children aged between three and six years receiving herniorrhaphy in Japan. Children and caregivers who watched the video together as frequently as they want at home in a relaxed atmosphere were better informed and prepared, and they exhibited less anxiety regarding surgical hospitalization than those who watched the same video once at the outpatient clinic a week before surgery.[4]

Telling a child as much about the procedure as possible actually helps him not to be afraid. The more they watched the video, the less they were afraid.

SEX

The one subject that parents probably fear most to tell the truth about is sex. It is not such a long time since children in the "developed" world were told they were brought into the world by large birds, who carried them suspended from their beaks in cloths and dropped them in front of their houses. Compare this with the natural way children in so-called "primitive" societies are exposed to the physical processes of life and fully informed about them so as to be prepared when they are able to participate in them.

Fortunately nowadays many parents are becoming more open with their children and use real terminology when talking about the reproductive organs. Giving body parts a funny name does not really benefit children. Some people talk down to children and come up with childish words when they can just as easily use the correct term. We don't have funny names for our hands or feet, our hair or our teeth. Children may learn a pseudonym for the body part at one stage of their life and then hear his peers using the accepted term as a teenager. This can make the young adult feel embarrassed and awkward, while the young person who has grown up with the correct term will seem confident and unashamed. Realizing you've been kept in the dark while others know the truth can make a person feel vulnerable.

There are a lot of nice, beautifully illustrated books for young children showing how babies grow within the mother and are born. Young children have a great interest in knowing where they came from, and they have the right to know. From a very early age it is good to show a child books about how babies grow inside their mothers. Baby boomers may not have grown up with this kind of information freely available to them. Many of them will remember the shame involved in hearing about sexual reproduction from friends, as though it was a secret. Secrecy implies the notion that certain things are acceptable to the group and certain things are not. Generally a secret also implies that something is shameful. Children show no ill effects when they are exposed to the truth about where babies come from.

The next level of information is about sexual reproduction. Children will ask at one point or another, "But how did I get in there?" and parents need to decide at that point how to explain sexual reproduction. There are lots of books available to parents on how to explain this to their children, depending on the age of the child. The worst thing a parent can do is to distort the truth or withhold it from the child. I remember a friend of mine told me that at age ten she plucked up her courage and decided to confront her father to get the information she longed for. "Daddy, what is sex?" she asked him. Looking very uncomfortable he answered, "It's the difference between men and women," and promptly left the room. She felt let down by her father and was thrown back to the distinctly unreliable information of her friends. Unfortunately nowadays, young people who are naturally curious can find lots of unsavory sources of sexual information on the Internet, and the best protection a father or mother can give a child is information.

Another reason to give a child full information about reproduction is so that he or she will not engage in dangerous behavior or incur an unwanted pregnancy. Ignorance of biology can lead to consequences that impact one's entire life. There have been cases in the media of young girls who did not even know they were pregnant and had to give birth in a toilet. Full disclosure is best, even when a parent is talking about the need for precautions to prevent pregnancy. Though it is quite naturally difficult for a parent to think about the sexuality of the child and vice versa, these truthful discussions are a child's best protection against misinformation, shame, pregnancy, and even rape.

ADOPTION

Parents who adopt children face a number of dilemmas when it comes to telling the truth. There is the feeling of inadequacy that parents often confront—they could not have their own child. Do they want to convey this to the world and to their own child? In the past some parents have chosen to keep secrets and not tell anyone their child was adopted. Nowadays people are not quite so afraid of public opinion about fertility. However, adoptive parents can feel a lot of confusion about what to tell their child, how to tell it, and when to tell it.

A study done by Penney (2007) consisted of interviews of adults who had been adopted. These adults, aged thirty-five to fifty-five, talked about their feelings about adoption and the ways in which adoption had impacted them. Respondents were divided into different phases or categories, depending on their reactions and attitudes. There were some similarities and dissimilarities in people's feelings about being adopted. However, the one thing they all agreed on was their need for more information when they were young: "Phase 5 adoptees wished they could have talked more freely about adoption and that they could have had more information about their birth family as a child. This latter desire was the one regret shared by all adoptees except for those in Phase 1."[5] Strong negative emotions were shown by adoptees who were not fully informed. Being deprived of information or being treated as though they were not capable of hearing the truth affected all these adults for their entire lives and left them with a feeling of regret. Once again it seems clear that children have a need to know the truth.

PARENTS' RELATIONSHIPS/DIVORCE

How much do children need to know about their parents' relationships? What happens when parents are going through separation and divorce? How much should a child be included in the process? When things are going well in a relationship, parents have no problem kissing and hugging in front of children. Good feelings tend to include the whole family; when we are happy, it's time for group hugs. However, when parents begin to have problems in their relationship, there is the worry that those negative feelings are going to impact the children.

Fighting in front of children is not a good idea. Many people do it without realizing they are impacting the children, yet others try to hide negative interactions. However, children perceive sarcasm and coldness just as clearly as they hear yells and insults. When parents are not happy with each other children are affected. How much should children be told? Can parents cover the problem and keep the child innocent of the conflicts going on between them? How much can children handle?

One couple decided to separate but did not want their young child to know, fearing it would affect her. The father would sleep at his own apartment and arrive at the mother's apartment early in the morning before the child woke, pretending he had stayed there the night before. They were trying to keep the illusion of a strong family, thinking that at age three she would not be able to handle their separation and should be protected from the truth. However, she was soon getting in trouble in school. She was angry and aggressive. They did not realize that the child sensed the problems between them, overheard the strained phone calls, and perceived her parents' body language and tense interactions. Since she experienced the tension but had no way of understanding where it came from, she internalized it and acted it out. She probably felt very alone, since her parents were not sharing their feelings with her, and she could not share her feelings with them. They were pretending nothing was wrong, when the child knew that there was. Hiding the truth did not help but aggravated the problem.

Selvini (1997) discusses the relationship between his patient's mental illness and the secrets they concealed from him: "The parents' two-facedness, this ambiguity between what is denied and what is exhibited, creates a state of anxiety and confusion. There will be contradictions, shifts in behaviour, for which there is no rational explanation."[6] The child knew something was wrong but learned to mistrust his own instincts. This disconnect led to his polarized thinking. In an interview study of Australian children of divorced parents, Bagshaw (2007) reported that children expressed the need for the truth:

> The interviews with children identified a lack of communication between parents and their children about the reasons for the parental separation and what the separation meant for the children. All children interviewed stressed that they would have preferred to have had more information prior to their parents separating, in particular from their parents. This confirmed the findings of other studies. It is therefore recommended that service providers find ways to assist parents to talk with their children about the reasons behind the separation and the processes involved before, during, and after the separation.[7]

I think it is worth repeating the one striking comment: "All children . . . stressed they would have preferred to have had more information prior to their parents separating."

Though parents may feel they are protecting a child by hiding the truth, they are, in fact, causing difficulties for the child, and this study shows those difficulties may be long-lasting. They must, however, inform the child in a spirit of truthfulness. They should not allow their own anger or sense of betrayal or disappointment to color the way they present the truth. If they are aware they are angry, then they can help a child best if they present the situation in as neutral a way as possible. "Your mother and I are fighting a lot, and we think it is better if we are not together for a while," is of course better than "Your mother is being mean to me, and I have to get away from her." Both are different ways of representing the situation. Many of the respondents in the above study wished their parents had sat down together and talked to them as a couple, instead of presenting just one side of the problem. Children instinctively know there are two sides to every situation; no one person has a monopoly on the truth.

If parents are going through counseling and think there is a hope for reconciliation, they can tell the child they are having some problems and are getting help. Should they volunteer this information? If they can see the child's behavior is a little different than it has been previously, either quieter and more conciliatory or else more disruptive than usual, then there is a good chance the child is aware something is going on. In that case, parents should open the discussion, being careful to ask the child how he or she feels once they explain they are having problems. It is not a good idea to give too much information without asking a child for feedback.

SECRETS AND SOCIAL POWER

Secrets are a bad idea in general, for many reasons. The problem always seems greater when you don't know the limits of it, and most secrets are partial truths. In addition, children very often intuitively know the truth, and so they can often tell when something is being kept secret from them. Very young children cannot lie, as they are unable to know what another person is thinking. Similarly, very young children cannot keep secrets. Keeping a secret from someone is similar to withholding the truth, with the added aspect of allowing someone else in on the fact to the exclusion of the third person. In this way power can be shared between two people only by depriving the third person of it. Children may be easily drawn into this kind of manipulation since they often desire social power and will agree to keep secrets just to be included in the "in crowd." Adults should refrain from drawing children into secrets of any kind, unless they are the pleasant kind—springing a surprise party or buying a surprise gift for someone, or doing a secret good deed. Secrets, like gossip, are the refuge of those who do not have the courage to face the truth or tell it to those who need to hear it.

Family secrets are often preserved by parents, out of fear or misguided protectiveness. However, they can cause serious problems in children. Parents often try to submerge their own suffering by acting as if their problems did not exist. This is a misguided attempt at protecting. Instead of helping their children, they may cause them more problems. Selvini (1997) discusses his experience with patients when parents try to protect their children by disguising their own sufferings and acting as if they have the "perfect family":

> Our patients' parents try to show a facade, to themselves and to others, of which the secret if it were disclosed would present a formidable challenge. So, we find perfect husbands and fathers, real supermen, who must keep their extramarital affairs or their psychotic episodes under cover in order to maintain their fake image . . . When we examined our case histories we noticed a recurrent characteristic in parents of children with serious mental disturbances, namely their staunch denial of any significant suffering of their own, either marital or personal. The key conception here is the self-deception of a parent, which for the child will result in a dangerous confusion in his or her affections. (320)

Secrets can be used by peers or even abusive adults to keep children from disclosing wrongdoings. Children who are used to keeping secrets may be more likely to fall into these kinds of traps. A child who can say to a peer, "No, I don't like secrets," is to be greatly admired. A child who can tell his parent that an adult asked them to keep something secret has a good self-preservation instinct. We can help children to have this kind of confidence by rewarding them for truth-telling and discouraging family secrets. Secrets tend to imply shame. We all know politicians who have had their secrets revealed in public. These public figures usually fare worse if they have concealed the secret for a long time, and if they continue to deny them after they have been revealed. Admitting faults readily tends to bring people into favor again and hasten the forgiveness.

ENCOURAGING CHILDREN TO TELL THE TRUTH

Many families either overtly or covertly encourage their children to lie. Family gatherings may fail to be an occasion for real sharing of feelings, but instead be an arena where children see adults modeling disconnected behavior and being dishonest in their exchanges. Adults who want to "manage" the group situation can encourage children to be dishonest. "Don't say anything to Uncle Joe about what happened last time," or "I know you don't like your cousin but give her a hug anyway," or "If Aunt Sheila gives you another sweater, just say it's nice," and so on. Although parents may mean well, in point of fact this kind of suppression causes more negative feelings, which do not help the child but rather hinder him from developing real mastery of his emotions and making real connections with others. Parents in this instance could train the child in healthy self-assertion. If asked by Aunt Sheila whether you like the sweater, just tell her, "Thank you for taking the time to knit a sweater for me, but you are forgetting to make them bigger for me. I am not six any more; I need a bigger size."

I remember one time in school I had not done my homework. When the teacher came into the room, I was quite scared. The teacher was in a strange mood that day. We were expecting her to check the homework as usual. She didn't. She just stood there beside the window and said, "Listen, I am tired of being a police officer. The homework is for your benefit and not mine. I feel I should be able to trust you and not check up on your homework every time. I will just ask the question: Did anyone NOT do their homework?" For a minute I thought I was lucky; I could just keep quiet and get away with it. But then I realized the teacher was planning to trust me, and I had the choice of telling the truth and getting into trouble, or telling a lie and feeling deceitful. At that point I knew I could not breach her trust, and so I stood up and said, "I did not do my homework." She looked at me for what seemed like a long time, and then she said, "Thank you. I appreciate your honesty, and I know it took courage. That means more to me than doing the homework. However, you need to stay after class and do it." I felt great. I had told the truth and had been rewarded for it with praise, and that meant a great deal. That teacher taught a wonderful lesson that day. I will never remember what the homework was I didn't do, but the lesson about courage and honesty was something that has stayed with me to this day.

Ultimately, keeping and safeguarding secrets is a way of preserving or enhancing power. It is a very time- and energy-consuming process, however, and the power is very fragile, since once the secrets are revealed the power is lost and a person's reputation is often damaged permanently. Children should be encouraged to have the confidence to tell the truth and not keep secrets.

CENSORING CHILDREN

Children have a right to be told the truth, but children also have the right to tell the truth as they see it. Many adults are afraid of the truth and afraid how it will impact others. Without thinking they often stifle a child's honesty in order to protect the feelings of other people. While it is very important for children to value the feelings of others, it is also very important for children to feel their natural expressions are valued, and that they do have a right to express the truth as they see it. If this truth is hurtful to others, then the child can be taught how to say it in a not so hurtful way, but children's honesty should not be compromised in order to save other people's feelings. When children are brutally honest to other children, adults can intervene, since children need to be protected. However, when another child is not being affected, then adults need to listen without judgment.

One parent said, "What should I do? My son said to me, 'Mommy, I hate your mother!' I told him it was a horrible thing to say, and I sent him to his room." Parents often react strongly to strong words. Children have deep feelings; we cannot take that away or prevent it. A child may indeed hate something or somebody, and if he is censored, his feelings don't go away; they just go underground. However, hate is just another feeling for a child. A child may hate zucchini with the same intensity he hates your mother. Over the course of time those hates may change, or they may not, depending on the child's continued experiences. If a parent reacts by saying, "Oh, that's not true. You don't hate my mother!" or "Don't say that. It's a horrible thing to say," the doors of communication are shut down. If the parent simply says, "Oh, you hate my mother. Why is that?" then the child might answer, "Because whenever she comes over you spend the whole time talking to her and not to me." Then there is room for discussion.

It is a good idea to allow children to say what they think in the privacy of their own home. Some people play the "Hate Game" with their children, and this can be a very revealing and healthy exercise. Everyone takes a turn at saying five things they hate to hear. People might come up with things like, "I hate loud motorcycles" or "I hate when someone is crying" and so on. Then they move on to five things they hate to smell, taste, feel, and so on. These exercises are helpful because they allow a child to figure out who he is and what his dislikes and likes are. More important, he is learning that his hates are accepted and that he doesn't have to love everything in the world all the time. The Hate Game is useful also because the parent can pick up on things that bother the child. Recently when playing this game with some children I was surprised when a little boy went straight to "I hate when I have to leave my dad's house on the weekend." It was a perfect opportunity to let him talk about his feelings. It was a chance for him to talk about his parents' separation. Children should have an arena where they can speak about their negative feelings without fear of censorship.

Another parent wonders, "What do I do when my child says, 'I hate you'?" Once again the thing *not* to say is, "Don't say that. I am your mother!" because then you will never find out why she is angry. It's perfectly possible for a child to hate her mother and vice versa; it doesn't mean it's a permanent condition. We can hate someone and love them too. In the *Encyclopedia of Human Behavior*, Schoenewolf (1994) defines hate:

> A state of arousal or excitation in humans in which anger, negative judgments and impulses of destruction predominate. This state is produced by a combination of biological and environmental factors. Manifestations of hate are numerous, ranging from subtle, individual reactions expression to outright violence and war. However, not all hate is bad. Some hate is destructive while other hate can be constructive and beneficial.[8]

Hating can indeed be beneficial; for instance, it is a good idea to hate feeling sick, to hate disgusting smells, to hate germs, or to hate having a mosquito bite you, since it is healthy to be repulsed by invasive and negative forces that may present a danger to you. A child's hate is not systemic, and it is not a worldview, as in "hate crime." A child's hate is an impulsive and visceral reaction. Instead of suppressing its expression, the adult needs to hear and interpret it and reflect it back to the child. By allowing the child to tell the truth, the adult can prevent hatred from becoming entrenched or from finding a physical outlet.

Adults often react to the child's spontaneous truths with embarrassment. This is because the adult is trying to protect the feelings of others. Many parents have stories of how they were embarrassed by a child's honesty. A woman I know was on the bus when her child said very clearly about a heavily made-up woman in a large colored dress sitting directly across from them, "Mommy, look at the clown!" These are difficult situations since parents want children to be sensitive to others' needs, and no one likes to cause embarrassment. An embarrassed parent might want to silence or shame her child, when in fact everyone on the bus can see that the woman does, indeed, look like a clown. Is it fair to punish a child for saying what everyone else is thinking? It is possible to give the child insights into other people's feelings by saying something later on in private like, "That lady might not think she looks like a clown. Her feelings might be hurt if she thought that." It is quite a complicated concept for a child to understand how other people see themselves in relation to how they appear in reality, but children can slowly develop insights into these issues.

TOO MUCH TRUTH

It is possible to give information in a way that can cause pain to a child, and in this case it is possible to have too much truth. This can be the case when parents share information with children that is not helpful to them. For instance, the question arises: Should parents divulge stories of their own sexual lives? What if it is a cautionary tale that could help their child? Parents who are contemplating talking about their own sexuality should ask themselves how they would feel if their own parents talked to them in this way. If it doesn't feel comfortable, then it isn't right. Does that mean the parent is withholding the truth from their child? What if the parent had experimented sexually or had a bad experience? Could the child benefit from these anecdotes? In this case it is doubtful whether telling the child a painful truth is going to be helpful. It is even more doubtful that children are able to learn from their parents' mistakes. The only thing they may take from the story is that their parent is vulnerable, which may be frightening, and in that case too much truth can be counterproductive. A child only needs information and positive guidance; he or she does not need to hear details that could be intimidating or cause excessive fear.

The same is true when it comes to speaking with your child about drugs. Is it beneficial to divulge to a child that you thought taking drugs was a cool thing to do when you were in college? Even if you have a cautionary tale to tell, it still is doubtful if that information is necessary or helpful to communicate. Volunteering information to your child about things you shouldn't have done may in fact make him or her *more* likely to try those things too. After all, you are the role model, and if you tried it then it might be a cool thing to do. Parents need to be careful about sharing information that the child has not asked about, and parents can be selective in what they answer. If a parent wants to keep her mistakes private she has the right to do so as long as the child is not adversely affected by the secrecy.

Other people feel they need to tell the child the whole truth when, in fact, they are using the truth for their own purposes. One woman I know took care of her nephew when his mother was not able to do so. She prided herself on being a better parent than her wayward sister. When the boy was a little older she confided in him: "The reason you spent Christmas with us that year was that your mother was running around doing drugs. I was the only one who cared for you." The boy was very shocked and very hurt. This out-of-the-blue revelation didn't make him think more highly of his aunt. It damaged his self-esteem, since it made him feel that the only reason his aunt took him in was because she felt sorry for him, since his mother was not able to take care of him. In this case telling the truth was done out of self-interest, not in the interest of the child. The aunt wanted to prove what a good person she was but did not think of the child's reaction.

While it is clear that showing your weaknesses to children is helpful, and that even crying in front of your child can be a bonding experience, it is not a good idea for parents to divulge all they are suffering. The truth is subjective, and when a parent is suffering intensely, it is a subjective experience, it is not 'the truth' about the situation necessarily. Therefore it is not a good idea to tell a child all you are going through. That is not really sharing the truth, it is sharing your own problems, which can be too much for a child to bear. Truth telling should have no purpose other than the purpose of the child's good. People often tell hard truths just to get the information off their chest. However, they may be unloading it onto someone who cannot carry that burden. If you are in doubt about how much truth to tell a child, ask yourself, "What is my intent?" If it can affect the happiness of a child, then keep it from him and share it with someone who can help.

Notes

1. Cooper, D. (2008). "Teaching and Truthfulness." *Studies in Philosophy and Education* 27:79–87 (p.82)

2. Shenk, J. W. (2005. *Lincoln's Melancholy*. New York, NY: Houghton Mifflin (168).

3. Bettelheim, B. (2010) *The Uses of Enchantment.* New York, NY: Random House.

4. Wakimizu, R. and Kamibeppu, K. (2009). "A randomized controlled trial of an at-home preparation programme for Japanese preschool children: effects on children's and caregivers' anxiety associated with surgery." *Journal of Evaluation in Clinical Practice.* Tokyo, HK (400).

5. Penney, J., et al. (2007). "Reconstruction of Adoption Issues: Delineation of Five Phases Among Adult Adoptees." *Journal of Counseling and Development*, 85.

6. Selvini, M. (1997). "Family Secrets: The Case of the Patient Kept in the Dark." *Contemporary Family Therapy* 19(3), 315. September.

7. Bagshaw, D. (2007). "Reshaping Responses to Children When Parents are Separating: Hearing Children's Voices in the Transition." *Australian Social Work* 60:4, 450.

8. Schoenewolf, G. (1994). "Hate." In *Ramachandran, V. S. (ed.), The Encyclopedia of Human Behavior*. New York, NY: Academic Press, 501.

Chapter 3

Children Have the Right to Develop as Individuals

Humans are not robots. The human race is made up of individuals, each of whom is different from the other. Though we share common features, and though we are similar in many ways, not one human being is the same as another. Even in our DNA, the building blocks of our bodies, we are unique. Every human being is born with different abilities, different tendencies, different likes and dislikes. Babies are born with the potential to develop in any given direction and the innate capacity to achieve greatness if they so desire. A baby possesses huge stores of energy, drive, excitement, and delight in the world. In too many adults, these riches have been depleted or robbed by people who blocked their growth and expression when they were children.

Margaret Mahler was one of the first to document the process whereby a child separates emotionally and psychologically from the parents and becomes an individual. This process is known as individuation. On this journey a child takes a series of steps away from the parent, combined with a series of returns for "refueling" or support. The goal of every child, and every person, is individuation. Part of the process of individuation for a child is coming to recognize that others are also individuals. In this way, a well-developed human can fulfill himself and allow others to fulfill themselves too, thereby creating a healthy family and, by extension, a healthy society.

Children have the right to develop to their fullest potential as individuals. They should not be defined by the goals and aspirations of others; they should not be limited by the critical judgment of others; and they should not be compared and contrasted with others. Rather, they should be respected as wholly unique persons with the capacity to achieve great things and the vision to change the world. Children's innate qualities should be allowed to develop along their own individual paths and, in so doing, enrich not only their own lives, but also the lives of others.

IN THE FAMILY

Parents often make the mistake of seeing their child as a reflection of themselves. The tiny baby they have brought into the world seems weak and vulnerable, and a parent's good instinct is to protect and guide the child. In so doing, however, parents often project their own insecurities onto their child. They may think one child is not smart enough and needs to be pushed harder. Another child may be too shy and needs to join more groups, while another child may be too much of a dreamer and needs to focus more on schoolwork. All of these thoughts that occur to parents are based on their concern for the child's welfare. However, they are also based on their own perception of the world, which of course is based on their personal experience and their own childhood.

The truth is that though children may be vulnerable and immature, they are fully people, even on the day they are born. Their feelings and their desires are just as valid as adults' feelings and desires. The only difference is their lack of experience and knowledge about the world. So, when a little boy wants to jump off the couch because he thinks he is Batman, his desire and motivation are valid, and his ideas are worthy of respect; the only part lacking is experience. He does not yet appreciate the danger involved in jumping off the couch. For the parent, the task is to validate the purpose and intent of the child, but to apprise him of the obstacles and protect him as he tries out his ideas.

Here is one approach a parent can take: "You don't know what you're doing. Stop jumping off the couch; that's a bad idea. You are not Batman. You will get hurt. Stop pretending; it's foolish, and I won't allow it. Take off that silly scarf; it's not even a real cape. Go and do something useful like cleaning your room." Here is another approach: "Hey, Batman, you're a great jumper, but the bookshelf is a little close so you might slam into it. Do you want to go outside and jump in the back yard? I can show you a place that's better to jump from." The difference in the two approaches is that the second parent respects the child's vision. He wishes to be a superhero, and she allows him to be one. When obstacles are in the way, she helps him find another way to do it. He is using his imagination and has created a story. He is putting his story into action. He is allowed to complete his goal.

The parent of the first child will probably find that when he becomes a young man he will be afraid to take chances. He will feel his ideas are not worth doing. He won't think much of his own individual dreams, as he will now have an inner voice telling him, "It's foolish, and I won't allow it." He may not achieve all the potential he had when he was born. Sadly, his parents have not allowed him to develop fully as a unique person. The parent of the second child will probably be very proud since her son is now a movie director or a CEO of a large company, where he is able to use his vision to create new exciting projects. He believes in himself as an individual who has a right to develop all his talents and abilities, and a duty to the world, and to himself, to accomplish all he can. When obstacles come his way, his inner voice tells him, "Come on, we can find a better way to do this."

SEEING CHILDREN AS REFLECTIONS OF OURSELVES

Parents often feel disappointed when their child is not what they imagine a child of theirs should be. Perhaps they feel their child is too withdrawn. He does not join in when they bring him to a group situation. One father may feel that he was too shy himself when he was little, and now he feels his son needs to be more outgoing, otherwise he will end up having the same problems. The father may fail to see the boy is actually very observant; he is watching and listening to everything people are doing and saying. At the park he finds tiny seeds and notices the little stripes on them and wonders why they are different from the other seeds. At story time he makes wonderful comments about why characters in a story do certain things. When someone makes a joke, he gets it right away and laughs heartily. He is not shy; he is observant and scientific in his approach and loves to figure out why things happen and why people do things the way they do. If the father recognizes and encourages his boy's individual talents, he may turn out to be a scientist, a writer, a psychotherapist, an architect, or something else—something that makes him happy and enriches the world.

Parents can see their child may look like them, may have some of the same physical attributes, and may also be endowed with some genetic gifts or weaknesses that their family carries from generation to generation. However, it is a parent's task to step back and accept that this little child, though she came directly from her body and is formed of her genetic material, is a completely whole person who may or may not follow in her parents' footsteps. Good parents all wish their child to have the same values they have. They will teach their child how to look at others and how to treat others. They will want the best for their child. They will almost always want her to have a better life than they themselves had. In their attempt to get that good life for their child, they must realize that the child will have the right to make decisions about what he or she wants and who she wants to become. Parents need to accept that their child has her own individual talents and dreams, which may be completely different from the dreams of her parents.

Parents should make every effort to realize they may have goals and fears, which belong rightly to them, not to their child. Many parents do not recognize that they are projecting their own hopes and anxieties on their children. As Jung said: "Nothing has a stronger influence psychologically on their environment and especially on their children than the unlived life of the parent." It is never a child's job to live that unlived life for her parents. We are all familiar with the "stage mother" who pushes her child to achieve success she herself did not have. Teachers are well acquainted with the father who does the child's school project for him. These parents are giving a not-so-subtle message to their children: "Your ideas are not as valuable as mine." This message is enough to hinder the child in his process of individuation. On the other hand, many loving parents support and nurture their child's talents and help them fulfill their individual potential. Leopold Mozart recognized the talents of his son Wolfgang and promoted his career unstintingly. Without his father's support, Wolfgang may not have blossomed the way he did.

Parents should try to be objective and see who their child really is. When they see their child express his opinions, they should validate those opinions. When a child says, "I hate pizza," a parent should not say, "No, you don't; everyone loves pizza!" When he says, "I don't want to play soccer," they should not say, "Why not? Don't you want to play like your brother?" When she says, "I love worms," they should not say, "Ugh, don't pick them up. They're disgusting." In every expression a child makes, a parent should try to see the nature of his likes and his dislikes and reflect them back to him. "Jill is very interested in worms, right Jill?" would be a good comment at family time. "Bobby likes soccer but Frank doesn't care for it," would be a great way for parents to talk about their children in each other's presence. In this way parents can validate who a child really is by his likes and dislikes, and differentiate between the siblings' likes and dislikes. Reflecting children's individual tastes and interests helps them see who they are and how they are unique. However, parents should not compare children unfavorably with each other or comment on their children's performance in such a way as to set them in competition with one another.

Families sometimes foster competitiveness between siblings. Some parents might think it a good idea to tell a younger child she needs to be more like her older sister. However, fostering competitiveness is not healthy for family relationships, it does not bring about lasting happiness, nor does it guarantee success. The Kennedys were notorious for the prevailing culture of competition in the family. According to Lawrence: "Competitiveness, in the world and against each other, was the overriding Kennedy family value." She says this may have led to the death of one of the family members, Joe Jr. She writes about the incident in which Jack (JFK) became a hero through his actions on a torpedo boat, where he saved the lives of twelve men. This heroic action, however, triggered a horrible chain of events:

> Jack returned to a hero's welcome. Bzdek says a friend found Joe Jr. crying upstairs in his room while downstairs the family was celebrating Jack's valor. Joe, a naval aviator, "started volunteering for riskier and riskier missions even after he was supposed to come home," Bzdek says. "He wanted to show his courage and really outshine his brother." Joe Jr. had been groomed to be the family's first political star. But in 1944, his explosives-laden plane detonated in flight, and he was killed. . . . Still determined to launch the Kennedy political brand, Joe (Sr.) moved on to Jack.[1]

The family competitiveness may or may not have caused Joe's death, but at the very least it damaged the relationship between the two brothers, since one could not celebrate the heroism of the other. Furthermore, this anecdote shows that Joe could not even empathize with his brother's injuries—JFK had been badly injured in the war incident and would suffer the rest of his life in pain because of it. Yet all that concerned Joe at that point was that his brother had outshone him. Parents who create this kind of family atmosphere should realize that setting one child in competition with another is the antithesis of family.

In a family, each member should be appreciated for who he or she is. And each member should be entitled to the love and support of the others, whatever life brings along. Siblings cannot support each other if their own self-esteem rises and falls in relation to the accomplishment of others. Children in these kinds of families must feel a very fragile sense of success even when they do accomplish something, for after all they must feel that they may be outdone by others at any time. Children who are appreciated by their parents for who they really are do not need to feel in danger of losing the support of others, because they will have internalized their parents approval into their own supportive ego. They will always feel they are good enough, even when they don't achieve fame or material success.

Competitiveness is a good thing, and children are naturally competitive. However, children tend to challenge themselves, not in relation to others, but to their own goals. If you watch children in a playground, you can see them testing their strength, practicing various moves and repeating things over and over in order to challenge themselves and improve their performance. They will often say things like, "Watch me! I can climb to the top now!" No one has told them they are expected to climb to the top. No one has asked them to please improve their performance and go one step further the next time. And yet, it is what they do. They are self-motivated improvers. They set their own goals and work hard to achieve them, without adults—and often even despite adults. Children can take on difficult tasks and follow through with amazing drive. The inner motivation of children will surprise those who allow them to take on difficult tasks.

Children can accomplish the most difficult tasks when they are motivated. I know one young boy whose father was often busy because of his work demands. When he was seven years old, he was disappointed because his bicycle had a flat tire, and he couldn't go riding. Since his father wasn't around to help he suddenly realized there was only one option if he wanted to use his bike—he could do it himself. So he called on his memories of watching his father fix a tire, and he followed all the steps, taking off the tire and tube and locating the puncture. He remembered how to apply the patch and put everything back into place, a difficult task for young hands. To this day he remembers the pride he felt on accomplishing this task without any guidance, and the exuberance he felt taking off on the bike he had fixed all by himself. Few people would even think of asking a seven-year-old child to fix a bicycle tire, and yet the boy set this difficult goal for himself and accomplished it. He did it by challenging himself and pushing himself harder than an adult would have pushed him.

What children need from adults is not advice, and not an overload of instruction, but the kind of support often called "scaffolding." Scaffolding is a supportive network of comments and guidance a parent or teacher can give a child. It is not invasive or directive. Scaffolding means keeping in mind the child's goal and supporting and guiding him as he reaches his goal. Sometimes this kind of support is also called "empathic attunement." This means the adult recognizes the child has a destination in mind and helps the child to find ways of getting there. This attunement might involve saying things like, "You're building a tower. You're putting the blocks on top of each other." When the blocks fall, the parent can say, "Maybe we need to see what's making them fall over. What do you think is happening here?" and "How could we fix this?"

Scaffolding interactions validate the child's goal and the child's individual approach to problems. They also make the child think more about what he wants to achieve and how to achieve it, and they allow a child to develop his own method of critical thinking. Parents can supply materials, show children where to find materials or how to look in books and find answers. All these supportive techniques help a child to develop his individual projects and to keep on challenging himself. Telling a child, "No you can't do that. It keeps falling down; you'll get hurt," or "Let me help you. I know how it's done," or "That's not working. Why don't you do something else?" or "I have a better idea: Let's make a house instead," are all ways of diverting the child from his goal or failing to support him and give him the tools to succeed in reaching that goal.

How many budding scientists, engineers, or architects have been diverted from their path in life by unsupportive adults? How many people lead frustrating lives because they are afraid to go for a job they would really love? How many people are filled with regret about the path not taken? They in all likelihood did not have the scaffolding they needed to help them understand that their talents can lead them in the direction they want to go, and the support to know they can do it despite the obstacles.

IN SCHOOL

In some schools children are treated as if they are not individuals. In fact, being an individual is often highly discouraged in particular kinds of schools. Most schools are driven by curriculum goals and have cultural goals. Children are expected to accumulate shared knowledge and attain certain cultural standards. This is often done in school. However, in some cultures, schools not only inculcate, they indoctrinate. In these kinds of schools, children are trained not to think as individuals but as members of a group. In certain countries, at certain times in history, schools have served to foster political goals and train children for their roles in society. In the early part of the twentieth century, British schools reinforced not only gender roles but also political goals. Marsden (2000) mentions the songs sung by young pupils on Empire Day during World War I:

> Even the babies' class had a contribution to make in setting an example, as illustrated in verse, song and play: "I want to be a soldier,/ With bayonet and gun,/ I want to cross the Channel,/ And fight this cruel Hun./ I'm much too old for playthings,/ Like whips and tops and bricks,/ I want to be a soldier,/ For, listen! I am six!"[2]

Japan's compulsory education system began in 1868, and its purpose was moral education. Children had to recite daily the various civic virtues, which they were expected to incorporate, such as filial piety, thriftiness, and subservience to the Emperor. When World War II began, the Japanese government turned the school system into a means of indoctrination. They did this through the manipulation of textbook contents and the daily recitation of virtues. There was a Bureau of Thought Supervision, now known as the Institute of National Training (Kokumin Renseijo), and this bureau supervised textbook content. The children were indoctrinated about the superiority of the Japanese and the proper role of Japan in the world. Immediately after the war, European occupation forces destroyed textbooks and introduced new, more international-minded virtues into the curriculum.

The Nazi regime in Germany also realized the importance of school in de-individualizing children. They developed the *Nazi Primer* for educating Hitler Youth. This book went further than other school primers since it did not allow for individual variations, not even physical ones. Hitler Youth not only had to think alike, but also had to look alike. Individuals were made to feel they had to belong to a group and to look like everyone else. They were told to judge themselves and others by how similar they were, even down to the texture of their hair. The results of this depersonalization are well documented. Rational humans when deprived of their power to exert their individuality often act irrationally.

These examples are from a time when political extremism reigned. Clearly, none of our schools today are busy developing a youth militia. However, they do indicate the danger of uniformity. Though they are dedicated to the welfare of the child, many schools tend to encourage uniform behavior and uniform standards. Certain schools stress uniform characteristics that pupils must have, and in so doing they minimize the importance of individual differences. It is true that inculcating shared values can build a strong and healthy community. On the other hand, when teachers and administrators balk at the idea of allowing children to be individuals, then children may not feel empowered to express their individual thoughts or voice their dissent.

Variety should be encouraged in schools just as it is in nature. When people are allowed to express their individual differences, the group becomes stronger. The more individual variations or differences of opinion a group can tolerate, the healthier the group will be. Darwin introduced the notion that "outbreeding," or genetic variance, improved the health and future survival capability of the species. Charlesworth and Willis (2009) explain that studies bear out Darwin's conclusion about variety:

> The survival and fertility of individuals in experimentally produced inbred lines is frequently so low that many such lines go extinct. When surviving lines are intercrossed, the "hybrids" often have higher quality than their inbred parents and frequently exceed the best parent values for several characters. This

> increased performance of first filial generation hybrids is called heterosis, or hybrid vigour.[3]

Nature itself desires variation, and plants, animals, and humans, all benefit from incorporating new or "foreign" elements. Intellectually there is no doubt that individuals who bring new ideas to a group can add to the group's store of knowledge and can add new perspectives to a discussion. If a group remains fiercely homogenous, and individuals are discouraged from query, dissent and divergence, then the group is likely to disintegrate or self-destruct, just as the Nazi regime did.

THE INDIVIDUAL IN THE GROUP

The school system should be dedicated to two purposes—allowing the individual to flourish and giving the individual strategies to work in a group. However, most school systems operate from a strictly "top-down" philosophy. This kind of system is designed to maintain order and control group dynamics so that the traditions, structure, and goals of the group are preserved over time. In these groups the individual knows at the outset or learns pretty quickly that the institution matters more than the individual.

Children who attend traditional schools with long histories find out right away that "We don't do things that way; we do things this way." This may not necessarily be a bad thing. For instance children who attend a school dedicated to social justice may be told, "We do things to help other people," and this is a good thing. However, even in a school with healthy goals, the individuality of the child must be respected. Let's say this school of social justice has a policy such as, "Individual children cannot come up with new ideas for helping others; they must only do it in the ways we have decided and on the days that we have decided." This is not a healthy school. If, on the other hand this kind of school believes that "We want children to come up with new ideas for helping others in the community; we want to keep changing and growing," then that is a school that is helping individuals be individuals within a group.

COMPLIANCE AND DISSENT

One of the problems of "top-down" educational systems is that critical thinking is not encouraged, and children are encouraged to be compliant members of the group. It is understandable that teachers need to have control of group situations. Children by nature can be egocentric, and like an orchestra conductor, a teacher has to understand that there are many different voices that need to be heard within the group, some loud and dominant, and some weak and timid. This group management is not an easy task for a teacher. Many schools avoid the challenge altogether. They prefer to keep the orchestra silent and allow the conductor to be the voice of the class. There is no time for questioning, and dissent is not encouraged. In this way teachers cover a lot of territory, and the children just have to keep up. There is a serious problem with this kind of system, since many children feel they are not a part of the class and feel they are not recognized as individuals. They also don't feel involved in what the teacher is trying to teach.

In good schools, usually where there is plenty of funding, teachers are able to allow more time for individual attention to students. In other schools, children quickly grow to feel they are not a part of school, and school becomes boring to them. School dropout rates are increasing, particularly in the wake of increased emphasis on school testing. For many children, school is not a place where they feel like participants. If individual students felt they were included in the classroom or that their needs were being met, they would undoubtedly feel less detached and more likely to remain in school.

COMPETITIVENESS AND COOPERATION

Another problem with this kind of schooling in which individual variation is not valued is that competitiveness with other students is encouraged. The pattern in these schools is that there is a "right" answer that the teacher is in possession of, and the children are expected to participate in frequent competitions to supply this answer. The one who gets the answer the teacher seeks is praised. This Q&A format is common in most schools, and often there is a system of numerical or alphabetic grading—some people are considered "A" students; some are labeled "D" students. This kind of system is not designed to develop critical thinking; rather, it is designed to develop quick response and the ability to access information in response to challenge. Critical thinking and a questioning attitude are healthy in any organization. When schools are too concerned with children meeting set standards, there is little time for reflection and analysis.

In itself this system has many failings. The first thing wrong with it is the way children are set in competition with each other. If competitiveness in the family is bad, it is also bad for the classroom. If indeed school is meant to acculturate and prepare children to be members of society, then teaching them to compete against each other is not a good plan. Teaching children how to work well with others and gain their cooperation in order to achieve agreed-upon goals would be a much better plan. Most people work, not in isolation, but in conjunction with others, and most people need to get along with others in their daily work routines. Getting along with others, motivating others, supervising others, collaborating with others, communicating well with others, asserting your needs with others, hearing others' needs—all these abilities are important to people in their daily lives. Children need to learn how to communicate effectively with others, and since school is where children interact in groups, then school would be the ideal place to teach these social skills.

Setting children in competition with each other does not allow for the individual to develop her own abilities to the fullest, nor does it allow her to develop as a healthy member of a group. In fact, setting one child up against others by saying, "You're the best girl in the class," or "You're at the bottom of the class," is a way of creating problems for her, whether she is the "best" or the "worst." When a child feels she has to be in competition with others, then she cannot admit her weakness.

If a child thinks she has to be the best in class, then she can never say, "I don't know the answer," and she can't say, "I didn't understand that. Could you explain it again?" Similarly, if a child feels she is the worst in class, she can't ask those questions either. This is a problem, since children should be able to ask questions in class. Being able to know what you don't understand and being able to put your finger on what you don't know, are necessary talents for intellectual pursuit. I recently attended a board meeting in which a new board member said, "I feel stupid asking, but what does this line mean here in the budget?" Once she asked it, another board member said, "You know, I always wondered what that was, but I thought everyone else knew, so I was afraid to ask." That board member had attended for years, and though he was an adult, he was afraid to question something just because he thought he was the only one who didn't get it. The new board member had the courage to admit there was something she didn't know, and her doubt helped others to learn something.

When pupils ask questions, teachers can benefit from knowing how well they are getting the lesson across. Feedback from students should be encouraged and factored into the daily routine. If a child felt able to say to a teacher, "What did you mean by that?" or "I understood everything except the part at the end," the teacher would be able to refine her techniques and communicate better the next time. In addition, the child will come to understand the lesson. If there is an atmosphere of competitiveness, children will be motivated by fear of failure. Children will be afraid to show others what they don't know. In these kinds of classrooms, cheating will be seen as a way to survive. If a child feels his individual qualities are being valued he will be less likely to cheat. If he feels he is being judged only on what he knows of the material, he may try to get one over on the system.

When children are under pressure to compete with others, rather than allowed to use their own natural desire to excel, they can suffer psychologically. Some schools promote this intense competition. Teens can be under a great deal of pressure socially and emotionally. If they are also under pressure to perform at school, this may add to their burden. Drug and alcohol abuse are on the rise in teenagers. Suicide in teens has been rising steadily, and according to the Centers for Disease Control and Prevention, it is the third leading cause of death, behind accidents and homicide, of people aged fifteen to twenty-four, and it is the fourth leading cause of death for children between the ages of ten and fourteen. Children at these ages could benefit from a school system that recognized their individual talents and encouraged them in positive ways, rather than setting them in competition with others.

When children feel they have to prove they are better than others, they are not learning how to cooperate. It's every child for himself in that kind of environment. A friend who attended a top Ivy League university told me that students would tear pages out of library books so other students could not compete with them. In an environment where people learn how to cooperate, those students would not need to resort to vandalism to achieve their goals. When people desperately need to prove something to the world, they are not contributing much to society. When people realize they can gain strength from one another or that they have something to give other people, they are likely to live happy, productive lives.

A NEW DEFINITION OF INTELLIGENCE

The top-down, results-based, Q&A-style system is not congruent with how intelligence really works. Current thinking is that I.Q. testing is not a good indicator of intelligence. A new term widely used among educational researchers is "Executive Function." Executive Function is a description of the way human intelligence works at the highest level. The term describes the various most effective functions of intelligence—for instance, the ability to be flexible, the ability to prioritize tasks and categorize and manage information, the ability to manage emotions and the ability to vary one's reaction in order to respond in different ways to different situations.

A key part of Executive Function is knowing how to be flexible and to react appropriately, according to the situation. In other words, the intelligent thing to do is to respond to each individual crisis according to what is really happening. In the old days this function was known as "common sense." Common sense meant the ability to know that everything in the books might indicate one response, but an overriding sense of what works best might indicate a different response. This is similar to the way Executive Function works. When an individual uses her Executive Function, she can say that though she's read all the rules and knows all the facts, she is going to go in a different direction. At times there may be a human aspect involved in her decision, or she may be taking a long term view of a situation where others are taking the short term view. Or she may have to decide between the good of one person and the good of the majority.

There has been much discussion about left- and right-brain thinking. People can use their analytical powers and can use their intuitive powers. Law enforcement agents often read non-verbal cues instinctively, and this can lead them to find the truth, despite other apparently logical clues that lead in a different direction. Combining both kinds of thinking can be very effective. If an individual trusts in his own thought process and knows how to access all the aspects of his intelligence, he is more likely to come up with good solutions than one who relies on one kind of thinking. Thinking of intelligence as Executive Function brings us to realize the importance of the individual response.

INDIVIDUAL LEARNING STYLES

Since schools often focus on things like memorization and information acquisition, they tend to overlook other important aspects of intelligence, such as emotional intelligence, creativity, and critical thinking. These qualities are complex and present themselves in varied ways in children. So, teaching everyone the same thing, and in the same way, does not make sense. Children also have different study styles. Some children like to be up early, and these children function well first thing in the morning. Others like to stay up late and study. Some like to be organized and get homework done as soon as it is allocated. Others tend to leave it until the last minute. Some like to work in silence and others need to have music playing, some study well in a group, others in isolation. No style is right, and no style is wrong.

I remember beating myself up at school for my tendency to read the research material and put off doing the writing until the last minute. Sunday evenings were torture for me, since I felt so guilty at not having the paper done, and I would berate myself for being a bad student. No matter how bad I felt, I just could not force myself to do the writing until the eleventh hour. The only consolation was that the paper would arrive easily, almost formed, in need of a few revisions. It is only in the last few years that I realized what was going on. It was with great relief that I accepted that I had an internal process that had its own logic. Once the material was read, my brain was digesting the information, so to speak. The material was being organized and prioritized, classified, sorted, and edited.

Maybe this happened when I was asleep, or when I was walking or showering, etc. In any case, I came to the conclusion that my brain was busy working on my projects even when I was not aware of it. I was happy to realize I was not lazy at all; I was doing the right thing by responding to my internal voice, which told me, "Hold on. The paper is not ready yet; it's still cooking." Now that I understand my own method of working, I am more relaxed and more confident in my own abilities. It would be beneficial if children were taught about their individual differences. If children understood their own learning styles, the way their own individual brain works, they would be happier and better students. They would have more trust in themselves as students, and, being in touch with how they work, they could maximize productivity.

MULTIPLE INTELLIGENCES

A third failing of schools that suppress the individual is that intelligence is defined as one thing, and one thing only. Generally, in those schools, you are intelligent if you can read, write, and do math. In fact, there are many different personalities, and within each personality is a combination not only of temperament and style, but also of different kinds of intelligence. Howard Gardner is a well-known researcher and writer who came up with the concept of "multiple intelligences." He recognized that there are many different kinds of intelligence, including: logical-mathematical intelligence; linguistic intelligence; spatial intelligence; musical intelligence; kinesthetic intelligence; and personal intelligences—interpersonal feelings (understanding how others interact) and intrapersonal intelligence (understanding one's own feelings and motivations). He maintains that these kinds of intelligence can be present in any combination within any individual. Since all intelligences are valuable contributors to society, then none should be considered more important than another. He also believes that these different intelligences interact with each other in different ways within each individual.

A famous Irish writer, educator, and political leader, Padraic Pearse, founded a school in Dublin in the early part of the twentieth century. His treatise "The Murder Machine" describes his attitude to the British system of education then in force in Ireland. He was an innovator, very much ahead of his time, since he valued the individual talents of children. He felt that the educational system of the time was a machine that swallowed children up and turned them out like manufactured items ready for consumption. He believed children should develop along natural lines:

> I knew one boy who passed through several schools a dunce and a laughing-stock; the National Board and the Intermediate Board had sat in judgment upon him and had damned him as a failure before men and angels. Yet a friend and fellow-worker of mine discovered that he was gifted with a wondrous sympathy for nature, that he loved and understood the ways of plants, that he had a strange minuteness and subtlety of observation—that, in short, he was the sort of boy likely to become an accomplished botanist. I knew another boy of whom his father said to me, "He is no good at books, he is no good at work; he is good at nothing but playing a tin whistle. What am I to do with him?" I shocked the worthy man by replying (though really it was the obvious thing to reply), "Buy a tin whistle for him."[4]

It does seem quite obvious that if a child is good at something and enjoys doing something, then she should be encouraged to do it. Motivation is a key aspect of learning, and if a child is already motivated before she begins working on a subject she will be more likely to work harder and achieve more.

In most schools, children are not included in the learning process. They are not asked what they want to learn, and they are not consulted on how they feel they are doing or how they feel they need to improve. They are expected to aim at goals that are set for them and judged on how they achieve those goals. Since children have an internal motivation to begin with, it makes more sense to align the teaching with the child's motivation. For instance, if a child likes gathering sticks at recess time, wouldn't that be a good jumping-off point for a teacher? Teachers could look at various kinds of sticks, relate them to various kinds of trees, look at books about trees, read and write the names of trees, and jump on to a study of trees. Maybe the child would be interested in building with sticks and explore different kinds of architecture and construction, which can incorporate math and reading activities. This kind of teaching does occur in certain schools where the value of the individual child's interest is recognized.

If there are different kinds of intelligence, and each intelligence works in different combinations, and if each child has a different personality and different emotions, then it follows that each child is truly unique, and each child brings different interests and talents to the school setting. Each individual child is working in different ways to develop his talents and improve himself along his own unique path. Since most schools tend to prioritize certain subjects without regard for the child's interests and inclinations, it is no wonder most children think school is boring.

CREATIVE THINKERS

There are many individuals who do not take well to school at all. One of those people was Albert Einstein. Einstein had a series of creative insights into the relationships among the elements of the universe. These insights had a profound effect on scientific thought and changed some of science's basic assumptions. He was able to ask and answer a question most teachers at the time would have laughed at: "Why is the sky blue?" He proposed a notion most teachers would have sneered at and dismissed: "Is time relative?"

Einstein did not like the regimented atmosphere of school. According to his biographer Burnham (2005): "In school, Einstein stood apart from other students. He was slow in learning to talk, speaking with noticeable hesitation as late as nine years old. He had little interest in things apart from science and mathematics. More significantly, he rebelled, both quietly and openly, against the regimentation and authority common in German schools at the time."[5] Einstein's own words make abundantly clear how he felt. Abbott and Gillen (2000) report that Einstein recalled later in life that a progressive Swiss school he attended nurtured his intellect better than the more regimented German school:

> By its liberal spirit and by the simple seriousness of its teachers, unsupported as they were by any outward authority, this school has left unforgettable impressions on me. Comparison with six years' schooling at a German authoritarian *Gymnasium,* made me clearly recognise how much superior an education towards free action and personal responsibility is to one relying on outward authority and ambition. True democracy is no empty illusion.[6]

Einstein himself recognized the importance of a school that allowed individual development. His insights were so intensely intuitive, while at the same time analytical, and they could never have developed in an atmosphere of compliance. If Einstein had really believed that his teachers knew best, he would not have asked the kinds of questions he did. His famous quotes, such as "The only real valuable thing is intuition" and "Imagination is more important than knowledge," indicate that he knew the value of the individual in the intellectual process.

Thomas Edison was not happy in school either. He disrupted the teacher's agenda by his constant wondering, "Why?" His school was not designed to allow for the individual to express himself, much less to develop his incredible intelligence, and so he did his creative work in his own time. John Lennon, whose music has inspired millions, and who is known and loved worldwide as a uniquely creative individual, was considered a troublemaker and a failure in school. According to an article in the Daily Mail (2008), his teachers stated in his reports that he was: "Certainly on the road to failure . . . hopeless . . . rather a clown in class . . ."

This same article shows how his teacher thought of the poet and novelist Robert Graves. His final report says: "Well, goodbye, Graves, and remember that your best friend is the wastepaper basket." Winston Churchill's teacher said: "He has no ambition. If he were to exert himself he might yet be first at the end of term. Very truthful, but a regular 'pickle' in many ways at present . . . Is a constant trouble to everybody and is always in some scrape or other. He cannot be trusted to behave himself anywhere." These teachers did not notice the individual strengths possessed by these people, who all went on to contribute greatly to the world. From the tone of the reports they wrote, we can tell they were generally disappointed that the individuals involved did not fit into the system. It is even more unfortunate that these teachers did not have any insight into the emotional needs each of these children had and did not contribute at all to helping them work with their difficulties. One can only imagine how a good teacher could have channeled the boy who was a "clown in class" and helped him to develop his ability to make others laugh. Fortunately these three people had enough inner strength to survive school's negative feedback and allow their own individual qualities to shine.

There are many individuals who are termed "learning disabled," though in fact it should be said that they are differently abled. This is not just a politically correct term; it is a statistically correct term. It is a documented fact that a large number of children have difficulty learning in the ways that school systems dictate. According to the Dyslexia Health Web site, 15–20 percent of the population has dyslexia. We need to bear in mind that these are the cases that are diagnosed, for in many cases dyslexia is not diagnosed at all. If one in every five children has this "disability," then it properly should not be considered a disability. It should be considered a different ability, particularly as there is no relationship with intelligence, and many dyslexic children are high achievers and highly intelligent, innovative thinkers.

There are other obstacles a child may have to learning in a regular school environment, such as Attention Deficit Disorder. These children are also intelligent, and many of them, such as David Neeleman, founder of JetBlue Airways and inventor of the "e-ticket," have come to think of their "disability" as an asset. Neeleman actually believes his "ADHD" is what helps him to achieve. He "calls ADHD one of his greatest assets," according to Anne Underwood in an article called "The Gift of ADHD." The article goes on to document other examples of the benefits of this kind of personality: "'People with this kind of style make good entrepreneurs,' says another ADHD-diagnosed successful businessman who believes that making snap decisions can be a strength. He claims that people like him are successful 'because we think out of the box. . . . Impulsivity isn't always that bad.'" [7]

Craig Ventner hated school and felt he was no good at anything and, according to his biography, got C's and D's on his reports. He was so bored and disengaged that he left high school and became a surfer. After a while he felt an interest in completing his studies, so he returned to community college and pursued his natural interest in science. The rest of the story is well documented, as Craig went on to be the first person to sequence the human genome. Currently the Ventner Institute is working on the world's first replicating synthetic bacterial cell. This will be a somewhat miraculous breakthrough and will create options for the future that have seemed only possible in science fiction. Craig Ventner has repeatedly been listed as one of the most influential people in the world. In 2010 the British New Statesman Magazine listed him in the top fifty of the "World's Most Influential Figures." The story of Craig Ventner is another indicator of how our schools are often wildly out of touch with the value of individual differences and the limitless potential of children.

It seems logical to say that if a school caters only to 80 percent or fewer of the students and ignores the needs of the others, then that school or the entire school system itself may be considered disabled. Disabled schools are those in which the average dominates, the majority are motivated to maintain an attitude of superiority, and the individual is not encouraged to express his difference or dissent.

PROTECTING A CHILD'S RIGHT TO INDIVIDUAL DEVELOPMENT

In the Family

Parents should encourage children to understand their individual selves, both emotional and intellectual. They should reflect back to their children what they see and validate their child's unique self. Here are some things parents can do:

- Allow children to express likes and dislikes openly without criticism from the other family members. Never say, "No, you can't possibly like pink shoes," or "We all like swimming. Why don't you?"
- Reflect back the child's likes and dislikes in ways that show you permit the child to have likes and dislikes. For instance: "I love Jell-O, but you hate it. Right, John?"
- Allow for individual differences in the family but do not set children in competition with one another. When you refer to the individual differences it should be positive, non-judgmental and non-preferential. For instance: "Joyce finds reading very difficult. It seems to come easier to you, John."
- Allow that more than one family member can be good at the same thing. Avoid saying things like, "Joyce is the artistic one; John is the reader." In some families more than one child excels at the same thing. Though they are all different individuals, the Wayans brothers collaborated on the TV show *In Living Color* and were all great contributors. The Bronte sisters were all writers.
- At group family time, refer to each child's inner workings, not their performance or their outward appearance. For instance, refer to or ask what a child is feeling or thinking, what a child prefers or likes instead of how they performed in their school exam.
- Play the "Five Senses" game. This is where each person takes turns saying three things they love to hear, see, smell, taste, and touch. Then three things they dislike to smell, hear, etc. This process helps children know what they feel and gives them the confidence to trust their own instincts and feelings. In addition it can lead parents to understand what frightens or worries children. Children may say revelatory things like, "I hate that girl in school. She teases me every day," or even, "I hate when Mom and Dad yell"—things that let parents see what's going on inside.
- Family traditions are a good thing, since they bind people together and help make shared memories. However, traditions can be stifling if they are set from the top down and don't allow for divergence or individual needs. Children should be involved in helping to create the traditions, and they should be allowed to bring in changes. A tradition can only stay alive and meaningful if it includes all the individuals in the family, and if it changes and remains flexible as the individuals grow and change. If you ask your teenage child to come help pick out a Christmas tree and she would rather meet her boyfriend, then you need to let go of some old traditions and start to think of new ones. Your teenage daughter might be more ready to start a

new tradition, such as baking a cake for the holidays or picking out the tree by herself with her boyfriend's help.

- Discourage labels in the family and allow children to define themselves in their own terms. If you hear an aunt or grandparent saying to a child, "Oh, you are your mother all over again," make sure you comment that your child is an individual, and though she may resemble her mother, she is a unique person. Children can be made to feel small by relatives who compare them to other family members, and though this is done with good intent, it should be corrected so the child retains her feeling of individuality.
- Discourage stereotyping. "You are such a clown" or "You never get up on time" may not be intended to do so, but they are in effect ways of stifling an individual's growth. If a person feels she is a clown then she will feel that certain doors are closed to her and may not even try to have others take her seriously.

In School

When young children enter school, they have a real need to be seen as individuals. If a teacher makes an observation or positive comment about one child, others will often say, "Say that about me too." I remember saying to a three-year-old child, "James, your eyes are a beautiful shade of green." A little girl sitting next to him said, "What about me? What color are mine?" Pretty soon everyone wanted to hear a comment about how they looked. They very much want to know who they are in the eyes of the world, and they want to know the world sees their individuality and unique qualities. It is a basic need to be seen as unique and have your individuality validated. Teachers can help a great deal to make the child feel like a unique individual. It can be a struggle for children to develop their own individuality. They want to separate from their parents and become their own person. They do not understand how it is possible to be fully an individual, and yet at the same time accept another person's individuality. Teachers need to help children to work towards this goal.

- In the Early Childhood setting, teachers can make sure every child's name is displayed prominently—children love to see their own names.
- Children like to see their work displayed and should be consulted on where they want it to be hung if possible.
- Children should have their own cubbies and be able to decorate their cubbies with pictures of themselves and have their drawings displayed.

- Teachers can talk about differences and similarities, but they should stress not outward appearance but inner thoughts and feelings.
- Children should be encouraged to talk about their favorite things. Teachers can ask them to talk about games they like to play with parents, what things scare them, and how they feel about numbers, colors, foods, and so on.
- Young children often bring in "transitional objects" to preschool—perhaps a raggedy blanket or a cuddly toy. These objects are almost sacred objects to a small child, as they represent him and are outward images of him as an individual. They should be treated as important objects by the teacher, who can, however, set her own rules that limit use of the object in a reasonable way. For instance: "Play with Blankie for a while, and then put Blankie in your cubby till rest time." Or "Bunny can't sit at the table with you but she can sit on the shelf and watch you eat lunch."
- Children should be allowed to develop independence skills. Taking a few minutes and waiting for a child to put on his own shoes gives him a sense of being an individual with the growing ability to take care of himself.
- As children grow older, their talents and preferences will start to emerge. Sadly, school tends to get more restrictive, as children are pressed to learn to read, write and prepare for standardized tests. "Show and Tell" is a great old school tradition that allows time for children to talk about items that mean something special for them. One young boy I know wanted to be a paleontologist—he could say that word at age three. He brought in dinosaur toys and books at Show and Tell, and the other children became interested. The whole class became "paleontologists," digging in the sand table for "fossils." In the second half of the year he became a knight, and the class followed him and changed roles accordingly. Pretty soon their vocabulary included moats, gauntlets, and portcullises.
- Small groups could work on projects where each individual plays a different role—one child might draw, the other might write, a third might build or do calculations, and so on.
- Homework should not be a boring assignment that makes children feel stressed. Instead of having children repeat work done in school, teachers could have children do research projects or write personal reflections on the lessons. These personal reflections could be done in the form of collages, videos, or photographs, as well as written work. Children could be allowed to pick topics that relate to their life, family history, or ambitions.
- Children should be encouraged to think about what makes them different as a learner—what is the best place for them to study, do they like music playing or silence, what helps them to remember things, what things in school tend to stay with them, or do they study best in the morning or late in the evening?

- Children should be encouraged to ask questions. And they should be praised for asking, since it shows they are interested. Children should never be told, "That's a silly question." Generally speaking the teacher needs to see the intent behind the question.
- Teachers can help troubled children to turn their lives around by helping them to use their individual talents productively. I recently saw a documentary about a famous actor who was in trouble with the law as a teenager. He was lucky enough to have a teacher, a priest, who cared a great deal about him. The teacher attended his court appearance where he awaited sentencing for yet another petty crime. The boy cried in court and told the judge he had learned his lesson. He assured the judge that this was a turning point in his life, and he promised never to err again. The judge felt sorry for him and suspended his sentence. As he turned away, he winked at the priest and gave him a big grin, as if to say, "I pulled one over on him." The teacher later confronted the boy and told him he should be an actor, since he had given such a great performance in court. He followed the teacher's advice. Today he makes millions of dollars with his acting and returns a great deal of money to his teacher's charitable work. We need more teachers like this who truly help children to develop as individuals.
- Group-building exercises can allow children to comment on what they like about each other. This helps children to gain a sense of who they are and how they appear to others. Comments should be positive.

Everyone Is an Individual

When children feel truly unique, they feel truly human and can accept the humanity of others. While respecting a child's individuality, adults must help children respect the individuality of others. Children are unique individuals, but they need to learn that everyone else is an individual too.

Notes

1. Lawrence, J. abcnews.go.com/Politics/story?id=8422580&page=2. <AuQ: Accessed date?>

2. Marsden, W. (2000). "'Poisoned History': A Comparative Study of Nationalism, Propaganda and the Treatment of War and Peace in the Late Nineteenth and Early Twentieth Century School Curriculum." *History of Education* 29:1, 29–47.

3. Charlesworth, D., and Willis, J. (2009). "The Genetics of Inbreeding Depression." *Genetics* 10, 783–796.

4. Pearse, P. (1905). "*The Murder Machine: The Bodenstown Series No. 2.*" Dublin, UK: Irish Freedom Press.

5. Burnham, R. (2005). "The Man Who Remade the Universe." *Astronomy* 33:2, 38–45.

6. Abbott, L., and Gillen, J. (2000). "Put the Baby Genius Kits in the Bin." *Annual Meeting of the European Conference on Quality in Early Childhood Education*, London, UK.

7. Underwood, A. (2005). "The Gift of ADHD?" *Newsweek*, March 14.

Chapter 4

Children Have the Right to Boundaries

Children are human beings with the right to have their boundaries respected. When children are very young their bodies need to be cared for by others, and so they need to be picked up, fed, cleaned and dressed, held, and protected until such time as they are capable of supporting their own bodies and taking care of themselves. This need does not give any person the right to handle a child without regard to his personal integrity as a human being. Even very small children have a sense of their own dignity, and though they are usually powerless to protest, they do have a strong and lasting awareness of the injuries to self-esteem that come from being manhandled or disrespected.

A child's boundaries are of the same importance as an adult's boundaries. A child has the right to personal boundaries; his body is his alone, and he should be consulted and informed with regard to its treatment. A child has the right to personal property, and his property and sense of ownership should be respected. A child has the right to privacy and personal space. A child has his own sense of time; a child's sense of time should be respected while adults require him to coordinate with their schedules. A child has the right to learn about the boundaries of others. Children need to learn to respect the personal space, time, and property of others, and in order to do so they should be told when they are overstepping the line. Knowing how to respect others' boundaries will ultimately safeguard a child and prevent him from getting himself in trouble.

THE CHILD'S BODY

A child is born physically helpless. He cannot move around without assistance of others. He cannot even control his own body movements; his hands swing wildly around, scratching his own face. He can look at things he wants but cannot move toward them. He cannot obtain the sustenance necessary to keep himself alive, and when sustenance comes close, he cannot even grasp it but must have it inserted into his mouth for him. We cannot say for certain how a child feels about all this, but we can tell from our own feelings of helplessness that, when things go wrong in our lives, that lack of control is deeply disturbing to us. Anyone who has been hospitalized and unable to move can attest to the fact that being physically at the mercy of others is not an optimal situation. Many of us have nightmares where we are unable to walk or are trapped and unable to escape, and these feelings of panic show us how important our control over physical freedom really is.

When a mother handles a baby, she is giving him unspoken messages about his body. Babies can be handled carelessly or with respect. They can be carried under the arm like a football or cradled gently close to the mother's face. These ways of holding a baby give the baby information about how his body matters to his mother and, by extension, to the world. When a mother dresses a baby, she can pull the shirt hard over his face to get it off quickly, or she can wangle it gently and make eye contact with the baby to make sure he does not feel scared having his face covered by the shirt—something many babies find frightening.

As a baby grows, parents have a great deal of physical interaction with his body. They need to bathe, dress, carry, feed, and lift him from one place to another. During these interactions a child is sensing how his body is treated. He notices if he is thrown down into his crib without regard for how he might land. He notices if he is talked to gently while having his diaper changed. He notices if hands come in and grab him too often or someone comes too close to his face making loud noises. Parents are not perfect; none of us knows how a baby feels exactly, and well-meaning parents can make mistakes. A few years ago it was considered the right thing to do to place a baby on her stomach to sleep; now it is considered unsafe. Swaddling babies was considered the right thing to do in the past; now of course it is not recommended at all. Parents who try to do the right thing based on their own knowledge are not abusive parents, and they are not disrespecting the baby's personal boundaries. They are doing their best, based on the information they have at hand.

The difference between parents who engage in unsafe practices, thinking they are doing the right thing, and parents who disrespect a child's boundaries is a clear one. Respectful parents are those who make an effort to imagine how they themselves would feel if someone treated them in this way. A child will not suffer long-term harm from being laid on his stomach by a loving parent who thinks she is doing the right thing, but he will suffer emotional damage from being thrown rudely onto the crib or having his shirt yanked off roughly. Those actions tell the baby he does not matter. His body is not to be respected.

As a child grows, so should his independence and his sense of self-esteem. A child's self-esteem is intricately connected with his body. Though a child is created within a woman's body and is a part of her body at one point, when he is born, his body is now his own. Parents of young children need to respect and encourage a child's sense of ownership of his body. Ownership expresses itself in a desire for autonomy, which is very healthy and should be encouraged. There are few things more distressing than seeing parents walking children on a leash, and yet it still happens. Though it is a very difficult stage for parents to endure when a child thinks he can do anything and is invincible, parents must allow the child to have as much physical freedom as possible while also creating safe boundaries for him.

When I took my daughter into the swimming pool with me at age two, she was sure she could swim and kicked and flailed at me so she could get out of my arms and swim away. Naturally I could not let her do it since she might drown. On the other hand, I wanted to encourage her spirit of endeavor and desire for physical independence. It was a real struggle—I had to let go for short bursts and allow her to try to swim but keep my hands underneath to catch her all the while. It was a real balancing act—I had to balance my fear against my wish for her to be independent. Creating boundaries for a child of this age involves a lot of work for parents. You have to be extremely close but appear to be far away. You have to keep children in your sights but act as if you are not worried and as if they are doing it all by themselves.

Some parents do not respect a child's need for physical autonomy. This kind of parent will resort to grabbing rather than talking to a child. I have seen parents walk over to a child in the playground, tell him it's time to go and plonk him into a stroller and strap him in. However, this may not be disrespectful to the child at all. This action may have been the end of a long chain of negotiation. Perhaps the parent reminded the child they would be leaving soon; perhaps she gave the child a two-minute warning; perhaps she had asked the child once too many times. At that point it might be a parent's last resort to pick the child up and put him in the stroller. It would not be too startling to see such a child kick and scream and try to escape his imprisonment. This parent has tried to respect the child's boundaries by telling him they were leaving, preparing him for departure, and giving him choices. A parent who is put in the position of having to place the child in the stroller can still treat a child respectfully. She can say, "I don't like grabbing your body, but I have asked you to leave, and you are not listening to me, so I am going to count to three. If you can't cooperate I will have to pick you up and put you in the stroller." When she counts to three and nothing happens, she can just say, "I'm sorry to do this, but I need to put you in your stroller now." Making sure she expresses her dislike of manhandling takes the real sting out of it, and giving the child a choice makes him a partner in the action so his boundaries are intact. He has, in effect, made the choice to resist.

Real disrespect for a child's boundaries occurs when a child is busy playing in the park, and the parent comes along and grabs him without warning or previous discussion. No words are exchanged; the parents uses his own body to control his child's body and does not explain anything to the child. This child is probably used to being grabbed and often does not fight at all but just looks depressed or helpless and goes along with these aggressive actions passively. When a child is fighting or throwing a tantrum, he is demonstrating that he has the ability to fight back. He may lose, but at least he will go down kicking and screaming. A child whose physical boundaries are routinely disrespected is usually passive or depressive. Being used to having his boundaries crossed, he does not feel entitled to respect, and so he does not even fight.

When children begin to gather in groups—in playgrounds and in schools—they need to be taught that everyone has the right to have their body respected. Adults should validate their rights and let them know it is not acceptable for others to sit on top of them, step over them, or push them aside in order to get somewhere first. They also need to know not to put their hands too close to other people's faces or otherwise invade other people's circle of comfort. Parents and teachers can help children to express their right to that boundary. They can teach children to say, "Please don't touch me," if they are being touched and don't like it. Children can learn to say, "Can you move please?" if they want to get through someone else's space. And they can learn to yell, "Stop!" if someone is physically harassing them or their wrestling play goes too far.

PRIVACY AND THE BODY

Even though children cannot express this need until they get a little older, children have a right to privacy regarding their body. That simply means children should be consulted about being touched or having their clothes removed. A parent does not have to get written permission to put on a child's pajamas, but she should always make sure the child is treated with consideration of his boundaries. Parents can simply do "voiceovers" as they go along, for instance: "OK, let me help you with your top. Here we go. If you put your hands up, I can help pull this over your head. Oops . . . sorry. I didn't mean to scare you." Doing a "narration" helps to explain to a child how and why a parent is helping him dress or undress and shows the parent accepts that a child's body is his own, but he needs a little support until he can be independent. It also indicates to the child that a parent feels she owes it to the child to explain what is happening to him since it's his body, and he has a right to know what is going on. When a parent thinks it is fine to pull clothes on and off a child without words and explanation, it is a breach of a child's boundaries. A child needs to be consulted in matters of his body. When he is too young to be consulted, he should receive explanations and gentle treatment.

Children often don't like to go to the doctor's office. Though there are some wonderful and empathic pediatricians, there are also many medical practitioners who think nothing of coming close to a child and touching her body without asking permission. They would not even dream of doing this to an adult, and yet they feel it is perfectly fine to lift up a child's shirt and put a stethoscope on her chest without asking if it's OK or explaining the need for doing it. This kind of person will often rebuke a child for cringing away from him and remind her she shouldn't make a fuss since it's not going to hurt. A child is not only afraid of being hurt; she is also not comfortable at having strangers touch her body without permission. Going into the hospital can be traumatizing for young children, who have no control over what happens to their own bodies. If adults feel helpless in the hospital, a child must feel much more so. To a child, having adults reach over and grab you without your permission, and without warning, is threatening and uncomfortable.

Forcing children to kiss or hug others is overstepping their boundaries. While it is a terrific idea to teach children how to say hello and how to respond warmly when others say hello, enforced hugging and kissing is not a good thing. If a parent could step back for a second and ask himself if he would do this with his adult friends then he will know whether it's appropriate. Imagine you are at a party and your old school friend comes up. Ask yourself if you would say to your spouse, "Give this stranger here a kiss. I know you don't know him, but I do, so don't worry. Just go ahead and do it." If you wouldn't say it to an adult, then don't say it to a child. Most children have a healthy reserve and a suspicion of strangers, and making them hug and kiss people they don't know is tantamount to telling them to disregard their natural instincts. These same parents often put a lot of effort into teaching children to be wary of strangers when they grow older.

Some people might argue that children do not have a sense of their own physical boundaries until they get older. However, this is not true. Children do have an innate awareness of their own dignity, even though they cannot verbalize it. Recently a five-year-old boy I know started kindergarten. Though this school is considered not to be an enlightened school, the boy was distressed at the way his body was being shuffled around and the way he was not being treated with respect. Here are some excerpts from the notes he wrote and showed to me:

1. Why do you have to be in a line?
2. Why do you have to hold the same person's hand every time we go anywhere, even in the school?
3. It hurts your head to put your head on the desk but it doesn't to lie on mats. Why do the Pre-K get to lie down on mats and we don't? Because they are younger maybe; it could be just they're tired. Why can't we lie down on mats?
4. Why do they say, "Stop, look, and listen. OK"? Why can't they say, "Please can you listen?" or fire off a water pistol at the wall and the kids would all say, "I want to try that, I want to try that," and they would all get a turn.

When asked why he didn't want to put his head down on the desk (for rest period), he said it hurt, and he pointed to his cheek and said his teeth press against his mouth. When asked about the "Stop, look, and listen" rule, he said they were expected to repeat the teacher's words then clap to show they heard the teacher. He said they do it a lot throughout the day because children are not listening. When I asked him what he would prefer them to say, he said, "I would like them to say, "Please, can you listen?" It is quite surprising to have it so clearly confirmed that even a five-year-old child feels disrespected by being forced to clap when he hears the teacher, instead of being asked respectfully to listen. A boss would never insist on his employees putting their heads down on their desks or make them clap to show they understand. Children have the same feelings as adults, and their physical boundaries are just as important to them. The note written by the young child confirmed the idea that children have a sense of their own dignity and know when it being disregarded. Sadly, they also feel powerless to do anything about it. Fortunately, this young boy had a supportive mother who helped him write the note and share his feelings.

Some teachers may argue, "But that's what you have to do in school. Children don't listen unless you force them to." I would just answer that this boy was in preschool the previous year and was a real leader. He understood what the teacher wanted of him and was very happy to participate and cooperate without being told to clap. Children will listen if they are listened to. It is clear from his notes that he is trying very hard to understand what is going on, but no one is explaining anything to him.

Though teachers may have their reasons for the rules, they often fail to explain them to children. Adults should ask themselves how they would feel if they were forced to hold someone's hand—someone they may not necessarily like—day after day. Imagine if your boss told you to hold someone's hand with no questions asked. That would be considered a breach of your boundaries, and no one would dream of doing it. If children do need to hold hands, e.g. on school trips, and if they are resistant, their feelings should be considered, and they should be allowed some choice in the matter, or at the very least be given the opportunity to discuss the issue and voice their opinion. At the very minimum, a teacher can say, "Listen, I know you may not like to hold hands with each other every time, but we have found it's a good way for people to walk because . . ." and explain the logic behind their thinking. This would be an acknowledgment that children have a right to be informed about rules affecting their bodies.

PERSONAL PROPERTY

Children have the right to personal property. Very young children go through a developmental stage where they fall in love with the world and become attached to objects. They may have toys that they make a special bond with, and at nighttime they often have a "blankie" or soft touching object that is important to them. Some children become so attached to the object that they cannot go anywhere without it. Though this might seem obsessive, it is good for children to have "transitional" objects, which they take to bed with them or bring with them when they go to preschool. Making this connection with the special toy or touching object is a healthy part of a child's development. Not everyone has a blankie. However, all children become attached to objects, and they have a right to feel that way. People get attached to things. If a child is not attached to anything, and things can be removed from him without protest, then something is seriously wrong with him.

When children begin to socialize together, usually between one and two years old, for instance in "Mommy and me" groups, or in playgrounds and other common areas, parents tend to believe their child should learn to share with others. They are often shocked when a child will not allow another child to pick up his toy and play with it. They are even more shocked at the primal conflict that often ensues. More than likely there will be pulling and tugging, which can escalate into assault and battery. A young child's reaction to having his toy taken away, even if it's not his favorite toy, is to defend it with tooth and nail. Literally. Most parents take this as a horrible omen. Their child is selfish and will be like this for the rest of his life if they don't step in and do something. In the heat of the moment parents will say, "That's not nice. Let the little boy play with your toy. You should learn to share. You'll get it back in a few minutes." They may even take the toy away and give it to the other boy.

Here again, it might be useful for parents to ask themselves if they would behave like this with an adult. Let's say you are at the park with your friend and she has a lovely handbag. Another friend of yours comes along and picks up the handbag and starts rifling through it. Your friend reacts in horror and snatches at her bag to get it back. Imagine you say to your friend, "That's not nice. Let her take your bag and look through it. You should learn to share. You'll get it back in a few minutes." You grab the bag and take it away from your friend, and you give it to the other woman so she can continue rifling through it. Most sane people would never dream of doing that. Thinking about it this way can help parents understand that a child is entitled to have something that has been given to him and to keep it for himself. Learning how to share is done in a different kind of situation and definitely not through enforced sharing.

A child has the right to personal property. Teaching a child to share can be done in many ways. However, when a child is in the park and has a toy with him, or when another child comes into his house for a play date, expecting him to share it is not the right setting for teaching children to share. Most children will share with others once they learn the joy of doing so spontaneously. Forcing a child to share will make him more insecure and more afraid of having other children in close proximity when he has a toy.

Giving is a very healthy aspect of human behavior, and it is usually modeled for the child by the parents. The more you give your child the more he or she will give to others. It does not have to be a gift of material things; it is more meaningful to children when parents give their time, their attention, their understanding. That is real sharing. A parent can make a point of giving a child something he knows other children will like: for instance, a box of snacks to bring to school for everyone. A child can make gifts for others, a child can do simple favors, and those are ways a child can learn to share. Many children will respond well when their peers ask them to share something they have, and they can be extremely generous. When this generous impulse comes from inside a child rather than from the parent or teacher's direction, then it should be praised.

A child has a right to possess things. Personal property a child has a right to own include: her clothes, her toys, her bed, her books, her stroller, her pacifier, her toothbrush, and her hairbrush, and if she has her own spoon and dish or any things that are for her alone, they should all be considered her personal property. Usually adults consider personal property things they have paid for or earned themselves. However, a child does not have money and so has to be bestowed with these things. Once bestowed, they should not be taken away. Taking away a child's property is akin to stealing. Giving away a child's property is also wrong. Some well-intentioned parents bring in their child's toys to the classroom, thinking the child has tired of them and the rest of the class may like to use them. The child who used to own the toys can become very upset. The object that was once exclusively hers now belongs to everyone. Children cannot be expected to share in this way.

A child's clothing matters to his self-image. Even young children know when they are wearing something attractive or new. I have had experience meeting young children for the first time, many of them under two years of age. Though they may not answer when you say hello or ask their name, they often present what they think to be their most important feature. They may say nothing and look shy, but their body language shows you what they want you to notice. They may point their foot forward, and when you look down you can see they are wearing new shoes. Once you remark on their lovely shoes, they will smile, and shortly afterward they will tell you their name. It is obvious that even at this age, they are extremely conscious of how they look and how proud they are of what they are wearing. It is quite clear they know their clothing is a part of who they are, since they are proud of how they look and they are putting their best foot, or shoe, forward.

Hand-me-downs may be necessary but they can be demeaning, depending on how they are presented to a child. If an older sibling consistently gets new clothes and the younger sibling always wears the older child's castoffs, this can be upsetting. If both children wear hand-me-downs then that is different. Some parents buy clothes that do not fit a child properly. I know one family that consistently bought the child shoes that were too big, thinking this was good economy, since he would have the shoes longer and grow into them. Unfortunately, the child could not maneuver with the bigger shoes, and this slowed him down. Having things that fit you or look good on you is a contributing factor to the development of a child's healthy ego.

The ego is the self-image that helps a child to steer a steady course through the world, avoiding pitfalls such as depression or self-doubt on one side, and narcissism or self-absorption on the other. When a child knows she has clothing that is just right for her, she is able to internalize a nice image of her self. She sees herself as entitled to be dressed in something that defines who she is. If it is a well-fitting shirt, she feels good, if it is too loose or too tight, unwashed or borrowed from her brother, she may not feel presentable or attractive. In addition, she probably feels she is not good enough to have clothing that is just right for her. Children are very aware that others may have clothes that are nicer or better fitting. When a child has to outgrow a bed or donate her stroller to a younger sibling, she may be very disturbed. Parents need to take special care to discuss at length with a child the need to pass things on to others. At these points of giving, a child should feel compensated. If she is moving out of her bed, she should be going into a bigger bed with new special covers. If she gives up her stroller to the new baby she should get a scooter.

OWNERSHIP AND COLLECTING

Ownership of things for a child is a very deep experience. When a child feels a special attachment to something, it means a number of things to him. Having his own cup can mean he takes up a space in the world and plays a role in it. The cup is an outward symbol of his place in the world. There it is on the shelf along with the other cups, but it is different from all the other cups because it is his alone. In a way it represents him. Objects can take on a meaning, based on who owned it previously. When we look at the possession of someone who is dead, we can feel his personality or his memory is somehow contained in or transmitted by that object. Humans often think of objects in this way, to represent something about themselves.

Think of how fond you can feel of your own special coffee cup, or imagine how you would feel if your favorite dish broke. In ancient cultures, certain objects took on the spirit of people or animals and represented far more than the inanimate material from which they were made. We use the words "tokens," "symbols," and "totems" to express the idea that possessions can come to be imbued with value or significance. This notion may have its roots in childhood, when a child imbues a bottle with the same feeling he has towards the mother and extends this feeling toward other items given him by people who love him. Items become tokens for the child, and his attachment to those items is real and deep. When a child possesses things, his boundaries should be respected, and he should be entitled to a sense of ownership.

Children often grow to enjoy collecting objects, and this collecting habit can be a very creative hobby. It is not a materialistic trend and does not mean a child will grow up to be a hoarder or greedy. There are many things a child can learn from collecting. She can learn patience, since it takes time to build up a good collection. She can develop math skills, since collections can be organized, sorted, listed, subdivided and categorized. She can develop research skills in how to find other elements for her collection and also learn about value and exchanging. A child who collects things can be very focused. Children need to be allowed to make collections. They should be encouraged in this natural habit, as it may lead on to a wonderful career. Someone who collects stones can turn out to be a naturalist. Someone who collects fabric scraps might be an expert quilter. Margaret Mahler, who made such important contributions to our understanding of young children, had a less than satisfactory relationship with her own mother. Her mother once promised her a birthday party, a rare occurrence. However, she made the promise on the condition that her daughter give up her collection of chocolate animal figures so everyone at the party could have one. This invasion of her boundaries affected Mahler deeply and remained a painful memory throughout her life.

When a child is allowed to make her own private collection of anything, that collection becomes important to her in a number of ways. It helps her develop her own identity: for instance a child may think of herself as someone who collects dolls, and that sets her apart from other children who do not collect dolls and also bonds her with other children who do collect dolls. It is a way for her to make a connection with the world and with other people while expressing her own particular preferences. Children should be allowed the time and space and given access to the resources needed for collecting. Collecting can help children to save money since they have individual goals for their money. When a parent squashes a child's wish to collect by throwing his baseball cards in the garbage or won't allow him to look at catalogs in case he might be greedy, then that parent is not allowing the child to have his own relationship with objects, a relationship which can be a very positive feature of a child's life. Parents can encourage collections by providing children with a shelf to display dolls, a box to keep toy cars in, or a subscription to a collector's magazine.

PERSONAL SPACE

A child has the right to personal space. Even plants cannot grow unless they have the space to expand and develop. Nature provides winged seeds so new trees can grow at a distance from the parent. Even if you have a small amount of space in which to live, a child should be given some part of that space that is considered his alone. His bed can be the first place that he occupies. Extending outward from that he may have a room that is his, or he may have to share a room with others. If he is sharing a room, his sense of personal space should be respected. Perhaps he can have certain times when the space is his alone, and the door can be closed. Perhaps he can have a curtain so his area is cordoned off, giving him a theater in which to play or daydream or read without fear of interruption. Perhaps he can have a chair that is his. The child's personal space should be respected. Parents can help to enforce the boundaries of the child by letting other family members know they cannot jump on his bed without permission; they cannot burst open the door and should knock first if they want to enter when he is in possession of the room for his allotted time.

Parents should respect a child's personal space. However, parents should never leave young children unsupervised for any extended periods of time. Allowing a child to have private space should begin slowly. Gradually parents can withdraw from the child's space so their child is still within their range of vision but is able to feel a sense of privacy. Then a parent may move out of range of vision but be within earshot. Over the course of time, parents are able to allow their child to be alone for longer periods of time. For instance, a parent can allow a child to be in her room while the parent is in the other room doing various tasks. A child will be content knowing she has an "invisible boundary" around her—she knows the parent is near and is protective but is trusting enough to allow her to have ownership of her own space without fear of interruption. Parents should always have a good sense of what is going on, even when they are not directly observing the child. It is possible to skim past the child's room without him feeling spied on and tell at a glance what he is doing, whether he is calm and involved, or whether he is on the brink of doing something dangerous. Most parents will have emotional radar so they know what their child is likely to be doing, more or less, when he is alone. Most good parents can tell a good silence from a bad silence.

BARRIERS ARE NOT BOUNDARIES

When children are older, they should be allowed more and more time alone in their own space. Parents should never stop monitoring their child's mood and activities, even when they are teenagers. They should always know in general what is going within the room in the same way they knew when the child was small—is he calm and involved, or is he on the brink of something dangerous? Though parents may have anxieties during the child's teen years, they should always maintain respect for his boundaries. Parents should not burst into a child's room, take the door off the hinges, go through a child's diary or emails, or ask his friends about what is going on in his life.

Those things cross a child's boundaries and make him feel he is not deserving of trust. A parent should always knock before entering the child's room. A parent should demonstrate by her attitude and behavior towards a child's space that she trusts the child completely. This trust should be informed by the parent's knowledge of a child's emotional state.

A child at times may set up negative or destructive barriers around himself. If he is depressed he may go into his room and close the door. Though he is desperately in need of human connection and wants his parents to help him, he may not be able to pull himself out of this dark place. It is a parent's duty not to let those barriers stand. She must break through the barriers and help the child to open up the discussion about what he is feeling. Parents should be respectful, but if a child is in a precarious emotional state a parent should not be afraid to say, "Look, I want to respect your privacy, but I am concerned about you, and I want to tell you how much I care. I would like to talk, and I want to know if you would like to talk to me." In extreme cases, if a parent is seriously concerned about a child—if she worries he is addicted to drugs or feeling suicidal—then the boundaries are no longer boundaries; they are barriers and need to be crossed so the child can receive urgent care.

WHEN PARENTS SEPARATE

When parents decide to live in different places, children are often expected to do a lot of moving around. They may have to go to one parent's house on the weekend, or on every other week, and so on. They will have to bring their possessions with them, their homework, their favorite teddy bear, their clothing. They will have to undergo an added number of physical transitions as well as the emotional transitions they are already enduring. Parents need to set up some new boundaries for children. If a child is staying with Dad on the weekend he should have a special space that is the child's alone, so that he will find a place in Dad's new apartment that feels like home. Parents can help with this by creating an area for the child that is specially his.

A friend of mine suggested that moving children from one place to another seems like an unfair burden, added to the stress of divorce. "Why can't the children stay in one place and the adults come and go?" she asked. The parents could share a second apartment on a rotational basis and come and go in the "children's apartment." This way the children would not have to go from one place to another, and the parents would experience what it feels like to have to move around from one apartment to the other. Though in practice this may be impossible, in theory it is true that children often suffer from having to recreate boundaries in a number of places.

TIME

A child also has the right to her own sense of and relationship to time. Young children have their own concept of time. Children do not make commitments or take on responsibilities, and so they approach time differently. Most adults conduct their lives based on expectations they have of themselves and others, goals they want to attain, deadlines they have to meet, and rules they have to keep. Children do not function in the same way. They are task-oriented; they become deeply focused on their activities, and the most important activity to a child may be daydreaming or play.

We can think of it in this way: adults tend to operate horizontally, going from point A to point Z, and the best way to do that is to proceed quickly in a straight line. A child is operating vertically. He is going "into" the activity rather than skimming over it. This excerpt from a poem by William Blake is his attempt to express a spiritual ideal. However it also expresses the way a child approaches the world: "To see the world in a grain of sand, and to see heaven in a wild flower, hold infinity in the palm of your hands, and eternity in an hour."[1] The sense of timelessness expressed here is how a child experiences the world when he is absorbed in contemplation of something. There is an old fable about the tortoise and the hare. This fable is a good illustration of the difference between an adult and a child. The adult is racing as fast as he can, hopping over obstacles and keeping his goal in mind. The child proceeds slowly, taking in every pebble along the way. And at the end of the story, the tortoise wins. Another parent I know made a very wise comment: "It's OK to travel to the zoo just to look at the ants on the ground."

Most parents know how difficult mornings are. And most teachers will attest to this too since they will observe that many children arrive in school quite stressed. Morning routines for parents are difficult because the morning is the intermediate space between the night and the day. It is the point after the dreams are over and before the activities have begun. A parent's task often becomes very burdensome to him in the morning. This is because a parent is trying to transition the child from a state of dreaming and timelessness to a state of engagement with the outside world. In the parent's mind the child must "get with the program." This means the parent must get the child to move quickly, to accomplish many tasks in a short period of time—dressing, washing, eating breakfast, brushing teeth—and get out of the house and get to school. However, the child has another agenda.

When a child wakes up, she often does not know the difference between dream and reality. If she has had a nightmare, she may be still experiencing that feeling. When she does eventually come out of that state of consciousness, she is full of the sensations of the morning. Most adults have forgotten this feeling, but when a child is new to the world, everything is interesting—the way the morning light makes patterns on the ceiling, the specks of dust twirling and sparkling in the air, the sound of wheels outside the window, the distant train whistle, the feeling in your fingers as the muscles begin to awake. Since everything is new, the child is enjoying this sensational meal, absorbing all the details slowly and savoring the flavor of this unique morning. The parent, on the other hand, has long forgotten to savor each moment and feels that his tasks have to take priority; he must get his child up out of bed and on the way.

One parent told me of the moment in which she realized that mornings with children are the clashing of two different worlds. She had two young boys and was trying to get them both dressed so she could get them out to school. She left the older one to put his socks on, while she took care of the younger one. The morning, like most mornings in her house, had become more and more stressful as time ticked on, and she had already become tired of her own voice giving one instruction after another to the children. She was aware that if things went on this way she would be arriving late to school again, and this was making her even more anxious. Finally, she returned to the room where the older boy was supposed to be putting his socks on. Instead of putting his socks on his feet, he was sitting on the floor, throwing his socks up at the bookshelf. She felt an overwhelming sense of rage and helplessness.

She stood in the doorway and had her mouth open, ready to scream at him and let all her anxieties vent, when she suddenly saw the world from a different point of view—his. In a flash of insight, she realized her child was trying very intently, and very happily, to make the socks land on the top of the bookshelf. He wasn't trying to make her angry. He wasn't thinking about getting dressed. He was focused on a goal he had set for himself, and his goal was all-absorbing. He was engaged in a physics experiment that occupied his attention completely. When she realized that this is where his mind was, and that this was how he was using his time, she said she felt she had a "Zen moment." At that point she knew that yelling at him was not the right thing to do. She knew she needed, if even for one second, to acknowledge that he had his own agenda. She took a deep breath, and she told him he was a good shot; he almost made it to the top with his socks. Then she sat down on the floor with him and promised that, when he came home from school, they would play that game together, and she would throw the socks too, and they would have a contest. The boy was delighted and put his socks on right away. I have no doubt he thought about the sock-throwing contest all day long. And I have no doubt that with his mother's support he could indeed be a physicist one day. Or a sock-throwing Olympic champion.

Parents and teachers do need to respect a child's time and to respect that a child has her own agenda. The child certainly needs to slowly learn compromises. She needs to work her way into the world where other people have agendas. Parents and teachers need to be patient and allow her to compromise slowly. Most schools operate on the basis that children need to fit into the school schedule, and very few operate on the basis that school schedules should coordinate with a child's sense of time. Children can become very involved in activities they like and can spend long periods of time and develop a very strong focus while working at these activities. Instead of encouraging this deep sense of focus, many schools are dominated by the clock and the bell. Even if a child is engrossed in building something or taking something apart, she must stop and move on to the next activity. By the time she has transitioned and become absorbed in the next activity, she may have to stop again and move on. This kind of scheduling can sidetrack or even crush creativity and may not be the best way to encourage children to love work.

Bill Gates, who is well known as a highly achieving and successful entrepreneur, often spent long periods of time just thinking. Isaacson (1997), talks about how much that irritated Gates' mother:

> When Bill Gates was in the sixth grade, his parents decided he needed counseling. He was at war with his mother Mary, an outgoing woman who harbored the belief that he should do what she told him. She would call him to dinner from his basement bedroom, which she had given up trying to make him clean, and he wouldn't respond. "What are you doing?" she once demanded over the intercom. "I'm thinking," he shouted back. "You're thinking?" "Yes, Mom, I'm thinking," he said fiercely. "Have you ever tried thinking?"[2]

Clearly that thinking paid off, since Gates went on to be a very successful and philanthropic individual whose work has impacted the lives of many people. It is also interesting to note that his mother had an intercom. She could communicate with her son while he was alone in his room and check in periodically to see he was doing fine, and yet she gave him the place and time where he could, in fact, think.

ADVENTURE

One of the most exciting aspects of childhood is the sense of adventure. Most of us will recall how we felt great freedom when we took off on an adventure with our friends. This adventure might only be a trip around the block on a spaceship or a journey to the island at the bottom of the garden. On those adventures, the whole world seemed huge and endless, and the possibilities were infinite. This sense of infinity, when we recall it in contemplative moments, holds great peace and great excitement, all at the same time. In those adventures, a child can feel she is at the forefront of an expedition, that she is the discoverer of a new world, that she is able to see over the horizon to a world of endless morning. None of those journeys are possible without privacy. A child can take off and conquer the world in the space of a half-hour, but that half-hour should be hers alone. She should have no demands and no constraints. She should feel completely free.

When a writer sits down to write or an inventor sits down to invent, he cannot do so with people interrupting him. He must have the solitude and peace that is needed to take off on the inward journey. He cannot find the treasure if he is distracted by someone else's needs. And so a child cannot focus on the work of imagining or analyzing, which he needs to do, if he is being called to do certain tasks. Parents and teachers must give the child a safe space and time in which to do imaginative and contemplative work. This means they must recognize that a child has boundaries of space and time that should be respected in order for him to grow in a healthy way. Children need the freedom from supervision that is required to have an adventure. Parents and teachers should create an atmosphere of freedom where boundaries are loose and children can explore, experiment and invent. Play is often the arena where children take off on these kinds of mental journeys, and parents and teachers should loosen the boundaries of a child's play so these imaginary adventures can go as far as possible.

Nowadays we have access to new methods of invading a child's private world. Cell phones, as well as Internet social media, are part of almost everyone's life. The use of cell phones has expanded to the point where many children now have their own phone. The cell phone has become a great asset for children, and it gives parents a sense of security—they can get in contact with their child easily, and so it is possible to allow them more freedom of movement. However, cell phones can also be used invasively. Parents who would have otherwise had to let go and trust that their child will be able to take care of herself, now often call constantly just to check up. This means that many children are now "on call" and do not have a sense of adventure or freedom.

Parents and educators need to value the time a child spends thinking, daydreaming, planning, and imagining. While it is healthy for a child to have routines and to adhere to those routines necessary for health, growth, and safety reasons, the child should be allowed to have his own boundaries of time. By letting children know their needs are being respected, an adult will achieve far more cooperation from a child. Children will be more likely to integrate themselves into the adult world if the adult world is seen as friendly and understanding.

SETTING THEIR OWN BOUNDARIES

When children grow to be adults, the benefits of respecting their boundaries as children will pay off. Many young men and women who have grown up in disrespectful households will not be able to define their own boundaries. In work relationships as well as personal relationships they may feel they do not have rights, and so they allow others to step over the line. They cannot assert their rights. If a child is allowed to feel his space is his alone, then when he grows to be an adult, he will have a healthy sense of his own boundaries. He will not allow people to invade that space. If a child feels her body is hers alone, she will not allow anyone to take advantage of her or touch her inappropriately. She will trust in her own natural instincts and feel a sense of ownership of her body and her feelings.

Girls or boys who have been sexually or physically abused are likely to feel that this is the way things have to be. Sadly, when they are grown, they can be liable to fall into the same kinds of relationships in which they allow others to take advantage of them sexually or to treat their bodies abusively. They have grown up thinking they do not matter, and their bodies do not really belong to them.

Children whose boundaries have been violated may create insurmountable boundaries of their own as a reaction to what has been done to them. A young woman I know had a mother who went into her room when she was not around and searched through her diaries, accessed her cell phone when she was asleep to see who she was talking to, and frequently went through her pockets. The mother was tortured by a sense of foreboding and mistrust and felt she had to try to manage the girl's life by finding out what she was doing at all times. The young woman left home when she was eighteen, got her own apartment, and did not tell her mother where she was living. She still has difficulties in relationships and is very reluctant to let people into her life. Her need for personal boundaries became transformed into a need to create barriers to prevent others from invading her space.

Children whose personal possessions have not been respected may grow up believing that they are not entitled to own things and may fail to achieve the financial success that could have been theirs. I know one young man who, when he was a young child, had a piggy bank where he saved his allowance diligently. He loved saving and loved feeling how heavy the piggy bank was getting. However, one day he found his bank broken into and emptied out. He felt certain his older brother had taken the money, and yet his parents did nothing to address the issue. His personal space had been invaded, and his personal property had been taken. No one had protected those boundaries for him. Needless to say, after his money was taken, he stopped saving in his piggy bank and did not get back into the habit of saving again.

To this day that man has difficulty in making ends meet, even though he earns a very good salary. He told me that even now he does not like to become attached to things, since they might be taken away from him. He is probably afraid he will feel a sense of loss and sadness all over again. And so he is careless with his personal property and often loses things, and when he buys clothes, he does not buy himself anything expensive, though he gives expensive gifts to others. In this case the child whose boundaries were not respected gave up on any attempts to set boundaries for himself. He felt helpless, and in order to avoid the feeling of being invaded, he made the decision not to care too much about anything.

Breaching a child's boundaries or preventing a child from asserting her own boundaries may have physical consequences. Rowa (2001) studied women with anorexia and found that there was a connection between anorexia and the breaching of boundaries in childhood: "More difficulties with parent-child boundary violations were reported by women with anorexia than by control group women, especially when father-daughter relationships were examined."[3] Though it is not clear why this correlation exists, it seems as though fathers play an important role in helping young women become independent adults. When girls begin to separate from their mothers in teen years, they effectively set up new boundaries for themselves that their mother cannot cross. At this time in life, the father can become an ally and support his daughter's new boundaries. If a father is needy and wants his daughter's support instead of the other way around, it seems to impact a girl's healthy development and create undue stress. Anorexia is one of those symptoms of stress, seen particularly in women.

OTHER PEOPLE'S BOUNDARIES

A boundary is a line that marks the edge of a person's space/time/property. Where a farmer's field ends, he may have a fence. That fence marks the beginning of another farmer's property. Similarly, where one person's boundary ends, another's begins. A child cannot feel safe or free, unless there are boundaries that surround him and make him feel enclosed. His boundaries are only as secure as the boundaries of others. For instance, if a mother gives a child his own space and time to enjoy his freedom and exploration of the world, and yet she allows him to invade her space whenever and however he wants, then he does not have real security within his boundaries. He will know his mother is not strong enough to protect his boundaries if she cannot protect her own. The child sees that this mother allows him to have what he wants, but she herself is not to be trusted.

The need for boundaries is a basic human need. Refugees who have had to leave their own environment and relocate to another space suffer greatly from the loss and often experience great difficulties adjusting to their new place. Humans have a tendency to want to find a space where they belong. Part of that belonging consists in having boundaries. People often like to belong to towns, to cities, and to countries, and the boundaries of their environment make them feel a sense of identity. Many place names refer to whether a place is in the east or the west, whether it is close to a lake, or at the bottom of a mountain. Knowing the boundaries of your world is important for a child, since children do not know what lies outside the small circle of their lives. For a young child, the world may consist of the street he lives on, the school he attends, the shop on the corner, the moon overhead, and his grandmother's house far away.

Those boundaries help a child feel safe. Seeing the same streets every day is reassuring for children. Having the pattern of dinner, then bath, then bed makes a child feel safe, even if he fights against it at times. Disruption of those routines can be frightening and leave a child feeling insecure. A child has the need to know he is limited and contained. Similarly a child needs to know that though he has a right to own things, he cannot own everything, and some things are outside his reach. He needs to know that time is limited and that bedtime is at the same time every night, there is a time he needs to stop playing and rest. He needs to know that other people feel hurt just like he does, and he can't step over them on his way to the other side of the room.

Let's suppose a parent does not encourage a child to respect the property of others. That child is allowed to climb and jump on the furniture, and when he visits other people's houses he climbs on their furniture. Soon he is not getting many invitations to play dates. The parent is limiting the child's world instead of expanding it for him. If a parent allows the child to invade her space or otherwise cross her boundaries, she is not helping but limiting him. I know one mother who had a poor relationship with her husband. She compensated for her lack in the marital relationship by doting on her son. She allowed him to have and do whatever he wanted. She put his needs before her own and allowed him to breach all rules.

When he turned up his nose at his meal, she took away the one she had lovingly prepared and cooked another one for him. When he didn't feel like going to school, she let him stay home. That boy grew up to be a very fearful individual. He soon refused to go to school altogether. After a while he stopped going out of the house. Pretty soon he did not come out of his room, and his mother served his meals to him in his bedroom. Ironically, since the mother did not set any boundaries for her son, he created a series of insurmountable barriers for himself and his whole life became confined to one small space. When his mother died, he began going out of the house again, got a job, and now lives an independent life.

In certain cases in which parents feel overwhelmed due to family crises, divorce, death, and so on, the parent may feel unable to function fully as a parent, and in this case young children may step into the parental role. These children are often referred to as "parentified" children. There are no boundaries between the roles of parent and child, and so the child is allowed to fall into a parent's role with all its privileges and responsibilities. The weakened parent, who lets the child take over his or her job, cannot create strong boundaries. This child may have extra privileges, can stay up late, can choose what she eats, may even be allowed to shop for what she wants to eat or what the family eats. She may have authority over younger siblings. She acts like a partner, or even a parent to the parent, and takes over the responsibilities the parent cannot currently handle. This kind of responsibility and loosening of boundaries takes a toll on children. Parentified children can have an abnormal level of authority—they may dictate to their siblings and tell their parents what to do. But they also have a very heavy burden of responsibility for which children are not equipped. When they become adults, they may have a very difficult time as parents, and many are reluctant to get into relationships or to have children.

Gloria Steinem (1983) talks about her relationship with her mother, who was 'someone to be worried about and cared for." Gloria had to develop resilience and self-reliance even to the point of not allowing herself to get sick:

> In these rooms behind a furnace, I made one last stab at being a child. By pretending to be much sicker with a cold than I really was, I hoped my mother would suddenly turn into a sane and cheerful woman bringing me chicken soup a la Hollywood. Of course, she could not. It only made her feel worse that she could not. I stopped pretending. I almost never got sick again.[4]

A depressed parent may be unable to set the kinds of boundaries necessary for a child to feel safe enough to be a child. Those children need to be more vigilant than other children and can suffer from the shame of not having strong parents to protect them, and can even feel guilty for being a burden on their parents. Steinem says: "If pressed hard enough she would add, 'But if I'd left (your father) you never would have been born.' I always thought but never had the courage to say, 'But you might have been born instead.'" Gloria herself never felt the desire to be a parent.

THE RIGHTS OF THE ADULT

Since children are vulnerable, they need their boundaries protected by adults. But some adults fail to set boundaries for themselves and for the children. I know one mother who allowed her child to hit and kick her, saying he just "doesn't know what he's doing." When he got to school and kicked the teachers, he found himself in a lot of trouble, which his mother could have prevented if she had asserted her right not to be kicked.

I remember when I was in school, we had a really pretty and very popular teacher. Though we were in high school and getting ready to take important exams, she did little teaching; instead she played games and did puzzles with us, saying that she trusted us to do the work at home. She assigned homework but did not check it. One of the games we would play in school involved drawing pictures of ourselves and then analyzing from the drawing what kind of person we were. Everyone looked forward to her class, including myself, as we knew it would be fun. I ignored my underlying anxieties, but in the end they proved to be real, since I failed the subject miserably, as did most of us in that class. Later I felt angry that she did not do her job and keep us on track. She trusted us too much—we were not capable of making those kinds of decisions at that age. She had the right to insist that we focus on the topic at hand, but she didn't assert that right, and she failed us all, literally. If an adult decides she would rather be a child's friend than be her guide, she is not helping the child.

Notes

1. Blake, W. (1988). "Auguries of Innocence." *The Complete Poetry and Prose of William Blake.* New York, NY: Random House, 490.
2. Isaacson, W. (1997). "In Search of the Real Bill Gates." *Time* 149:2, 44–56.
3. Rowa, et al. (2001). "The Family and Anorexia Nervosa: Examining Parent-Child Boundary Problems." *European Eating Disorders Review* 9, 97–114.
4. Steinem, G. (1983). *Outrageous Acts and Everyday Rebellions.* New York, NY: Henry Holt and Company, 144 and 150.

Chapter 5

Children Have the Right to Play

Children have the right to play. The United Nations Convention on the Rights of the Child affirmed this right: "States Parties recognize the right of the child to rest and leisure, to engage in play and recreational activities appropriate to the age of the child, and to participate freely in cultural life and the arts." Play is not a luxury for children. Children have an innate drive to play, and play contributes to their physical, emotional, social, and cognitive development. Children who are deprived of the opportunity to play are often maladjusted to social situations, and there is even a strong link between play deprivation and criminal behavior. Conversely, play is connected with creativity and innovation as well as flexibility and higher cognitive functioning.

How do we define play? Though there are many different kinds of play, such as competitive sports, board games, and so on, and these kinds of games have a lot of benefits, the kind of play we could describe as essential to a child's development would be the kind a child naturally plays—that is, self-directed play. Self-directed play is play a child chooses and directs, sometimes solitary and sometimes collaborative. It is play without a goal or time limit; it has no expected outcome, and it flows according to its own rules, which are often fluid and evolving. This kind of play occurs naturally, does not require adult participation, and is a fundamental need in childhood. It is often called "free play."

THE NEED TO PLAY

Donald Winnicott, the influential writer on children's development, believed that play occurs in a transitional space. Transitional space is a time and place where a child is capable of being apart from a parent and sustains himself emotionally through interaction with toys or without toys, through private speech (talking to himself), or engaged with other children. This activity of play exists in a world of its own. It is not the inner world of thought or dreams; it is not the outer world of functionality, e.g. eating, getting dressed. In this transitional space between reality and dream, a child practices, recaps, experiments, and creates solutions. These activities are essential for the child's emotional health, and the urge to play is a natural and healthy one.

A human cannot survive without dreaming; experiments have shown that lack of dreamtime can result in hallucination, disturbed behavior, and, finally, complete mental breakdown. Similarly, a child cannot survive without play—it is as if a child needs to have "waking dreams," and those dreams are play. Rochat (2009), in his wonderful book *Others in Mind,*[1], describes the different levels of human consciousness. These levels of consciousness develop as a human grows. Babies spend a great deal of time in sleep, which is one form of consciousness—the person is alive but not conscious of the outside world. There is the nascent consciousness of the infant, which gradually becomes consciousness of the self, then consciousness of others, and "co-consciousness," or consciousness of ourselves in relation to others.

I would suggest that play is another form of consciousness. When children are engaged in play, they are not fully conscious of the outside world but are deeply involved in another reality that is self-directed, a manipulation of experience and sensation combined with imagination. When adults are engrossed in hobbies or creative pursuits, they may also slip into this semiconscious world in which reality ceases to exist for a period of time. During these times, the player experiences the world as though she is directing all that happens, and time seems to stand still. The play activities that take place in childhood are much more frequent and are driven by necessity rather than choice, and they are an essential activity for emotional, social, and cognitive growth.

We have all seen, and hopefully most of us can remember, the way a child often can barely get to sleep at night because of the excitement of thinking and planning some game for the next day. When you open the gate to the playground and stand back and watch the way a child rushes in to play, you can see children are being pulled toward this activity. We can all probably remember being so engrossed in play activity that the concept of time ceased to be a concern. Parents can testify to this—try to get your child to stop playing and come eat dinner, and you will see how deeply involved a child can become in play activities—it is almost like trying to wake someone up. This engrossment is so pleasurable that it is the driving force behind the impulse to play. The child constantly seeks to recapture his involvement and feeling of focus, and so he is restless until he is able to play once more. We all enjoy that feeling, which Mihaly Csikszentmihalyi describes as a feeling of "flow," of oneness with the world, though sadly, as we age, it becomes more difficult to attain. Manning reports that Froebel, the founder of kindergarten, or "children's garden," describes this oneness as spiritual:

> Play is the highest phase of child development—of human development at this period. Play is the purest, most spiritual activity of man at this state, and at the same time, typical of human life as a whole—of the inner hidden natural life in man and in all things. It gives, therefore, joy, freedom, contentment, inner and outer rest, peace with the world. It holds the sources of all that is good.[2]

The word "spiritual" in this case might be defined not in a religious sense, but as something outside the mundane. It connotes a source from which humans may draw inspiration, energy or enlightenment. A spiritual activity, then, is an activity that is not done with the purpose of changing, advancing, or improving one's position in the world, like driving a car from one place to another, or selling a car in a car dealership. A spiritual activity is one that does not have a physical goal; it is done simply for the reason that doing it brings a connection with a source outside the self that is refreshing, relaxing, revitalizing, fulfilling. Playing can be defined as spiritual, since it brings that connection and achieves the functions of revitalizing and inspiring. If you decide to wash your car, you might find that relaxing and fulfilling. If you decide to build a toy car, that might also be relaxing and fulfilling. However, these activities are still goal-oriented and have predictable outcomes. You will probably not encounter any uncharted areas where you will be thrown on the mercy of your inspiration. If you decided to *pretend* you were driving a car, and you allowed yourself to become fully involved in the pretense, then you would be entering the world of play. There you would come to many unbridged passes, and you would have to make many leaps of faith. That is the use and transcendent joy of imagination.

PLAY CONNECTS CHILDREN

Imaginative play often takes the form of dramatic play. This is a naturally occurring type of play that children seem to choose over most other types of play. What occurs in this play is generally that children imagine themselves in a certain role. When in this role, they create scenarios around this persona. The play can be done when a child is alone or in conjunction with others, and this is often termed collaborative play. When children are playing in collaboration with one another, it is quite striking the way they communicate. If adults were to put on a play, they would probably say, "OK, let's pretend that you are the mother and I am the baby. You sit at the table and I will make food for you." When children play, they communicate in a much more rapid and intuitive way, and they also respond to each other in a very accepting way. The scene would likely go like this: One child will say, "I'm the mommy, OK?" and then the other child will lie on the floor and suck her finger. Unless there is a dispute about who plays which role, children do not need to explain to each other what to do or what to say; they intuitively and instantly get into the role. When the play takes an unexpected turn, the children always go with it and adapt themselves to the situation.

In the park one day, I saw a group of well-meaning adults organizing a group of young children with a colored "parachute." Much of the time was spent telling the children which side to hold, how to stand, and what to do, and the adults seemed to believe they were doing something wonderful for the children, who, gamely, went along with the idea. After a while the play ended, and the parachute was lying on the ground. The adults were chatting together, and the children began playing with the parachute. They took the corners of it and started running around the playground, holding onto the sides of it. They were laughing spontaneously, and new children who didn't even know each other joined in. The children seemed really excited in the way they were working in a group, weaving in and out of the trees and benches. The amount of joy on their face was astonishing. They kept looking at each other, checking in with each other's expressions, coordinating their movements, even though they had not known each other a few minutes before.

Once or twice someone fell on the parachute, and the others pulled it with surprising gentleness and everyone laughed. I was quite amazed at the way no one was getting hurt; there was a plan they all shared, a plan that was evolving as they were running around the playground, and each one of them was in tune with the plan. It was all a beautiful dance. The children were in the moment and alert—it reminded me of a flock of pigeons that flies over the park just like that, swooping and darting, flowing and following, ever changing, ever flexible. The children were alive and happy, and the play was leading them, and they were intensely connected to each other. Just then the adults came back and tried to reorganize the play. The children looked disappointed. Their joyful adventure was over. What a pity.

Trying to recapture what it is like to be a child is difficult for many adults. However, there is probably one thing all of us can remember, and that is the joy of play. Teachers and parents can provide evidence for this—we can all see that children are happy when they play and show sadness or disappointment when they have to leave play and go on to other activities. Parents can also attest to the fact that if you want a child to help you around the house, for instance tidy their room or wash the dishes, you can succeed if you turn it into a game. My two daughters spent about a year of their lives pretending to be dogs—Chippy and Buffy. If I wanted them to do a chore, such as washing dishes, I would pretend to be the owner and ask Chippy and Buffy if they could help wash the dishes—of course I would also need to participate in the play by using a special dog-owner voice: "Up, Chippy! Up, Buffy! Good dogs! Wash dishes!" Even though they hated washing dishes when they were "humans," never for a moment did they think of reasoning that dogs can't wash dishes; they simply loved play and would do anything if it was part of the game, and they were allowed to stay in the roles of Chippy and Buffy.

This engagement and willingness to forego all arguments or resistance and overcome all obstacles to play shows that children are truly driven to play, and that play is a need that is probably in the uppermost range of the hierarchy of needs. If we look at this from a developmental point of view, we need to recognize that if all children have the urgent desire to play, if all children appear to find satisfaction in play, if all children will ignore their own preferences and dislikes in order to play, then surely play must serve an evolutionary or sociological function. Therefore play must be considered a need rather than a luxury.

PLAY DEPRIVATION

Many adults resist the notion that play is a need. There is a common illusion that many adults have been led to believe: that play is something that must take a second place to "work." Even when certain adults accept that play has a function in a child's life, they do so only as long as they can say that "play is actually a child's work." They do not accept that play itself is an innate drive. A good way of assessing whether play is an innate drive, similar to the drive to eat, drink, or be connected with others, is to look at what happens when children are deprived of play. Stuart Brown, who is a great proponent of play in childhood and is author of the book *Play*, was motivated to champion play when he saw the connection between lack of play and psychic disturbance. According to an article by Wenner (2009) in *Scientific American Mind*:

> On August 1, 1966, the day psychiatrist Stuart Brown started his assistant professorship at the Baylor College of Medicine in Houston, twenty-five-year-old Charles Whitman climbed to the top of the University of Texas Tower on the Austin campus and shot forty-six people. Whitman, an engineering student and a former U.S. Marine sharpshooter, was the last person anyone expected to

> go on a killing spree. After Brown was assigned as the state's consulting psychiatrist to investigate the incident and later, when he interviewed twenty-six convicted Texas murderers for a small pilot study, he discovered that most of the killers, including Whitman, shared two things in common: they were from abusive families, and they never played as kids.[3]

The conclusion we could draw from these statistics might be that play deprivation may be the cause of disturbed behavior. However, since there are many other sociological factors that might be in effect, we cannot without further research conclude that lack of play is a cause of disturbed behavior. However, if we look at these studies, we can at the very least conclude with certainty that there is a correlation between abusive families and play deprivation. That in itself is an indicator that play is a normal healthy activity, since it exists to a greater extent in healthy families than it does in abusive families. If play exists as a normally arising activity in families in which children develop according to healthy developmental lines, then surely play is a requisite part of human development.

Play deprivation has been shown to be linked with social dysfunction. Obviously it would be unethical to conduct human experiments to find out the nature of this link, and it also is difficult to prove conclusively that play deprivation in humans causes social disturbance. However, there is evidence that play deprivation causes social malfunction in rats:

> Animal studies lend support to the idea that play deprivation leads to poor social skills. According to a study published in 1999 in *Behavioural Brain Research*, rats that are kept isolated during the two weeks of development when they most frequently play—the fourth and fifth weeks after birth—are much less socially active when they later encounter other rats as compared with rats that are not isolated during the same two-week period . . . . (Wenner 2009)

Other studies on rats show that play produces specific chemicals in the brain that encourage brain development:

> Another study suggests that play promotes neural development in "higher" brain areas involved in emotional reactions and social learning. Scientists reported in 2003 that play fighting releases brain-derived neurotrophic factor (BDNF)—a protein that stimulates the growth of new neurons—in these regions. The researchers allowed thirteen control rats to play freely with companions for three and a half days and kept fourteen other rats isolated for the same period. On examining the rats' brains, the researchers found that the cortex, hippocampus, amygdala, and pons of the rats that had played contained much higher levels of BDNF than those of the rats that had not. "I think play is the major mechanism

whereby higher regions of the brain get socialized," says Washington State University neuroscientist Jaak Panksepp, who co-authored the study. (Wenner 2009)

These studies, along with others, prove that play is connected with central and ancient parts of the brain, and therefore it must serve important functions. The fact that animals participate in play indicates that there is a universal and primal drive to play. Anyone who has a dog for a pet knows that dogs have a few basic needs: nourishment, companionship, and play. Young dogs in particular spend long periods of time playing.

Some adults do not understand that play should have a prominent place in a child's life. They think their child needs to be stimulated with flash cards or other aids to cognitive development. Even very small children are put under pressure by parents who think academic achievement is the most important thing in life. They also think academic achievement is best accomplished by forcing children to read before everyone else or constantly quizzing them instead of letting them think and process the things they do see. They are misguided. Play helps children to internalize information they are perceiving, and so it probably plays a greater role in learning than most people realize.

A recent book documented a parent's attempts to make her children "successful" by forcing them to practice a musical instrument until they were "perfect." This parent deprived her children of the time to play, including prohibiting playdates with other children, so that more of their time would be devoted to work. At one point she threatened to burn her child's precious toys if she didn't succeed at an assigned task. David Brooks (2010) responded to her tactics in a *New York Times* article: "Practicing a piece of music for four hours requires focused attention, but it is nowhere near as cognitively demanding as a sleepover with fourteen-year-old girls." He says that playing together builds important life skills:

> Researchers at the Massachusetts Institute of Technology and Carnegie Mellon have found that groups have a high collective intelligence when members of a group are good at reading each others' emotions—when they take turns speaking, when the inputs from each member are managed fluidly, when they detect each others' inclinations and strengths.[4]

Other parents rush their children to karate, to ballet, to chess, to swimming lessons, to French classes, thinking they are doing them a huge favor. When my children were little, I must admit that I thought the same way. I took my children to every class, every exhibit, and every event I thought would stimulate their intellectual growth. One day I dragged them away from their play with dolls and headed off for a museum exhibit I had read about. They were clearly not motivated, but I hurried along, holding both their hands, rushing to the bank so I could get some money before we went to the subway, which would get us to the museum. As they dragged their feet, I walked faster, feeling more and more exasperated. "Come on!" I would bark frequently, trying to get them to hurry. It was 90-degree weather, and it was hard to walk fast, but the voices in my head were saying, "It's your job to educate them. You need to get as much stuff into their heads as possible while they are young." As we neared the bank, my irritation was unbearable. "Why don't you two hurry up?" I snapped. "We'll never get there at this rate! What's wrong with you? I'm doing this for you!" My older daughter looked at me and said quietly, "But, Mom, we just want to play." Suddenly I felt really ashamed. "What am I doing?" I asked myself. At that moment, looking at her earnest face, hearing her simple plea, I had a real breakthrough. I knew that I was working against their natural drive. We did go to the bank. I got some money out, bought ice cream and took them home to play. We were all much happier.

PLAY IN SCHOOLS

Some parents and teachers fall into the misconception that children need to work hard at academic subjects in order to succeed in life. The chain of argument is that if you don't squeeze a lot of information into your head, you won't succeed in school; if you don't succeed in school, you won't go to college; if you don't do well in college, you won't get a steady job; if you don't get a steady job, you won't be happy. Though many of the links in this chain are weak, it is a heavy chain. This kind of thinking can be very burdensome for parents and children—in particular for children who don't do well in school in specific subjects. A lot of stress is placed on "core subjects," which basically are math and reading, and most schools tend to fall into another misconception: the more you focus on these core subjects the better the child will do in school. The current trend in the United States is to cut back on time allotted for play both inside the classroom and also at recess. In addition there are huge cutbacks in the time allotted to subjects such as music, art, and drama, which are being considered peripheral and unproductive. Though it seems counterintuitive, focusing intently on certain activities for long periods of time will *not* improve one's liking of those subjects nor even one's performance at these subjects. Taking a break between subjects and studying subjects for short periods of time can be more conducive to retention. The joy of discovery and learning can also be diminished when the pressure of exams is applied.

Other countries seem more enlightened as to the most effective way to educate children. Let's take a look at Finland. Schoolchildren in Finland are not routinely tested in the way children in the United States are. There are no national tests. The Finnish National Board of Education takes a 10 percent sample group at each age in order to assess progress. At the end of their initial educational phase, when they are around fifteen years old, children are tested, but the results are kept confidential and schools are not compared with each other. And yet, Finnish children outperform children in many other countries. Interestingly, Finnish children take learning more seriously and become life-long readers. As Halinen (2005) points out in an article in Educational Leadership:

> Eighty-five percent of Finnish families subscribe to a daily newspaper. Only Norwegians and Japanese subscribe at a higher rate. A typical Finnish family starts its day at the breakfast table by reading the morning paper and commenting on the day's news. The number of books published annually in Finland is high given the size of the population, and each Finn borrows twenty-one library books, on average, each year.[5]

Schools in Finland do not pressurize children by focusing heavily on core subjects; their educational policies are in accord with a child's needs and natural drives. School administrators understand the need a child has to play. Finnish children do not start school as young children in the United States. In Finland, children are allowed to spend the first seven years of their life in play, both outdoors and indoors. And when they do go to school, Finnish children are allowed more time for relaxation and play during the day than are children in the United States.

Finnish schools also have a shorter school day than most U.S. schools. In Finland, the school day lasts from five to six hours, while most U.S. school schedules last from six to seven hours. This does not include after-school programs, which have recently been mandated for "underperforming" American students, and it does not include summer schools, in which U.S. children who did not fare well during the year are expected to attend in the (vain) hope that it will improve their performance.

The schedule in Finnish schools is lively and varied. In a school at Tuvila, the day begins at 8:30 a.m. and ends at 2:15 p.m., and the lunch period is for one hour, which includes outdoor play. In this school, there are a total of four and three quarter hours of work daily. Two and a quarter hours are spent on academic subjects, while two and a half hours daily are dedicated to non-academic subjects, including one period a day, four days a week, of storytelling. (Kimonen, 2001)[6]. In Suutarilla, outdoor play is scheduled at frequent intervals during the day, and the academic periods are kept to a limit of forty-five minutes. "The students, who number about 500, pad about in their socks. After every forty-five-minute lesson, they are let loose outside for fifteen minutes so they can burn off steam. Others are allowed to practice their music, and they file into classrooms, sling electric guitars across their chests, or grab drumsticks and jam." (Alvarez 2004)[7].

This "burning off steam" as Alvarez describes it in her *New York Times* report, is another way of describing play. Being able to strum a guitar and beat drumsticks is also another way to play. Play is scheduled into the child's day because Finnish educators think of play as an integral part of a successful school. Hyvonen (2008) describes the way in which Finnish schools place a high value on play:

> The Finnish educational system and curricula lay emphasis on play, collaboration, and equality. Modern educational practices allow the learning environment to be enlarged from indoor classrooms to outdoor playful learning environments (PLEs). PLEs have been constructed in schoolyards in Finland with the goal of increasing learning through play in curriculum-based education and augmenting collaborative play (ColPlay) between boys and girls.[8]

The Finnish concept of involving play in the school day works well, since these schoolchildren perform better academically than most children around the world. Finnish educators see the potential of play to help boys and girls communicate better. Though self-directed play arises without adults, and functions well without the presence of teachers or parents, many schools now realize that play should be integrated into classrooms.

PLAY AND COGNITIVE DEVELOPMENT

More and more studies confirm the fact that play enhances a child's cognitive development. When a child plays in self-directed ways, she is integrating what she knows of the world and what her own interior world dictates. Play allows a child to bring the outside world in, as well as allowing her to bring her internal construction to bear on the outside world, all done in the privacy of her own play space. Wenner presents some interesting studies that connect improved cognitive functioning with play:

> In a classic study published in *Developmental Psychology* in 1973, researchers divided 90 preschool children into three groups. One group was told to play freely with four common objects—among the choices were a pile of paper towels, a screwdriver, a wooden board, and a pile of paper clips. A second set

> was asked to imitate an experimenter using the four objects in common ways. The last group was told to sit at a table and draw whatever they wanted, without ever seeing the objects. Each scenario lasted ten minutes. Immediately afterward, the researchers asked the children to come up with ideas for how one of the objects could be used. The kids who had played with the objects named, on average, three times as many nonstandard, creative uses for the objects than the youths in either of the other two groups did. (Wenner 2009)

It seems that playing allows the brain to come up with a wide variety of solutions and ideas and may be the foundation of "brainstorming." In play, the critical voice is put on hold, and ideas flow freely. Many writers and artists use this method of free writing or free association, and this allows them to tap into a spring of ideas. Once the ideas are produced, the analytical function of the brain can help to shape them.

Another study outlined by Wenner showed, surprisingly, that rough play, or free-form wrestling, can play a part in cognitive development. Very few parents or teachers think that when boys or girls wrestle, they may be learning strategies that will help them in other areas of their life:

> Play fighting also improves problem solving. According to a paper published by Pellegrini in 1989, the more elementary school boys engaged in roughhousing, the better they scored on a test of social problem solving. During the test, researchers presented kids with five pictures of a child trying to get a toy from a peer and five pictures of a child trying to avoid being reprimanded by his mother. The subjects were then asked to come up with as many possible solutions to each social problem; their score was based on the variety of strategies they mentioned, and children who play fought regularly tended to score much better. (Wenner 2009)

Play itself tends to have a large scientific component. When children play with water and sand, for instance, they are measuring, weighing, and so on. As they develop, they tend to move from simple pouring and moving activities to devising scientific experiments. You can see children aged as young as three years old setting up slides and funnels while they attempt to make water or sand run from one part of the table to the other. They are using an intuitive form of scientific research: create a hypothesis, conduct an experiment, and draw conclusions. And this is fun. Piaget, one of the most widely respected educators, concluded that real mathematical learning cannot exist without this play exploration of materials. Children who learn multiplication tables may develop good memories, and that is not a bad thing in itself, but they may not grasp math concepts in the way children who experiment frequently do.

PLAY, FLOW, AND CREATIVITY

When children are playing they experience a sense of "flow," or deep engagement. As Rathnude and Csikzentmihalyi (2005) state: "The central concept in the theory is flow: an intrinsically motivated, task-focused state characterized by full concentration, a change in the awareness of time (e.g. time passing quickly), feelings of clarity and control, a merging of action and awareness, and a lack of self-consciousness.[9]

Maria Montessori, like the other influential educators before her, based her unique method on the fact that a child needs to play with materials. She is in accordance with the other thinkers in her belief that once a child is engaged, he or she becomes so motivated that the activity takes on a life of its own. Since the child is playing, concentration becomes absolute, and an engaged student often spends long periods of time in work. In addition, the work will be memorable and meaningful to the child, through the process of self-engagement. Like her predecessors, she believed that the teacher's role is to facilitate rather than to demonstrate, to stand back and allow a child to integrate the world into her own thought processes. This is a good definition of play.

When children are absorbed in an activity, playing with materials, they may be pulled away from that activity by teachers who have a specific agenda. When children find joy in engagement with materials and spend long periods of time in a certain task, they are, in fact, developing their powers of concentration. Most schools do not honor the child's need to be absorbed in projects and instead require a child to stop what he or she is doing and move to the next activity, whether ready or not. Play behavior tends to be such that a child focuses for long periods of time on one activity and takes that activity to its fullest extent. When a child is allowed to do so, he or she strengthens focusing ability and obtains a sense of fulfillment.

Many parents and teachers try to force children to learn through traditional methods, rather than allowing them the time and space they need to learn. They fail to recognize that play is not a desire to escape; it is a way of fully engaging with the world. Very few children enjoy the regimentation of school. Though most children manage to get through school, many drop out or become alienated because they cannot function in the way that is expected of them. They appear to be failures because they cannot learn in traditional ways. Thomas Edison did not fare well in school, and yet his inventions changed the world in many ways—not least of which was the creation of the first motion picture machine. He was extremely creative and inventive and interested in the world, and most of his learning went on not in the classroom. Frost, his biographer, describes some of the techniques he used to learn outside of school: "He preferred to discover the world on his own. He hiked to railroad yards, foundries and lumber mills, observed the activities for hours, made sketches, and then went home to his workshop to build a model railway, a toy cannon, and a water mill. He found deep satisfaction in using his hands to create." (104) When Edison became a successful inventor, even as an adult, he retained the joy of play, and used play as a core of his scientific method:

> He would sit at one of the lab tables, chew tobacco, and make a little drawing of a new component. He'd ponder it, pass it around among his staff, and wander off to read a couple of technical manuals [. . .] . He'd browse among his supplies, toying with the piles of magnets, generators, batteries, condensers, pumps, wire, and coil with the grace of an artist and the zest of a child. Then he would take a short snooze. A dedicated napper, Edison may have found inspiration and ideas in his dreams. He'd wake up and wolf down a few bites of pie. He'd light a cigar, study his original sketch, and add a few squiggles. He and his team would then build a prototype and experiment with it for days, weeks, months—whatever it took to perfect the design.[10]

It is interesting that Edison continued to play, and that in his working life, his play life and his dream life were closely integrated. He was able to move smoothly in and out of different levels of consciousness and effectively draw these areas together by creating new ideas that had not been hitherto conceptualized, or may have been conceptualized but never before actualized. His play activities created a bridge to his unconscious, where he accessed new ideas through his imagination.

Play is a theater where children can rewrite the script. Freud (1908) makes a connection between a writer's work and the play of children:

> The child's best loved and most absorbing occupation is play. Perhaps we may say that every child at play behaves like an imaginative writer, in that he creates a world of his own or, more truly, he rearranges the things of his world and orders it in a new way that pleases him better. It would be incorrect to think that he does not take this world seriously; on the contrary, he takes his play very seriously and expends a great deal of emotion on it.[11]

An artist continues the work children do in their play by connecting us with the feelings and fantasies that often have to take a back seat in our daily lives.

PLAY AND EMOTIONAL DEVELOPMENT

Probably the most important aspect of play is that it helps a child in her emotional development. Play is an adaptive activity. Parents of young children may overhear their child in her "transitional space" at bedtime or other quiet times, talking to herself either with or without the use of toys or other props, narrating some story. They will observe words and phrases that have particular meaning in the child's life. This "private speech" often includes snippets from "real life" and may include phrases that the parents have recently used with the child, and the child is now using with a doll, for instance. The child may use words from stories she has read, and the drama that is unfolding between the child and the toy may be very similar to a drama that is going on in the child's life. For instance the child may be re-enacting a mother having a new baby, or a girl going to school for the first time, or a child going on an airplane trip to visit her grandmother. The story will be changed, and roles may be reversed.

One young girl I know pretended she was having a baby and that the baby was also her sister. Her mother in the story was transformed into her older sister. In this way she played the role of mother, big sister, and younger sister and was trying out all aspects of these relationships and what it might feel like to be in each person's skin before the baby was even born. Her mother participated fully in the role-playing and allowed the child to be the play director. It is not surprising that this child adapted very well to the baby and her role as big sister.

How does this play serve a child's needs? In her play, the child is trying to come to terms with events in her life. It is dramatic play. The child is playing a role, or playing at playing a role. The function of role-playing is adaptive. If someone plays the role of the aggressor in a play, he or she will know what it feels like to be aggressive. If someone plays the role of victim in a play, then he or she will know what it feels like to be the victim of aggression. Empathy is a vital for a child's socialization. Children who are empathetic will be less likely to act out hostility on other children. Since there appears to be link between lack of play and criminal activity, perhaps the link is here, in the failure to role-play and a failure to develop an understanding of the inner world of others, and even a lack of understanding of the self in relation to others.

GETTING OUTSIDE THE SELF

Shakespeare said: "All the world's a stage." When people are faced with difficult tasks or difficult situations to deal with, things can be easier to bear if one is conscious of oneself as playing a role, even if it's pretense. For instance, if you are at the gym and using the rowing machine, and you feel tired and have resistance in your body, you might feel like giving up. However, you can use your imagination to help you break through the resistance. For instance, you can imagine you are rowing across a beautiful lake to your castle on the other side, where a fine meal awaits you; only a few more strokes to go, and you will be there. Some athletes visualize themselves with a gold medal around their necks while they are doing the difficult work of preparing physically for the challenges that lie ahead. Pretending you have achieved your goal can help you to achieve your goal more easily.

One friend of mine who used to be carsick would picture herself on the outside of the car running alongside and looking in at herself. This out-of-body pretense helped to stop the carsickness. Young children often hear the voice of a sports commentator while they play sports. Although they are alone, they can conjure up and get into the role of an outside person who sees and comments on their achievements. In this way they are objectifying themselves in the world, or developing meta-awareness, and at the same time they are also projecting themselves forward in time to when these events could occur. Through play, children see themselves as part of a story in which they are a character. Being able to do this is a great coping skill. People who face adversity in life can get through difficulties by projecting a good ending on their story and then aim for that happy ending. There is a film called *Life is Beautiful*, which tells the story of a father and son who are in a concentration camp. The father tells the son stories so they can imagine they are in a different place, and the stories help them to bear their suffering.

THE THERAPEUTIC VALUE OF PLAY

Seeing yourself as another person, or being able to step outside and see yourself playing a role, can be very releasing and restorative. When children are pretending, engaging in dramatic play, they are doing just that. They are arming themselves with coping strategies for things that may happen in the future or adapting to events currently happening in their lives. One young child I knew was extremely aggressive with other children and had a turbulent relationship with his father. However, he changed his behavior completely at the sand table when he played the role of father and the teacher played the child. His voice altered, his demeanor calmed, and he suddenly embodied the good qualities of his imagined benevolent father. As "father," he spoke gently and tenderly to his son (the teacher), something he probably longed for in his real life. He wanted to play this drama over and over again.

Therapists often use play to diagnose the issues children face or to help them to develop strategies to cope. Based on the idea that children are naturally capable of self-healing, play therapy aims at allowing the child's creativity to come to bear on his or her problems. Play therapists provide a setting for the child to work, much like a producer gives a stage for the director and performers to do their magic. Children create their own theater during their play, and in that theater they become director, writer, and actor. Through their play they reinvent their experiences in a way that helps them gain mastery over them.

Robson (2008) describes her therapy with a nine-year old boy, Leigh, whose fifteen-year old brother, Sam, (not their real names) died of heart failure. The child plays with play dough, sand, and also art materials, and through his games he works through his feelings—sadness, fear, anger, and helplessness:

> He pummelled the evil man with his fist and put the play dough back in the box. The two cousins were squished back into their containers, but Sam was put in very gently with just his hair being rolled down so he could fit. He then decided to paint Sam and painted a sunny day with grass and soil underneath. Sam was standing with his arms out and passing a football to Leigh, who also had his arms out as if they were both about to give each other a hug. I felt a very strong sense of sadness, although Leigh didn't say anything. He finished his picture and went back to the sand to fill up the big wheel. He wanted to put enough sand in so the bottom wheels stopped turning and asked my help to fill the bucket. He then gave me the other wheel but helped fill it. He found a man and put him under the smaller wheel and took delight in him being completely covered. He then got two more men and put them under the two wheels of the big sand machine and covered those. He then "rescued" them with the sieve. Was he trying to stop time and rescue his brother?[12]

Therapists allow children to direct the play, to have the power they lack in their own lives, and this helps them to conquer the feeling of helplessness many children feel, especially when they are dealing with bereavement of this kind. Children who have been involved in war or witnessed or experienced traumatic events often reflect these events in their games. Play has such powerful restorative properties that it is part of many child therapists' techniques. Therapists tap into the natural healing force the child possesses.

Chazan (2002) videotapes segments of play and then analyzes the structure of the play, including cognitive and affective elements, as well as the function of the play for the child. Her scientific analysis demonstrates her awareness of play as a naturally occurring process, which functions in the development of the child: "Playing and growing are synonymous with life itself. Playfulness bespeaks creativity and action, change and the possibility of transformation. Play activity thus reflects the very existence of the self, that part of the organism that exists both independently and interdependently, that can reflect upon itself and be aware of its own existence."[13]

PLAY AND SOCIAL DEVELOPMENT

In a regular classroom or a home setting, play that is facilitated by teachers can help emotional development. When children pretend in the presence of other children, scenarios are collaborative. Both sides need to give and take, to listen, and to cooperate, or the play will disintegrate. Studies show that children who play more advanced cooperative type games are socially more adept, more liked, and more successful in group situations. Reciprocality in play is an indication that children are able to understand the thought processes of others. Being able to play well with others bodes well for children's future social relationships.

Even when children play alone, they often rehearse social situations and practice dialog. In this way they are going over past events and trying to understand them, and also they are practicing strategies for future encounters. There are a number of studies of children with social difficulties, including autism spectrum disorders, who have been "taught" to play, or helped to strengthen their own play skills. The goal of these interventions is to increase reciprocality and strengthen the child's ability to relate well to others.

When children play together their level of communication is strong, and the language they use to communicate is sophisticated. Children in most schools do not have the opportunity for interpersonal learning. Desks are often placed in rows facing the teacher, and these children spend most of their day facing forward, seeing their friends only from the back or sides. Chatting is generally prohibited since teachers are under pressure to cover as much material as possible and are also being judged on the performance of their students in mandated exams. Social interaction is limited to recess time. This is unfortunate, since children tend to learn a great deal from their peers.

The more time that is spent in play with others, the more communication can occur. Language, including overtones and undertones, implicit and explicit meanings, cultural inflections, similarities, and variations, can be enriched through interpersonal communication. If schools can foster, protect, and encourage children's play, then children will be happier, more related, and will be more enriched cognitively. Children learn social skills when playing with others—sharing, patience, cooperation, negotiation, communication, organization, resourcefulness, supportiveness, and interdependence.

Many classrooms thrive on an atmosphere of competitiveness. Teachers often single out the best child, reward the one "correct" answer. This Q&A method may encourage memorization of data and goal-setting, which are helpful skills. The negative aspect of this is that many children learn to perform only as long as they are supervised and as long as there is some kind of reward or feedback. There is no autonomy in the learning, and the focus is on attaining goals set by the authority figure. On the other hand, when children play together, they are learning skills such as flexibility, mental agility, divergent thinking, independence, and the ability to collaborate. Loners, children who do not play with others, can grow up on the margins of society and develop unhealthy attitudes to others, which may be dangerous to others as well as themselves. The lonely scientist is just as dangerous as the lonely assembly worker. Playing well with others and being able to be hurt and recover are good preparation for a healthy and happy social life. Children who are driven by the need to please adults and be high achievers can suffer from stress and can be subject to depression and, sadly, even suicide if they do not succeed.

When children play together, conflict always appears. Rather than avoiding conflict, teachers can use this conflict to help children to learn how to deal with it. If two children are fighting over a block, a teacher can say, "Hmm, both girls want that block. What should we do?" If children are putting on a play and two boys are fighting over who is the chief pirate, a teacher can say, "Does anyone have any good ideas about this situation?" Since children want to keep playing, they will be motivated to solve the problem with a little guidance. A benefit of play is that it can cause conflict. Teachers should see this as an opportunity, not a failure.

PROTECTING A CHILD'S RIGHT TO PLAY

At Home

Parents should:

- Play with children.
- Let the child direct the play.
- Let the child come up with ideas.
- Hold back the adult critical voice (e.g., "This won't work") until the child has tried and found out for himself.
- Supervise group play so conflict doesn't destroy the fun.
- Reflect a child's difficulties back to him so he can overcome them: "I see you two boys want the same block. What could you do?"
- Provide simple and natural toys.
- Allow long periods of time for play.
- Provide private space for a child to play.
- Allow children to experiment with many materials.
- Allow children to make a mess or loud noises.

- Take children outside to play in playgrounds and in nature.
- Stand back and allow children to take risks while observing from close by.
- Create games so chores will be enjoyable.
- Use games as an aid during transition times.

Play should be encouraged in the home from the very earliest ages. Infants like to engage in simple play that fosters reciprocal relationships. This bonding through play is vital for emotional and cognitive development. Parents who make faces for their babies and talk in baby voices are naturally responding to their child's wish to be mirrored. Though parents may not notice the fleeting expressions of their baby, he or she is also imitating the parent's expression. Studies show that this interaction between baby and parent is the first game and serves the function of bonding parent and child.

There are many games that very young children love to engage in, such as peek-a-boo, another game in which babies are learning that when something goes away, it will return. Parents should play as often as they can in this way. Hiding and revealing games further assure children that there is constancy in his changing world. "Back and forth" games can help a child to bond with adults. These can include rolling a ball from parent to child. In doing this, eye contact with parents will strengthen, and the child will develop the ability to predict how others will respond to his advances as well as developing his skills at responding to his playmate.

As children develop their fine motor skills from the age of six months onward, parents can provide simple toys for them to manipulate. At this point parents need to stand back and allow the child to practice and explore. Educational toys should be kept simple, putting spheres and cubes into appropriate shaped holes is fine, and children learn a lot about the world in this way. However, studies have shown that children are learning about the properties of the world by putting toys in their mouths, so even if expensive educational toys are not available, a child has the innate ability to explore simple toys in his or her own way in order to get what she needs, and minimal guidance is required.

What is not appropriate for young children is trying to teach them to read or learn math by quizzing them and showing them flashcards. This kind of play is not enjoyable for children, who participate only to get the feedback and approval of parents. It is invasive and stressful and does not pay off in the long run. Young children should be given safe and natural materials—water, spoons, sand, cups, blocks, and be allowed to explore. This is not the time to worry about cleaning up the mess. Parents have to try not to worry about mess despite all they've learned through the years and to try not to be upset at noise, as children love to bang things and make loud noises as they play.

As children begin to walk, they will engage in pretend play and should be allowed to have the space and time to do so without interruption or pressure. They love kitchen and cookware as well as dolls and building toys. While children interact with others, issues of sharing and aggression will come up. Parents cannot sit back and allow two- or three-year-old children to work things out. They must stay in the background and yet be close enough and ready to step in and give the children emotional and social guidance so their struggles can work out positively.

At age four or so, children will be developing their social abilities and will be able to do more and more advanced play with others. Parents will still need to be close and supportive, as conflict will present itself and children need help. Toys can be provided for children in this age range, but they should be the kinds of toys that allow the imagination to expand—doll houses, dress-up clothes, sand, water, sticks, rocks, blocks, and other building toys, anything that permits the child to take the toy and use it rather than the other way around. Two good questions parents can ask themselves before buying a toy are: "Can my child do more than one thing with it?" and "Does this toy allow my child to use her imagination?" A toilet roll tube costs nothing and fits the criteria. A box of toilet roll tubes and a roll of tape can be a treasure trove for a little scientist or artist.

As children age, their play becomes more complex. Parents need to allow freedom for play, since homework often consumes a child's time, and well-meaning parents think the best thing for their child is to provide ballet classes, piano lessons, karate classes, swimming, and so on. Organized activities are fine, but should be kept to a minimum, since even an eight-year-old child can feel the pressure to succeed very keenly. If children are left to their own play, parents will notice they are naturally self-challenging. Watch a child learning to ride a bike or roller-skate. Provided the child has chosen to do this activity, he or she will work at it untiringly until the skill is mastered.

Hobbies or pastimes a child loves will play a large role in his life. One man I know collected eggs from wild birds' nests when he was a child and tried to incubate them in homemade nests hidden in the basement. When his parents discovered them, they were angry with him and threw them out, saying it was a foolish thing to do, nothing would ever hatch, and anyway what would he do with the birds if they did hatch? To this day that man wishes he'd been allowed to follow his interest. He works in an office job and still dreams about what it might be like to be a doctor or vet. Perhaps the parents could have encouraged his passion for nature instead of squashing it. He might have grown out of that interest and moved on to something else, but the point is that he will always feel regret and resentment that he was not allowed to find this out for himself.

Many parents today think computer games and video games are educational or entertaining for children, but they are not very healthy ways for a child to play. In his book *Last Child in the Woods*, Louv (2005)[14] points out the benefit of play outdoors. He refers to "nature-deficit disorder" as the lack of contact with nature which affects many children nowadays. Outdoor play is not only good for a child's physical health; it is also open-ended play since there are no rules on trees.

In School

Pre-K and kindergarten children are drawn to dramatic or free play in the same way as a ball thrown in the air is drawn back to the ground. Play is magnetically attractive to them; it is a real and natural need. There is extensive research in this field, demonstrating the benefits of play. Despite these results, many schools are cutting back severely on the amount of time allowed for play, even at the kindergarten level. Administrators and teachers who know better should hold firm on their conviction that children need to play. The first kindergarten was designed by Friedrich Froebel and was, as its name says, a garden for children to play in. It seems we have reverted to the time before Froebel.

If a three- or four-year-old child is in school for a six-hour day (and many are there longer), then the amount of free play should be at the very minimum two hours. Children should not be asked to sit still for long periods of time. An ideal day for children of this age should include at least two hours of play and a lot of varied activity, including art, music, and dance. This kind of variety allows for a child to have different kinds of stimulation while also allowing for academic activities along with satisfying the need to play. The child in this scenario has plenty of time for play, and teachers will notice that work time will be extremely focused and productive. A good experiment for teachers of young children is to take children outside to play for a half hour, then bring them in and give them focused tabletop work to do. Then try the experiment the other way around. They will find the children who have just played will be very quiet and interested in the focused work.

Children like to role-play, and teachers can take advantage of that play to expand on those themes. Based on children's interests, teachers can present books about firefighters or bring in skeletons or anatomy books at reading time and enhance the child's cognitive growth. Playing at being a knight can easily lead to building castles with blocks or learning complicated terms such as battlements, gauntlets, moat, and drawbridge, or learning emotional lessons such as how to manage your aggression by play fighting with swords and sticking to the rules of combat. Many good schools create a happy playful learning environment such as described here. Talk between the children during play increases their cooperative skills and fosters learning. I have seen many children develop an interest in a subject just because one of the other children brings in her passion to the classroom by sharing a toy or book from home. When teachers create a busy interactive environment such as this, there may be a lot of noise, but there is also a lot of excitement. With a classroom such as this, the child goes home happy, relaxed, and excited to return the next day to learn more.

In the older grades, time allocated to play tends to shrink since teachers feel more and more pressure to prepare children for exams. In first grade, hard work seems to be the order of the day. No more dress-up, no more interpersonal learning, and play is confined to recess time. From this point onward, children may learn various subjects to one degree or another, but they all learn one thing: school is a place where they have limited freedom and little power. When children are extrinsically motivated, they don't learn as much as when their motivation is intrinsic. In addition, children learn better when they are physically involved in the learning process. Good teachers or administrators could take the following steps to encourage children to be more openly playful and participate more:

- Involve children in classroom decisions, including set-up. This may allow a teacher to create a more interactive and playful classroom.
- Teach science through an experimental and interactive approach. Science should be playful and allow as many concrete experiences as possible.
- Teach math through play. Conduct hands-on experiments for mathematical activities so that children learn the real meaning of numbers. Math and music are also very connected, so pattern can be taught through the use of music. There are many games such as Sudoku, Connect Four, and games involving dice that can be used to illustrate various mathematical principles.
- Teach history through play. Teachers can put on plays and have children act out certain roles so they will come to understand history, which after all is a form of fiction involving characters and dramatic events.
- Teach reading and literacy study through play. In upper grades teachers can use drama to enhance children's grasp of plots, character, and events. In the lower grades teachers can play games such as "find the word" and hide words around the classroom or matching word games, etc.

- Teach literacy through creative writing. If a child writes about his own life, he will be more likely to read biographies of other people.
- Use music and art as teaching aids. One creative teacher I know used paintings as a way of studying various periods in history.
- Use popular media and art materials instead of traditional educational tools. A pupil could be asked to make a short movie for homework instead of writing a paper, or make a collage about a historic era, for instance. Homework does not need to be dreary or onerous.

Adults can do a lot to protect a child's right to play, from giving space and time to a child to play by himself, to encouraging and supporting a child's playfulness throughout his childhood. Adults can also fight against repressive philosophies that try to cut back on the normal activities of childhood and deprive children of their access to the world of their own imagination.

Play is universal. It exists in animals and humans. Play has been observed for many years to be the prerogative of children. Toys are a feature of life in cultures all over the world. Even animals play. Play is a natural activity for children, and it is one to which they are drawn as though by a magnet. This almost magical activity brings children into a special area of consciousness in which the child becomes a deeply engrossed participant. Studies show that the more a child plays, the more advanced his skills become—cognitive, social, and emotional. Other studies show that children who have not been allowed to play grow up to have disturbed personalities.

When children play at outdoor games—climbing, riding, roller-skating—they are harnessing their physical energy and achieving harmony between body and mind. When they play in conjunction with others, that harmony extends to others, their defenses decrease, and collaboration increases. Along with collaboration and social interaction comes cognitive growth. When they wrestle and challenge themselves in physical play with others, children develop mental flexibility and good-humored acceptance. When children play with others in dramatic role-playing, they learn skills that help them learn adaptive and collaborative skills. When children play alone in self-directed dramas, they learn coping skills so they may adapt to their changing lives and the vicissitudes that befall them.

We need to protect and defend the child's right to the space and time in which to do what the child wants. We need to stand back and allow children to come up with their own wonderful ideas, and when we do play along with them, we need to let them direct the play, since play is the one area in which children can be the powerful people they want to be. If we deprive them of that power when they are young, we may feel the repercussions of their anger or depression later on in life.

Notes

1. Rochat, P. (2009). *Others in Mind.* New York: Cambridge University Press.

2. Manning, J. (2005). "Rediscovering Froebel: A Call to Re-examine his Life and Gifts." *Early Childhood Education Journal* 32:6, 371–376. June.

3. Wenner, M. (2009). "The Serious Need for Play." *Scientific American Mind,* 23–29

4. Brooks, David. (2011). "Amy Chua is a Wimp." *New York Times Op Ed,* January 17.

5. Halinen, et al. (2005). "A Land of Readers." *Educational Leadership* 63:2, 72–75.

6. Kimonen, E. (2001). "Ed. Curriculum Approaches: Readings and Activities for Educational Studies." *Jyvaskyla University Institute for Educational Research.* Jyvaskala, FI: 2–278.

7. Alvarez, L. (2004). "Educators Flocking to Finland, Land of Literate Children." *New York Times* Vol. 153, Issue 52814: A4, April 9.

8. Hyvönen, P. (2008). "Teachers' perceptions of boys' and girls' shared activities in the school context: towards a theory of collaborative play." *Teachers and Teaching: Theory and Practice* 14: 5–6, 391–409.

9. Rathnude, K., and Csikzentmihalyi M. (2005). "Middle School Students' Motivation and Quality of Experience: A Comparison of Montessori and Traditional School Environments." *American Journal of Education* 111: 341–371.

10. Frost, B. (1999). "Thomas Edison: The Man Who Brought the Twentieth Century to Light." *Biography* 3:10, 104–112.

11. Freud, S. (1908). *Character and Culture.* New York, NY: Macmillan Publishing, 35.

12. Robson, M. (2008). "The driver whose heart was full of sand: Leigh's story: a play therapy case study of a bereaved child." *British Journal of Guidance and Counselling* 36:1, 71–80.

13. Chazan, S. (2002). *Profiles of Play.* London, UK: Jessica Kingsley Publishers, 198.

14. Louv, R. (2005). *Last Child in the Woods.* New York, NY: Workman Publishing.

Chapter 6

Children Have the Right to Be Protected from Bullying

Children are naturally vulnerable individuals and as such are liable to be hurt physically or emotionally by those who are bigger or have more power than them. Therefore they must be protected. Seedlings are often grown indoors so they can become strong enough to survive outside in the elements. In the same way, young children cannot be left to fend for themselves physically or emotionally when they are in danger of being bullied, harassed, intimidated, or humiliated by others. They must be sheltered by nurturing adults and given techniques of self-defense. It is a child's right to have that protection, and parents and teachers have a duty to protect them.

Bullying is the act of intimidating or mistreating other people. Bullying can take many forms. Unfortunately it is almost a primal instinct for some people to intimidate others and use their power to make others feel less powerful. Usually this happens when the person who is doing the bullying has herself been bullied, or feels inadequate or threatened in some way and needs to feel superior. These individuals often gratify their egos by trying to make others feel intimidated and may band into groups in order to gain support in their bullying activities.

The definitive aspect of bullying, as contrasted with other forms of negative behavior such as arguing or fighting, is the express intent to hurt. The bully intends to elicit fear or acquire subjugation. Bullying may take place over a course of time and may be a pattern of behavior, but it can also consist of only one episode that results in eliciting intense fear, which is the goal of the bully. When a young child experiences bullying, he may feel able to withstand the bullying and defend himself. More often than not, a young child tends to feel helpless in the face of bullying. Bullying is very common, and it is probably safe to say that every one of us has experienced it at one time or another. Parents who have experienced bullying as young children may react by feeling helpless and angry when they hear their child has been bullied and may instruct their child to act aggressively or seek revenge, and that is not necessarily a good strategy for a child. Adults can help children to defend themselves in better ways.

PHYSICAL BULLYING

It is easy for adults to physically intimidate young people since they are small and unable to fight back. That is why parents and guardians should be careful about the people to whom they entrust their child, especially when the child is very young and cannot tell the parents about what is happening in their absence. Physical bullying may be quite subtle and may not be the same as physical abuse. An adult can bully a child by grabbing and pushing, and although this kind of treatment does not leave bruises, it does make the child feel intimidated and coerced. Sadly, this kind of rough handling, or physical bullying, is very common and can be seen on the streets, in buses, and aboard subways. Physical bullying of young children may be accompanied by verbal threats, and while verbal bullying is very damaging, it is different from physical bullying in certain ways.

The verbal threat that goes along with physical bullying is an extension of the physical bullying. I recently witnessed a woman in the street grabbing and shaking her child by the neck of her coat. As she did so, she warned the child about future physical actions: "Just wait till you get home!" That threat is really just an extension of the physical bullying and an attempt to extend the physical power, which the parent exerts over the child with her physical abuse. In that way, bullies might, for instance, hit a child just once. Thereafter they might need only to say something like, "Remember what happened last time?" In this way they get control over the other person by threatening to repeat the previous action. This may or may not be accompanied by verbal or emotional bullying. One girl I know had just started at junior high when another girl came up to her and said, "I could hurt you if I wanted to, but I won't." Though she didn't lay a hand on her, and her words even seemed to promise *not* to lay a hand on her, this was still a physical threat. The effect of the comment was to make the girl aware of imminent violence and to be afraid of it. The taunt was effective for the bully, as the girl experienced fear every time she saw her.

As children grow older, physical bullying can take various forms. There may be low-level bullying that is neither violent by nature nor malicious in intent. For instance, children may be grabbed and pulled by adults in order to keep them going along with the program. Teachers and parents may not even be consciously trying to bully children but may think it is their duty to get things done according to the schedule. Instead of letting children fasten their own coats or finish their lunches slowly, they may feel the pressure to move things along, and so they intimidate children by pulling and grabbing, putting their coats on for them, though they are quite capable of doing it. The goal of this kind of physical action is not malicious. This controlling behavior is not aimed at instilling fear, but it does take power away from the child in order to achieve the goal of the adult, who may himself feel harassed by his own inner or outer demands.

I remember seeing one parent who had a very gentle voice and a respectful manner towards her child. Her calm and relaxed manner made her child behave in a very controlled way. She would speak to him from across the room without even looking over at him and use the same kind of voice she would use for adults—"Harry, would you mind cleaning the blocks up?"—while she herself was busy doing her own work, and the child happily obliged. It seemed there was an invisible thread connecting them, a kind of trust. You could tell that the child was not hassled or bullied by the mother and obliged quickly because she was allowing him to have his own space and time to respond to her. She seemed to me to be an "unbully." Her trust in the child was paying off since she had all the cooperation she would like from him.

At homework time, some parents feel they need to physically intimidate the child so the work gets done. I know one highly intelligent and well-educated person who told me that when she was a young child doing homework at the table, her mother used to stand over her with a fly swatter in her hand. When she got a wrong answer, the fly swatter came down on top of her head with a loud crack. I am sure this parent thought she was doing the right thing for whatever reason. The result of her actions, however, was that the child grew up with a lot of anxiety and now struggles hard to manage her own mood swings. Though she is very accomplished, she does not feel at peace. Once again, this parent was not consciously trying to deprive the child of power, so her behavior does not fully fit the definition of bullying. However, she was intimidating the child. The result of the intimidating behavior is that the child was robbed of the enjoyment she should have had in doing her homework and she developed a life-long anxiety.

Parents and teachers who are themselves caught up in anxiety do these kinds of intimidating actions. They are done in order to achieve compliance from children. These adults probably do not realize the consequence of their actions. That is not to excuse this kind of behavior. Any intimidation of those weaker than us is morally wrong. However, the outcome is not an express intention of the person who is bullying.

There is a second level of physical bullying, and that is the kind of bullying in which the bully is conscious of his goal and deliberately seeks to inflict pain or humiliation. Physical bullying tends to occur at an early age. A child of two will grab a toy away from another child so he can have possession of it. If he can successfully hold on to it, he will. He may resist the previous owner's attempt to take it back by hitting, biting, or any other means he feels necessary. This is an early form of aggression. There is nothing personal in it. It is not even anger. It is a primal kind of aggression in which the child is driven by the need to possess something. The child is probably not even conscious of the effects of his actions. However, when we do look at children of this age, we may also see a form of sadistic aggression.

Some children may, for instance, step on another child's hand just to see their reaction or, perhaps from a form of innate sadism, to enjoy having power over another. A young girl may pinch her baby sister's leg because she is feeling jealous, but she may also do it because she enjoys inflicting pain on someone she feels has taken something away from her. This is a kind of vengeful aggression. Children will also try to seek revenge on other children who are hurting their friends. These kinds of normal and natural aggression are what parents work to tame. If this "taming" is not achieved, the result may be a child who likes to bully others. However, it should not be done by bullying the child into compliance.

Taming aggression is achieved by having the Id come into a workable arrangement with the Superego. During the first three or four years of a child's life, the adults in her world are working to socialize her to allow her to develop a healthy Ego. The healthy Ego is a balance between the Id, or primal aggressive impulses, and the Superego, or conscience. This process takes some time, and parents and teachers need to understand that two worlds are colliding: the world of "I want to" and the world of "I should." The authority figure has to come up with compromises so that a child is happy to give up the unsocial behavior and substitute acceptable behavior. Authority figures cannot be heavy-handed in this process, or the result will be a child who complies outwardly with the rules and inwardly feels aggressive. This child may feel the need to intimidate others the way she feels intimidated by adults.

In a normal healthy family situation, the child will come to realize that it is OK to feel aggressive. She does not need to feel too ashamed of her aggression; in other words, her Superego will not be dominant. On the other hand, she will not be overly aggressive; her Id will be under control. Alongside this development, a child should be becoming empathetic to others. With empathy, a child will feel the feelings of others and will learn that hurting others is not a good thing; however, she may still feel like doing it. A healthy child can admit to herself, "I would love to hurt that person, but I am not going to do it." A healthy family can allow a child to say these things openly, and parents can say to children, "I know you would love to hurt your baby sister. I can understand what you are feeling, but you know you can't do it." This kind of openness will help a child control feelings of sadism or anger and help her to refrain from bullying, even when the parents are not watching.

However, things don't always go so smoothly. Many families suffer difficulties and even trauma, and these factors may affect children adversely. If a husband is inflicting physical abuse on his wife, their child will likely have great difficulty in managing his own anxieties and his anger. John Lennon's killer, Mark David Chapman, grew up in such a household. The feelings of helplessness he felt on seeing his father bully his mother resulted in his own anger going underground. This anger surfaced later in life and caused him to commit the ultimate violence, murder—the assassination of someone who had nothing to do with the cause of his original pain.

SELF-DEFENSIVE BULLYING

School presents great difficulties for children whose peace has been violated, either through direct bullying and sadism of their own parents, or through witnessing bullying and violence done to others in the home. The typical child bully is someone who comes to a group situation with a great deal of anxiety and anger. He experiences the school group in the same way he experienced his family. No one will be there to protect him, so he can only rely on himself. Danger is all around him. People bigger than him have control over him and may hurt him. He feels helpless, and feeling helpless makes him feel angry. These factors make a child extremely defensive. If you picture an animal trapped in a corner, you can imagine that that animal will do anything it needs to do in order to protect itself. That is probably what a violated child feels inside.

A child of this kind has a weak Ego. He does not think of himself as capable of surviving without being on the defensive. He thinks that if he doesn't go over and grab a toy for himself, nobody will give it to him. And the only way for him to keep this one toy he has managed to get for himself is to fight off everyone who comes near. Contrast this with a child who has a strong Ego. This child has been comforted by adults and has a little interior voice that tells him, "Don't be afraid. You can handle this. You don't need to grab; just tell the person you would like a turn with the toy when he is finished."

The boy with the weak Ego cannot bear how vulnerable he feels. In order to regain some power and to make his Ego feel a (false) sense of power, this child will exert power over weaker children. The child who bullies comes to school feeling helpless and angry. His mother or his father may have struck him on the face that morning. And so, when he sees a little boy playing calmly with a toy, apparently happy and contented, his anger wells up, and he feels like hurting the little boy in the same way someone has hurt him. He will walk over to that little boy, take his toy, and slap him in the face. He is taking his first steps towards being a bully. At this point in time, an observant teacher can intervene and try to help the incipient bully to come to terms with his anger and helplessness. This early intervention could prevent bullying from developing into full-blown sadism. However, sadly, this seldom happens. More often than not, this kind of child tends to go from one level of bullying to the next. And this kind of behavior is not limited to any one social or economic group. Bullying happens in every school.

Boys tend to be more likely than girls to bully other children physically. And, oddly enough, boys tend to be the recipients of physical bullying more often than girls. Scheithauer (2006) reports on his study of German schoolchildren: "Significantly more boys reported bullying others, regardless of bullying form, and significantly more boys than girls were classified as bully/victims. Although there was no gender difference for victimisation at all, boys reported significantly more often than girls being bullied physically."[1]

In the very younger age groups, children are more overt in their bullying. The three-year-old who wants to hurt his peer may walk over and, lacking impulse control, just hit him with a toy. The other child will probably cry loudly, and so this kind of physical bullying is clearly visible. Since the action is overt, the teacher will most likely be able to see the bullying and take direct action. Young children may be more likely to be protected by teachers.

However, as children grow older, they become more able to deceive. Studies show that when children reach age four, they are able to know what others think. Perner (1997) explains that knowing what others think opens the door for deception:

> Another way to investigate children's understanding of how misinformation works is to look at their own use of it in deception. The bulk of the experimental evidence on children's ability to deceive clearly suggests that flexible and insightful deception does not emerge before the understanding of false belief at about four years . . . Also the opinion of mothers and nursery school teachers tends to converge on the age of four years as the onset of intentional deception . . . in which children understand that they are manipulating their victim's mental states and not just behaviour . . .[2]

Once children reach age four, they are able to be deceptive. The four-year-old bully has by this age learned that he will receive a consequence for his behavior. He also knows that if no one sees him, he may be able to avoid the consequence. A bully of this age may know how to step on someone's hand and, when confronted, say it was an accident. He may breeze past someone and, without looking at them, stick his elbow out and knock the other person onto the ground, then pretend it was an accident. At this point he is able to deceive. It might not be an effective deceit, since teachers may see a pattern—anyone who happens to be in this boy's way tends to get hurt. That is why teachers need to be vigilant, or the bully will develop more devious strategies. Adults need to spot the pattern, however subtle it might be, and try to take action as early as possible in a child's life. If the bully has learned to deceive and is quietly hurting people around him, he presents a threat not only to those around him but also to society at large. By the time this boy is seven or eight, his techniques will be more sophisticated. He needs help, or he will hurt a lot of people along the way.

DOMINATION BULLYING

In the higher grades, some children use "proactive" forms of aggression: for instance, taking something before someone else can get it or taking something away from someone else by force in order to establish dominance. This is a kind of physical bullying that is not so much aimed at inflicting pain or humiliation as it is to asserting one's leadership in the group. Leadership is taken and maintained by a pattern of aggression. The other children will tend to take a step back when a child of this type takes over. Since the individual involved may also gain a group of friends around him who like to operate in the shadow of a dominant person, quieter children may simply allow him to have what he wants and hope he doesn't bother them any more. Some children may gravitate to these dominant children because they are extroverted and may have qualities that they themselves do not have.

One man I know remembers to this day the terror he felt at being bullied. For no reason at all, one of the school bullies threatened to beat him up after lunch. Since he lived close to school, the boy ran home and spent the whole time barely able to think. He contemplated running away but finally decided that the best thing to do was to wait until it was late and everyone had already gone into the school. Then he dashed across the yard and out of his eye's corner saw the bully coming after him. Luckily for him, someone had told the teacher, who intervened and made the bully shake hands with him. But the fear did not go away. Most children in this position learn to live in fear, and many do not confide in their parents.

Teachers, unless someone speaks up, often don't see the extent of this aggression, as children are more able to confine their aggressive behavior to occasions when they are not being observed. They may also be able to keep their aggression at a certain level that does not exceed the standards imposed by the school. In other words, there may be a certain level of physical aggression tolerated by schools, either because it is not overt, not excessive, or not easy to prove, even if others report it. This kind of bully may be quite personable. He may speak out more in class, and he may have a way of making himself attractive to the teacher. The teacher may not even notice that he is dominating every conversation. And since the other children take a back seat and allow him to talk, the teacher may not perceive it as a problem. Some schoolteachers may classify children of this kind as "leaders" and write on their school reports that they have leadership qualities, though this is not real leadership at all but domination.

SADISTIC BULLYING

There is a higher level of physical bullying in which aggression is not solely aimed at keeping the bully in a position of power, but the bully is operating from the sadistic desire to see other people hurt or humiliated. I remember walking home by myself as a young child when a group of older children surrounded me in a circle. They started to talk to each other about me as if I were a mouse they had caught in a trap and were wondering what they should do with me. I started to cry, and one of them felt sorry for me and said, "Let her go," at which point I ran home. That incident did not involve any physical pain; no one hurt me. But to this day, I can remember the terror of being physically surrounded by a group of people who have power over you and want to hurt you. I can only guess that having that kind of power over a smaller person must have given some sadistic satisfaction to the individuals concerned. Perhaps also the enjoyment was increased by the fact that other people were witnesses to the triumph the bully had over the victim, or to the fact that the individuals in the group were gaining satisfaction from having strength by being in a group. I have no doubt that some of these individuals were themselves victims of abuse or humiliation, and that this was a way for them to restore some power to their own egos.

Some children use physical aggression and threats of physical aggression as a form of domination. They seem to enjoy having power and work hard to maintain it by routine acts of aggression. In many schools there is a small group, usually boys, who assert their physical strength—or, more accurately, a willingness to be aggressive—early on in the school year. In so doing, they assert their dominance, for no other reason than to be superior. These bullies seem to have a good instinct as to who will be afraid to fight back, and they select these people expressly for bullying. Strangely, though these bullies are in the minority, they are able to dominate the majority of others who seem to feel isolated and alone. I know one boy who, in middle school, found out it was better not to fight back.

At that time, boys were obliged to take a shower after Physical Education class. This meant that they had to undress in front of others in the locker room, wrap their towels around them, and proceed to the shower. The small group of bullies consisted in only three or four boys who were more physically developed and more muscular than the other boys. Their presence alone was intimidating to the boys who were not as physically developed; they appeared to be like men, while the others seemed more like boys. The bullies would use this opportunity in which others were physically vulnerable to go around the room and whip them with their wet towels. The boy in question was not as physically developed as the others and tried to change his clothing as quickly as possible without being seen. He was a perfect target for the bullies, who whipped him in the buttocks. The towel not only hurt his buttocks but inflicted pain on his testicles. The physical pain and feelings of humiliation were intense, but the feeling of fear overrode the whole episode. Not only was he unable to retaliate or defend himself, he could not even show pain in case he would become further prey for them. The experience of going to PE became terrifying for him. He developed physical symptoms that were undoubtedly psychosomatic and was excused from PE on some days. On other days, he avoided school altogether so he did not have to go to the shower. To this day, though he loves swimming, he refuses to join a health club or go to a public swimming pool, since the experience of going into the locker room brings back all the feelings of anger, humiliation, and fear he felt when he was at a very vulnerable age.

For myself, as a victim, the experience of being dominated by a group is still painful and difficult to think about, since it gives the ego a sense of vulnerability, and no one likes to think of herself as a victim. People who are victims of bullying may suffer damage to their self-esteem and may come to think of themselves as weak. They may also suffer depression later in life, since they have feelings of anger that have not been dealt with. Angry feelings, along with feelings of helplessness, can cause victims of bullying to react in different ways. They may direct their feelings of anger and helplessness inwardly and may become depressed or even suicidal. Alternatively, they may become bullies themselves, and they may engage in violent acts of aggression directed at innocent victims. We are all too familiar with how this works.

The word "Columbine" can be used alone, and most people in America, if not the world, will know what is meant by the term. Columbine High School in Colorado was the site of a terrible massacre in 1999. Two students entered the school and started shooting. They killed thirteen students and injured dozens more, and they finally killed themselves. They had intended to kill hundreds of people with bombs, which fortunately did not go off. After their deaths, contributory factors came to light about the young men. They had troubled personalities; one of them was diagnosed as psychopathic, the other depressive. However, another contributing factor came to light: the two boys were bullied at school and felt a lot of anger towards their classmates. In an article on the tenth anniversary of the shooting, Toppo (2009) reports that Eric Harris, the mastermind of the attack, felt rejected by his fellow students: " . . . one of Harris' last journal entries read: 'I hate you people for leaving me out of so many fun things. And no don't . . . say, 'Well that's your fault,' because it isn't, you people had my phone #, and I asked and all, but no. No no no don't let the weird-looking Eric KID come along.'"[3]

The article goes on to state that these kinds of school attacks, which have become increasingly common, tend to be committed by children who are bullied or rejected by their peers: "Princeton sociologist Katherine Newman . . . says young people such as Harris and Klebold are not loners—they're just not accepted by the kids who count. Getting attention by becoming notorious is better than being a failure."

The violence that is evident in this incident and other similar incidents often does not have its roots in physical bullying. Apparently Harris and his collaborator, Dylan Klebold, were not physically threatened by other children and did not feel in physical danger from other students. However, they were rejected and called names by others, which is probably a more deadly form of bullying—emotional bullying.

EMOTIONAL BULLYING

Emotional bullying is a very powerful form of bullying. The old saying about sticks and stones being more hurtful than words is not true. The use of words or the use of power in relationships can be far more hurtful to a child than violence or the threat of violence. Emotional bullying begins very early on. Children have a good grasp of the skill of threatening. It is not clear whether they learn this from their parents or not, since many parents like to use threats. But by the age of four, children know how to react to frustration by saying, "If you don't give me that toy, I will not invite you to my birthday party." The person who receives this kind of threat almost always gives in. Very few children can retaliate with, "I don't care about your birthday party. I don't need to be included in a group to feel important. I am an individual who is completely self-reliant." When children try another threat, for instance: "If you don't give me your toy, I won't share mine," the response can be very different. Children seldom relinquish a loved toy for a different one unless the one being traded is vastly superior. However, they will give up even the most exciting toy in order to be invited to a birthday party that will happen in the vague and distant future. Why is that? It is because children cannot bear to be ostracized. It is quite astonishing that children who live in the moment can feel the threat of social rejection so keenly that they would rather give up a delightful toy than be left out of a group of peers. The need to belong is apparently as important as any other need and more important than most other needs.

EXCLUSION

Many children like to play in small groups and frequently will reject a newcomer. "You can't come in here; we're firefighters," they will argue. When the other child says, "I want to be a firefighter too," they may or may not open up and let him in. They are likely to say things like, "You're not a firefighter. You're too small," or "You're a girl; you can't play with us." These are the beginnings of exclusive behavior. It is difficult to say why children do this. Children enjoy membership in groups with defined rules, for instance the "firefighter" group. However, they apparently enjoy the power to exclude others, and they seem to enjoy colluding with others in excluding. The child who sets the rules for the group—for instance, "We're monsters, and girls can't be monsters," —will find many followers.

Members of the group seem to enjoy the fact that others are excluded from this group. A child within the group will seldom protest this rule purely from a sense of justice. The response to sweeping statements such as "Girls can't be monsters" is always a resounding, "Right!" For some reason, children enjoy creating and adhering to social rules. A three-year-old will seldom think that an abstract and arbitrary rule can be wrong. He will never say, "I disagree; girls might make good monsters," He will never use logic such as, "Yesterday a girl was a monster. What about that?" And he will never ask the question, "Why not?" Generally, he will go along with whatever rule has been handed down by the most vocal member of the group. That is not to say that children are heartless. If a girl comes along and asks if she can join in the monster game, someone might ask the others to bend the rules on her behalf. And often they do. However, at other times these self-created groups appear to not welcome change once the group is established.

Some people might say that's fine. Children should be allowed to group themselves the way they want to, and in all fairness, why can't they have a game with a small group of players. Why do they have to allow others to join in? That's a very valid point and one that has been discussed at length in a wonderful book by Vivian Gussin Paley, entitled *You Can't Say You Can't Play*.[4] Children do have the right to play in small groups, and sharing everything you have is not always possible. However, we are talking about the role of the school in educating young children about exclusivity, fairness, and group dynamics. As adults, it is our duty to protect the weak, and teachers should not allow children to hurt others.

If we are not sure about whether children should be allowed to exclude others, we might once again take the situation and see if we can apply it to an adult setting. We can ask the question, "Would you accept this behavior if adults were doing it?" If a nation decides to reject or segregate one group because of their appearance, their age, their gender, or because they are recent immigrants, that is clearly discrimination. Not allowing others to join certain organizations is a form of exclusion. If children play games in which they deliberately exclude others, then that is an early form of bullying. Teachers and parents should not allow this kind of behavior to go unnoticed. They should discuss it openly and ask children to come up with a good solution themselves.

One problem of exclusion is that it can escalate. Once a child feels the power of having a group of children listen to her and follow her directives, she may want to maintain that feeling. On top of the satisfaction of having a group follow her rules, she may find that she can gain more authority by keeping some people out. Perhaps she is jealous of another girl. She can now exclude that girl from her group. Perhaps she will enjoy making that girl cry or look hurt when she is left out. Perhaps she will enjoy having other children tease her and, in this way, inflict pain without having the responsibility of doing it herself. Obviously, this kind of behavior does not happen all the time, and leaving a child out of a game does not always lead to exclusive behavior; however, it can. If teachers and parents ignore this behavior they may in effect be condoning bullying, since they are failing to protect the children who are being left out of the group. It is an adult's duty to try to help the children to come up with compromises and solutions to dilemmas such as the desire to play with certain people conflicting with the allegiance to others.

In one elementary school, children gathered at recess time in the playground and played, as is common at recess, without much teacher supervision. They played a game called "Cat and Mouse." The mice were almost always girls, and they hid inside a hollow area under a climbing dome. The cats were usually boys, and they enjoyed hunting for the mice, who huddled inside, safe in a group. They would surround the dome and pretend to prey on the "mice." Everyone loved the game. One girl told me that when she wanted to get inside the "mouse house" with the girls, she was told, "You can't come in here. There's no room for you," even though there was. She was humiliated not only by feeling left out of the "family" of mice, but also by being relegated to the group of boys. This is a kind of "gender bullying." The girls were aware of having a gender-specific group and aware that they had the power to exclude other girls from this group. Doing so made the girls less "girly" and have less status in the hierarchy of girls. Boys can do this too by indicating that some boys are less "masculine" than others, e.g. they are not wearing the right kind of shirt or shoes, or are smaller than other boys.

As children grow older, this kind of emotional bullying can escalate. Many people remember their middle school days as being filled with emotional pain. And most of that pain comes not from struggles with academic problems, but with dealing with difficult social situations. The primal needs for nourishment and shelter being satisfied, the next highest human need is the need for relating to other humans. Studies have shown that babies who have adequate nourishment and shelter but no human relationship will decline, suffer emotional and physical damage, and even die. So the need to relate to others may credibly be described as the most important human need of all. Being rejected is a very painful feeling to children.

SELF-DEFEATING BEHAVIOR

Some children are excluded because of their inability to develop good social skills. They develop self-defeating behavior that encourages others to dismiss or exclude them, and this can be a self-fulfilling prophecy. They are often rejected because they elicit rejection with their behavior. This kind of child may report to teachers or parents that "Nobody likes me." Parents and teachers may actually enable the child to remain in his self-defeating pattern. A teacher who intervenes and says, "Now, please play with this boy," can cause more harm than good. The child will be confirmed in his image of himself as weak and needy, and the group will be irritated by him. Nobody wants to *have* to play with someone.

One little boy complained to me, "Nobody will play with me." I observed his interaction with the group, and it followed a definite pattern. He would see a group of children playing together—for instance, building with blocks. He stood over them as they played, and said in a slightly whiny voice to no one in particular, "I want to play too." The children may or may not have heard him, but they ignored his whining and went on with their play. Possibly none of the children felt he was talking to them personally, so none of them responded. He then gave up and came to me to complain about being left out. He also went home and told his parents the same thing, and they in turn complained to me that their son was being left out.

I decided that he needed to learn how to present himself better. When he said to me, "Nobody will play with me," I explained to him, "You don't need to ask them. That's not how it works. You need to get down on the ground beside them and just join in." I went over with him and showed him. "Bring over that block and just put it on top where they are playing," I said. "If they don't want the bock there, ask them where they want you to put it." I encouraged him to stop asking for permission and to instead see what the others were doing and join in. I told him that if he wanted someone's attention, he should not say, "I want to play," but instead pick one person and say, "Hey, Jack, can I play too?" I also explained to his parents how I was handling his difficulty so that we could all work to help him instead of feeling sorry for him.

Another boy who was not very popular had a habit of telling other children what they should do. When the teacher told everyone to put toys away, he felt the need to be the teacher's chief enforcement officer. He put his hands on his hips and yelled at the other children to put things away. When they didn't move fast enough, he grabbed the toys and put them away himself. I noticed that he often stayed with the teacher and didn't find friends. One day I asked him if he wanted more friends, and he said that he did. I brought him over to a young boy who is very kind and articulate. "Why don't you play more with Justin?" I asked. "Because he always bosses me around," the boy answered. "When?" I asked. "When we're putting toys away, he grabs them," the child answered. I looked at Justin. "People don't seem to like it when you yell at them to put the toys away," I said. I continued to guide the boy away from unsociable behavior by pointing out the things he did that people didn't like and by telling him nice things about himself that people did like. Gradually he stopped his habit of bossing others around and moved out of the shadow of the teachers and into group play. Hearing feedback from other children is a good way to learn how to belong to a group. When children exclude, they may have reasons for doing so.

One day I was conducting a lesson on exclusion in a Fours Class. One of the boys pointed at another boy and said, "I think everyone leaves out him." "Why do you think that is?" I asked. "I think it's because every time we are having transitions or going out somewhere, he starts crying and doing silly stuff." The other boy's eyes grew wider. "No, I don't!" he said. "Well, actually

I think he is right," I said gently. "I have seen you doing it myself. Maybe you need to listen to what your friend is telling you." I was very pleased that this child had pointed out to his friend why he might be excluded. This particular boy had a lot of behavioral issues that the teachers and his parents were struggling with. Yet having it pointed out by another child in a neutral and objective way was very helpful. Though the boy found it hard to accept at first, his behavior did change after that encounter. When he did revert to throwing himself on the floor or running away, the teachers were able to say, "I don't think your friends enjoy this behavior." In this way, a child can learn a lot from hearing how he comes across to others. Getting feedback from others is a good way for children to learn how to be accepted and how to get rid of self-defeating behaviors. Teaching children social skills, especially ways of connecting positively with a group, can help to minimize the problem of exclusion.

TEASING

Children in groups attach to each other in complex ways. Language is one way of bonding within the group. Language can be used to provide information, or it can be used to withhold it. It can be used to communicate feelings or to withhold them. It can be used to provide access to resources or to withhold that access. Language can be used to transmit values and norms and set expectations for the group. As children grow older, they learn more about how information is transmitted and learn how other people think, and so they can be more and more astute in their use of language in social situations. Since humans cannot read each other's minds, and language is limited in its power to express all we think and feel, misunderstandings abound in human relationships. Therefore bullying can happen when some children understand more fully than others how to manipulate language and control information—or control the *access* to information, to resources, or to other relationships. Teasing can start out completely unintentionally.

One day at lunch time a boy said to another boy, "Your lunch is yucky. I hate ham!" The other boy said nothing, but it was clear that he felt hurt. Another boy joined in: "Me too. I hate ham." They both started laughing. I stepped in. "How does that make you feel when someone says they hate your lunch?" I asked. "Bad," the boy answered. "Look, it makes him feel bad when you say you hate his lunch," I said to the others. "But I don't like it. I hate what he has," the other boy said. "Yes, I know that you don't like it. But he does. His mommy made that for him, and he likes it. Two people can like different things. When you say his lunch is yucky, it makes him feel bad because he likes it." That revelation seemed to confound everyone at the table. It seemed like a new insight to them that people can be different, that people can like things you don't like, and that you can allow them to like what they like. In our school, we like to give children information about how other people feel and react. That seems to be a good weapon against teasing.

Some children use words with the intent to put themselves in a more favorable position. One day at lunch time, a child said to another child, "My sandwich is bigger than yours." In this case, we put a name to the comment. I said, "That's teasing. Teasing is when someone says that they are better than you, or bigger than you, or they have more than you." As soon as I said that, a little girl said, "My sister always says that her dress is nicer than mine." "Do you like when she says that?" I asked her. "No, I hate it," she answered. "Well, that's called teasing, and it is hurtful," I responded. Every time we hear teasing, we try to make the children aware that is what it is called. Now they recognize it themselves, and they reflect it back to each other. "You're teasing me," they say to each other, and we feel proud that they can do it. This is a good way to safeguard against bullying, as it gives children techniques for recognizing teasing and responding to it at an early age, and it also helps eliminate it in the classroom.

PREEMPTING BULLYING

Some people who are afraid of being bullied learn to use their wits to scare people away from them. The young boy who was terrorized by the lunchtime bully learned how to use sharp and witty comments to ward off bullying. He was able to draw a crowd around himself—they liked the way he used his wit to put people down. In this way they created their own coterie. They did not go out of their way to attack others verbally, but they learned to use language in a way that would defend them against others. They created their own "cool" group. I know another young girl who felt intimidated at school and managed to draw a group of "outsiders" to herself. She became the leader of these unaccepted individuals, and they formed their own group and developed their own insider jokes. This became a real safety net for all the members of the group.

Other people find older or bigger children who act as "bodyguards." These children are not afraid of the bullies and are happy to play a protective role to smaller or more timid children. Playing this role can be very satisfying for them, as they may not be accepted by children of their own age. The movie *My Bodyguard* tells the story of how an older boy helps a younger boy and coaches him on how to protect himself.

BEING ACCEPTED

Children seem to realize that others have a need to be accepted, and they can use that knowledge to hurt. Older children who wish to intimidate will wait until a child is alone or is outnumbered or unprotected by an adult, and they will use words to make her feel she is not good enough. "Did I ever tell you your ears are way too big?" one seven-year-old girl said to another girl when they were out of earshot of parents and teachers but in the presence of another friend. Since it was a loaded question, there was no way to answer. The presence of a witness was even more embarrassing. Since the little girl believed the bully, she didn't tell her parents, as she thought they also knew her ears were too big.

Children often feel a sense of shame when they have been bullied, and this shame may prevent them from telling others about the incident. They would rather preserve their sense of integrity than confide to others that they have been shamed. Bullies often force their victim to keep something secret under threat of retribution. These secrets may be very powerful ways of preventing a child from reporting bullying. This kind of bullying may have a sexual element, in which a child is forced to do something or witness something and then compelled to keep the experience a secret.

As children grow older, words are used increasingly to define group membership and bond members of the group together. However, they are also used more and more to give importance to social structures in order to increase personal power and inflict dominance over and even pain to others. Girls are more likely in the teen years to use words as a way of social bonding. This can take very positive forms. Girls tend to express their feelings more often than boys and can actually use their weakness as a way of connecting with others. Showing weakness to others can be a powerful way of connecting with the group and being accepted and obtaining support. Boys often lack this ability and tend not to use words to connect with others. Studies show that boys seem to fear exposing their feelings and consider emotional expression as a sign of weakness and vulnerability in group situations.

When children enter middle school, around age twelve or so, they are becoming more emotionally separated from their parents. They are less and less interested in the opinions of adults and more and more interested in the support from and opinion of their peers. They are also developing physically in such a way that their whole identity seems in flux. They enter this stage of their lives feeling uncertain, vulnerable, and needy of the good opinion of others. This is the age at which bullying becomes most virulent. At this age, children are able to use language in a very sophisticated way. However, they are still not always completely conscious of the power they exert over others.

Many children who have bullied and terrorized others in junior high often express complete surprise when their victims confront them later on in life. They inflicted a great deal of suffering without being aware of the effect of their words. Others, however, do have the intent to humiliate others.

APPEARANCE

The main target of emotional bullying at this age is appearance. Children make fun of others' weight or height, their skin (many children suffer from acne at this age) or hair, their sexual development, or their ethnic backgrounds. But, unfortunately, no one can win. A child may be teased if she is too fat, or she may be teased if she is too thin. She may have no breasts, or her breasts may be too big. She may be too short, or she may be too tall. The weapon used is teasing, but the point is to put other people into an inferior position, and the standards of physical perfection can be varied according to the target. Children at this age are aware of the insecurity other children feel. They seem to know that even beautiful people do not feel that they are beautiful. Many beautiful and successful people will say that they were bullied and felt ugly at this age.

In addition to their appearance, children at this age are judged and criticized by others based on their clothing. One young girl told me she was approached by a boy she didn't even know at gym class, and he asked her, "What's the brand on your sneakers?" When she replied, he sneered at her, "Where did you get those? Payless?" The result is a feeling of being not good enough, and this evokes shame. This kind of bullying is aimed at making other children feel impoverished or not stylish. Children can be teased by others who create a standard of clothing or style for everyone to follow. Stepping outside the fashion norms of certain schools can mean complete humiliation. One young man with long hair who attended a provincial school was called "Goldilocks" and shunned by the other boys. When his family moved to the city, he attended a more creative school, where he was accepted and thought of as "cool," and he became part of the "in" crowd. Another young girl arrived at a middle school dance and a boy came up to her and asked her, "What's that you're wearing?" That is a question to which there is no good answer. It is a criticism to which it is difficult to respond since it is phrased passively. Teasing and bullying about clothing often includes teasing about a person's socio-economic standing. Since teenagers are keenly aware of the failings of their parents, this kind of taunt is all the more hurtful.

I myself attended private high school where we had to wear uniforms. I was grateful for that, since I was a scholarship student and most of the other girls came from wealthy families. The uniform was a kind of protection for me since I didn't have to show my lack of expensive clothes. However, the uniform did not prevent a group of girls from asking me where I bought my shoes. They focused on the one item of clothing that was optional and used my choice of shoes to judge my financial standing. It was clear they guessed I was not as well off as they were, and they wanted to be able to judge and exclude.

SEXUAL BULLYING

Children of four and five are interested in understanding their bodies and the bodies of others, and this is perfectly natural. Children may play games in which they show each other their genitals. Again, this is a normal activity and should not lead to anything further. However, it can take the form of bullying if one child compels another to do something that makes him feel uncomfortable. If an older child pushes a younger child to show his genitals or do anything else against his better judgment, that is sexual bullying. If a child feels he does not have a choice or that his own instincts must be overlooked in the interest of preserving the good opinion or friendship of another child, then he is being bullied. Parents and teachers should be vigilant in this regard.

When puberty begins, sexual bullying seems to occur more often. One twelve-year-old girl had to listen to this comment over and over: "Can't tell if it's your front or your back," because her breasts had not developed. One boy asked another girl in front of the whole class, "What's that on your shirt?" She answered, "It's a cat." "What do you mean a cat?" he asked. "Isn't there another word for that?" She did not know what he meant. "Don't you know it's called a pussy?" he asked. She blushed while everyone laughed. He had succeeded in making her feel embarrassed and sexually unaware, while making himself look knowledgeable and clever. This is sexual bullying, and it is designed to make people feel uncomfortable in their sexuality or to make the bully seem mature and "in the know."

Sexual bullying can take many forms. It can take the form of calling people "gay" or making people feel they are not sexually developed or not sexually knowledgeable. It can also be used to imply people are sexually promiscuous and attempt to damage their reputation. This kind of harassment can be devastating to teens who are not sure what is happening with their bodies, their hormones or their emotions. Being called gay hurts if you are gay, and it hurts if you are not gay. The comment is malicious either way, since it is intended to exclude one person from the group and line others up against him, and that seems to be the point behind much bullying.

Some recent episodes that have hit the headlines because of their tragic nature illustrate just how devastating this kind of bullying can be. One young man who attended Yale University recently jumped off the George Washington Bridge because of being sexually bullied. His roommate used his computer to tape him having a sexual encounter with another young man and spied on him along with others. When the young man found out that his sexual encounter was broadcast in this way, his humiliation was so intensely painful that he killed himself. It appears that he had already reported his roommate to the school authorities, but nothing had happened to protect him.

ETHNIC BULLYING

Racial or ethnic bullying is unfortunately very prevalent in a lot of junior high and high schools. People who arrive from another country or another region are often targeted. Even teachers can be guilty of this kind of targeting. When I attended middle school, the nun who taught us mercilessly bullied an English girl who had come to Ireland and was new to the school. She was not only different from everyone in the class because she was English but also a Protestant. Day after day the nun called the girl a "spineless jellyfish" and a "sleveen." At that point we did not know what that word meant, but it sounded mean. Later I discovered it meant "a sly, obsequious, smooth-tongued person." When she was asked to go to the board to do a math problem, the girl quaked and her hand shook so that she could hardly write at all. But we could all see she was not spineless but terrified—and made all the more nervous by the nun's constant insults and harassment. She was not sly or obsequious but attempted to keep herself below the radar so she would not draw any more unwanted attention. I wanted to protect her, but to this day I am ashamed that I was too afraid to stand up to the nun who hated the English and hated Protestants with no exceptions.

I never did anything to help the girl; none of us did, since we were all afraid of being bullied by the nun ourselves. That is another problem with bullies: few people have the courage to stand up to them. In this case the teacher was doing the bullying, but even when other children do the bullying, few peers stand up for each other. That is why those in power have to step in and help. Many teachers have been criticized recently for not stepping in to stop bullying. In the past, when school children wanted to gossip about others, they used to pass notes in the classroom or whisper in the school cafeteria. Now, however, gossip is a full-time occupation of many young people because of Internet social media. People can say anything they want on these sites and cause a lot of emotional pain to others.

One fifteen-year-old girl committed suicide because of the bullying that took place in her school. She had recently arrived in the United States from

Ireland, and since she was a newcomer she became a target of bullying. The bullying took place on the Internet as well as in school. In Facebook comments about her, a campaign of relentless bullying took place. In school she was the brunt of physical bullying and threats. Although her parents complained to the school, none of the teachers took action. The girl's life became a living hell, and she ultimately committed suicide. In another case, a thirteen-year-old girl committed suicide following a campaign of deceit and harassment conducted by her former friend and actively aided by her friend's mother. Malicious gossip spread on the Internet made the girl's life torture, and she killed herself.

Bullying may begin as a simple kind of teasing, where one person's lunch is better than another's, and it can escalate into full-blown teasing in middle and high school, where one person's way of life is better than another's. In society, bullying may become a political weapon. During the 1980s in Colombia, Pablo Escobar was the head of a group of drug dealers who exported cocaine into the United States. His power expanded greatly through his use of bullying. There was a popular phrase used about him at that time, that he ruled by the "lead and the silver," meaning that he would bribe you with silver, and if you did not comply, you would be shot (with lead bullets). Since the bribery he used was grandiose, he became very popular—he donated money to communities and built amenities for the poor, making him a local hero. His bullying even extended to the top levels of government, and he used political assassination in order to deter others from going against him. Bullying, when left unchallenged, can cripple entire nations. The history books are full of examples of small groups of bullies who dominate large groups of people. Ultimately, Escobar was deprived of power when the United States collaborated with Colombia. There is a lesson here for all of us: peer support can eliminate bullying. If schools can encourage children to find support from each other and resist bullying, then children can become empowered.

Bullying needs to be eliminated from our families and our schools, and it cannot be done without the direct intervention of caring adults, parents, and teachers, whose job it is to supervise children while they interact in groups.

PROTECTING A CHILD FROM BULLYING

In the Family

The best weapon against bullying is a supportive family. The Columbine killers were bullied at school, but apparently they did not have a strong support system behind them. The difference between children who are bullied in school and survive, and the children who are bullied in school and are traumatized, is the support of a loving family in which they can confide. Some parents think they should tell their child to seek revenge, teach them how to fight back, and encourage them to engage in combat with others. However, this is not a good solution. Violence breeds violence, and the cycle continues and grows.

A man I know complained to his mother when he was a child about bullies coming after him in the street. "You go back out there and punch them! You show them!" she said. He must have felt terrified and alone, and his only weapon was aggression. His mother could have taken the time to explain to him how to handle his feelings, how to avoid these people, or how not to be sucked into conflicts. She could have made him feel safe by keeping him home and talking to him about how it felt to be victimized. She could have explained to him that the bullies needed forgiveness themselves and that he could be bigger than them if he could understand that. She could have helped him to react to stress by remaining calm and thinking about how he was feeling. She could have taken action herself and spoken to the other children's parents. Instead of protecting him, she threw him to the wolves and expected him to fight back.

This man grew up to be a bully himself. He had no insight into his own feelings and did not know how to be cool in a crisis. He beat his children for their mistakes. When things went wrong in the family, he yelled at his children. One time when he got lost en route to their vacation destination, he panicked and started yelling at the children for making him lose his concentration—and since he was yelling so much, the car ran into a ditch. Then he yelled at them again and blamed them for what he did. Parents can teach a child to box, to wrestle, to become physically confident; there is nothing wrong with that, since a child can feel less vulnerable if she is sure of her own ability—if not to fight, then at least to run fast. However, gaining the emotional strength to deal with being bullied is more effective than retaliating. Here are some techniques a family can use to help children:

- Dinnertime should be an opportunity for group discussion. At the dinner table parents should create an atmosphere in which children can discuss their daily experiences. This safe space should be the arena in which children can talk about problems at school and get good feedback from their parents and siblings.
- When children play alone together, whether they are siblings or playmates, parents should be vigilant. They should consider sweeping by a playroom unobtrusively from time to time to make sure no one child is being dominated by the other, either physically or emotionally.

- Siblings should very rarely have authority over each other without a parent's direct supervision. Young children often lack the ability to be objective enough to administer family rules. When a parent needs to leave an older sibling in charge of a younger one, both children should be allowed to give feedback on how the experience was for them. If the younger sibling expresses feelings of being bullied, parents should step in immediately and take action. If the older child shows anxiety about the responsibility, parents should think seriously about leaving him or her alone with the younger child. Anxiety may cause older children to bully younger children.
- Babysitters should be carefully chosen. If parents feel the need to install a "nanny-cam," they should do so.
- Parents should openly discuss the various parts of a child's body and which parts should be considered "private." They should encourage a child to know what feels right and what does not feel right, and let them know that no one has the right to touch their body without their permission or to make inappropriate comments about their body.
- Children should know they have the right to have boundaries. Children should be encouraged to listen to their own instincts and understand that they will know when something is not appropriate.
- Parents should talk to children about "secrets" and let them know that most secrets are not good. If someone has told them to keep a secret they should *always* confide that in a parent, no matter what the secret-teller has said to them.
- If a child reports being bullied in school, a parent may often wish to run to the phone and call the school or even speak to the other parents. The parent may also encourage the child to use physical violence against the bully. However, these may not be the best ways to handle the problem. Depending on the severity of the problem or the age of the child, the best way to handle the situation at first is to give the child techniques to handle these kinds of people, since the child will likely encounter this kind of situation throughout his life.
- If the problem does not go away, and especially if a child has been threatened physically or attacked by another child, a parent should approach the teacher or school administrator immediately, since that is extremely serious.
- Parents should not encourage a child to fight back. No child should have to go to school and engage in battle with others. It is the adults' jobs to protect children from physical harm. School should always be a safe place. If the schoolyard becomes a battleground, teachers are not doing a good job and need help and support to do so.

- If a child shows sudden reluctance in going to school when she has enjoyed it previously, parents should have private discussions with the child and find out if there is bullying going on. This should happen at all ages, from the very youngest child to the high school level.

For lower levels of bullying, which can nevertheless be very damaging, parents should try to equip their children with the ability to cope. Parents should consider the following techniques:

Tell a child to think of the teacher as a resource. He should report bullying directly to the teacher and not feel ashamed to do so. The parent should keep a note of the incident on paper and check in to make sure the child has indeed talked to the teacher. This will encourage the child to think of his teacher as a support system. If the teacher does not take action and the bullying continues, the parent needs to meet with the teacher. If the teacher does not take action, the parent needs to meet with the principal or school administrator. The parent should document all these meetings.

Tell the child to use other children as a resource. Encourage the child to talk to friends about the bully. If all are agreed, then they should stick together and come up with strategies. If the bully approaches, children can group together and say, "We don't like that." Children can approach the teacher as a group and say they don't like what's going on.

Talk to the child about an insulting remark that hurt and encourage her to realize that the bully's comment is not a reflection of reality but just an attempt to put her down. Ask the child if she really believes her ears are too big. Take a look in the mirror and do some esteem-building talk. Have the child reflect that this is only one person who has ever criticized her ears so the remark can be put into perspective.

Encourage the child to reflect about the other person. Ask the child empowering questions such as: Why would someone want to tell another person their ears are too big? What do you think the girl was trying to do when she told you your ears are too big? Why did she say it in front of the other girl? Why do you think some people bully others? Questions like this help a child realize it is the bully who feels insecure. There must be something wrong with her if she needs to put other people down. This helps the child redress the balance of power. Many people who are victims of violent crimes gain peace of mind when they come to understand their aggressors were themselves abused. Tell your child you think this bully needs some help, as she may not be getting enough attention at home. These reflective techniques help a child to gain a sense of perspective. An insulting remark from a bully does not need to be taken seriously but can be seen as an indication of the other person's weakness and their need to dominate.

Ask the child what she would have liked to say when she was bullied. Let her say anything she wants to say. She may say that what she wanted to respond was, "Well, you're a horrible, ugly witch!" Let her say it to you now. She will get a sense of relief just saying the angry thing that was in her mind, the words she was holding inside. She can vent all her anger in private. Let her hit a pillow and beat up the bully vicariously.

Ask the child what she could have said in response. Maybe she will come up with some appropriate ideas in case it happens again. You may suggest remarks that are not loaded with anger, since that is what a bully might enjoy. A child can say simple phrases such as, "I like myself just the way I am," or "I am sorry you feel that way," or "Other people like my ears," or "That's a hurtful remark." When children can have a set of simple statements and unemotional phrases like these, available and practice them so they come to mind quickly, they can feel armed against bullies.

Encourage the child to think of herself as having a team or belonging to a group of supportive like-minded people. If someone says, "Your ears are too big," remind her to say something like, "Lots of people like my ears." If someone says, "You're gay!" she can either say, "Plenty of people are gay, and I am too," or "I'm not gay, but some of my friends are. So what?"

If a child is a target of socio-economic bullying such as, "Where did you get that? Goodwill?" a child should be encouraged to reflect that many people in the world do not have enough food to eat and those who use wealth to feel superior are not responsible citizens. Another good response to that kind of remark would be, "Actually, yes. We can't afford more than that right now." The bully has nowhere else to go with that answer.

If the child is the brunt of sexual bullying it may be very difficult for her to confide in parents. However, if she can do so, parents can help her understand that many teens feel sexually uninformed and insecure themselves, and this is why they bully. The truth, and plenty of sexual information provided by the parents, can be the best weapon against sexual intimidation. If a girl can respond to a bully by saying, "The correct term is 'vulva,' but perhaps you are not aware of that," it might stop him in his tracks.

At school

Schools should be safe places for children. In reality, many schools do nothing to make children feel safe, and many schools around the world condone or ignore bullying on the part of students, and some schools in certain parts of the world even allow teachers to be bullies. Though school children bully each other on social media sites, schools are apparently not permitted to penalize their students for doing so, since the bullying takes place outside school hours. Schools could do a great deal to prevent bullying. Since bullying takes place in the school setting, there are many things teachers can do. Here are some ideas:

- Early childhood programs should develop social/emotional curricula for children. These lessons would guide children in developing healthy communication strategies. Children would learn to express anxiety, fear, jealousy, need, anger, and other negative emotions in healthy ways. When emotion is expressed in these ways, a child will not feel the need to dominate or bully. When children feel emotionally safe and connected to the feelings of others, they do not feel the fear that makes young children want to bully others.
- Early childhood teachers should identify children who have sociopathic tendencies—that is, children who lack empathy to the point that they are liable to hurt others physically and emotionally and feel no remorse, and may even experience pleasure. A lot can be done in the early years to help these children.
- Daily conflict resolution meetings in elementary school can allow children to work out solutions to conflicts verbally. In these classrooms, physical conflict tends to disappear as communication skills grow.
- Middle and high school seems to be a breeding ground for bullies. The kind of bullying that goes on there can cause great damage. This is very evident both in the number of suicides that are happening and in the fact that every person you ask seems to have stories about being bullied at this age. Bullying at this age has such impact that people who have left school many years ago still feel the pain acutely. This would indicate that greater intervention is needed.
- Teachers should be trained to spot the signs of bullying and have a set of guidelines so they know what is permissible and what is not.
- Children should be made aware of their rights, physical and emotional. These could be written up and placed on a visible sign. Children could collaborate in creating their own bill of rights for the classroom.
- Teachers should stop bullying at the first incident. A nasty remark should not be allowed to pass unnoticed. Teachers should be given permission to intervene when certain boundaries are crossed.
- Children should be trained in appropriate techniques for handling bullies.
- Children should be provided with avenues for presenting complaints to school authorities—for instance, daily or weekly report sheets that children fill out and hand to teachers. Teachers regularly prepare reports on children. Why can't children prepare reports for teachers on their own experiences? These reports could be confidential, and teachers would be aware of

trends—for instance, if everyone complained about Jeremy, then teachers would be alerted to a possible problem with Jeremy. Children would feel comfort in knowing they had a way to present their worries and be heard.

- Families should receive support in dealing with children who bully or with children who are being bullied. School could provide bullying workshops for parents and for children. This can be done with minimum effort and might only need to happen once or twice a year.
- Peer support should be encouraged, and children should learn that they can gain support from each other. Teachers can give children the vocabulary they need to communicate with their peers when asking for support. Children should be encouraged to think in terms of "we" and not "I," since bullies tend to pick on more than one person at a time. Children need to feel they are not alone.
- Schools should create contracts for children who attend their schools. These contracts should have sanctions attached to bullying behavior and would prohibit children from engaging in teasing or bullying each other on the Internet. Currently, schools do not have jurisdiction over cyberbullying but could do so if they insisted on contracts with their pupils' families.
- School administrators and district supervisors should ensure that every school has a written "no bullying" policy that is prominently displayed in school and distributed to parents and children at the beginning of the year. Many schools have dress codes; more importantly, schools should have behavior codes.

WHAT THE GOVERNMENT CAN DO

The Internet has become a very powerful social tool. People can make wonderful connections with each other and can reconnect with old friends, and even family members who have been lost or absent. However, the Internet is being used by bullies to further their work. It is the perfect tool for someone who likes to hide and do his dirty work from a safe distance. The term "cyberbullying" has been coined to describe what that means. There is a Web site called www.stopcyberbullying.org, and this Web site describes what cyberbullying is. At this point in time, the law is apparently not strong enough to prevent cyberbullies from causing a lot of pain to their victims.

In certain states, legislation is being introduced to help penalize those who bully others on the Internet. Currently, there are proposed laws that would make it illegal to use electronic means to cause substantial emotional distress or deliberately harass others. In 2008 in California, Assembly Bill 86 2008 was passed. This bill gives administrators the authority to discipline students for bullying others online. These laws and proposed laws seem to be the beginning of a movement to stop bullying among children.

At this point in time, laws are not stringent enough to prevent this form of harassment. New regulations should be introduced. People should not be allowed to harass or bully others on the Internet. There are some laws currently enacted—for instance, a law prohibiting anonymous targeting of others. Regulations still appear so loose as to allow people to torture others to the point of suicide, and these regulations should be changed. Similar regulations should be introduced to those used in the past for printed material. Laws pertaining to slander and libel should be applied to the Internet. Currently, people can blog anything they want about people and cause damage to others by the use of words. Written opinions can seem more important than verbal opinions, and once online they stay there forever. People tend to give weight to online comments, even though a blogger's agenda may be self-serving and his comments one-sided.

The problem about changing the law regarding cyberbullying is that in most countries, free speech is a valued right. That is something no one wants to compromise. In regard to children, however, free speech laws should probably be re-examined, since children and teenagers, in particular, are incapable of protecting themselves and are more vulnerable to the kind of damage harassing and defamatory speech can inflict. There should be a law enacted that protects children from hateful speech directed against them by others. Social media sites should themselves enforce stricter regulations. Cyberbullying could be reported, and the perpetrators could be banned from the site.

Bullying is rampant in schools and in society. There is probably no one who has not experienced the feeling of being bullied. Bullying can vary in extent from a low-level encounter to a full campaign of torture waged on a child by another or group of others. As parents and teachers, we need to realize that this kind of behavior can cause damage that can crush a child's spirit to the point that death is preferable to the pain he is enduring. We need to protect children from bullying, strengthen our laws, and give our children new strategies to protect themselves.

Notes

1. Scheithauer, H., et al. (2006). "Physical, Verbal, and Relational Forms of Bullying Among German Students: Age Trends, Gender Differences, and Correlates." *Aggressive Behaviour* 32, 261–275.

2. Perner, J. (1997). "Children's Competency in Understanding the Role of a Witness: Truth, Lies, and Moral Ties." *Applied Cognitive Psychology* 11, S21-S35.

3. Toppo, G. (2009). "10 Years Later the Real Story Behind Columbine." *USA Today*, April 13.

4. Paley, V. G. (1993). *You Can't Say You Can't Play.* Cambridge, MA: Harvard University Press.

Chapter 7

Children Have the Right to Forgiveness and Empathy

Children are apprentices, beginners, neophytes. They are new to the world and do not know its rules. They are smaller and less able than adults, and their emotions, as well as their physical actions, are not completely under their control. The human brain is not fully formed until the teen years are over, in particular the prefrontal cortex, which plays a part in regulating emotions, so even teenagers lack the ability to make fully rational decisions. Therefore, children and teenagers are likely to make mistakes, to fail to complete tasks, to have emotional outbursts, and to do things that adults may find disappointing, irritating, or even maddening.

Responsible adults who have authority over children need to understand that all children are born with goodwill and the desire for nothing more than happiness. Children have to go through a process of learning how to wait, to sacrifice, to share, and to substitute instant gratification for long-term happiness. It is our job to teach them how to accomplish these difficult tasks. At times children will not want to obey; they will try and test their parents, or they will attempt things and not succeed. In all of these events, children have the right to an empathetic response. In all of these events, children have the right to forgiveness for their failures and encouragement to keep trying. Adults need to have compassion for children, and if they do, children will, in turn, have compassion for others.

Adults often punish children by isolation, rejection, physical punishment, humiliation, or deprivation of benefits. These punishments are intended to reinforce the parent's position of authority in the hope the child will adjust his behavior through fear. Adults who punish and reprimand children harshly for their failures may reap a bitter harvest. Lack of forgiveness breeds anger and resentment, and undue or severe punishment can destroy a child's empathy and sense of justice. The way to develop an empathic and loving child is to show him empathy and love. A loving parent will forgive a child's missteps, pick him up, and help him to try once more. No one has the right to judge a child's actions unless he knows what is in the child's heart. No one has the right to punish a child who is trying his best. No one has the right to deny a child forgiveness.

Under the law, those who do not have the intent to harm are not considered guilty of a crime and deserve forgiveness. When there is intent, a person is guilty. In most countries, the highest punishment is reserved for those who commit a "first degree" crime—that is, those who deliberately intend harm and who plot and plan to commit a crime. Punishment varies in severity depending on the amount of premeditation of the perpetrator. When an offense occurs with no malice and no intent to harm, there is no punishment. It is vital we recognize that children, due to their limited experience and cognitive development, are often unaware of the consequences of their actions.

Even when a child wishes to hurt because of his anger, he may not fully comprehend the damage he is capable of causing. This is because young children may not be able to understand the feelings of others. Not until they reach four years of age are children capable of understanding that others have *different* thoughts than they do. There have been many studies of "Theory of Mind" in which experimenters try to find out what children know about what other people think. Under age four, children appear to think everyone has the same information. Therefore, children are often oblivious to the thoughts and the unspoken feelings of others. In the case of children who *do* understand the damage they can cause and *do* understand the feelings of others, they may be physically incapable of controlling their urges and their bodily impulses. Given these facts, children should be pardoned for the deviations they make from the path they are expected to walk. That is not to say that children should be treated as if they are completely irresponsible. As children grow and have more authority and power, they need to accept that each level of responsibility brings its consequences. But there can be no guilt where there is no intent to harm.

Most people regard babies with great compassion. They can see that a baby is helpless, and so no fault is attached to her actions. If a baby pulls your hair, you forgive her. If a baby throws up on your skirt, you make light of it. If a baby cries in the night, you may resent being woken up, but you forgive her because she is a baby and she is hungry. As babies grow into toddlers they become capable of agency. Adults want babies to be independent, and so we encourage them to learn how to gain mastery over concrete objects and to become mobile. However, now that they have learned to be independent and mobile, they have accrued some power. Once a child has power, the adult no longer thinks of him as helpless, and so he will now have some blame or responsibility attached to his actions. If a baby drops her bottle, her mother just picks it up. If a toddler drops his cup, her mother gets irritated. "I told you not to do that!" she may say. Power brings responsibility, and responsibility brings accountability.

When children seem to be capable of choice in what they do, that is the point at which parents demand accountability from their child. It is at this "turning point," around age two, that a lot of problems begin. Parents themselves struggle with rules and boundaries when their children are at this age. They often do not know whether they are being strict enough or too strict. One reason for the confusion is that they cannot be sure if their child is processing what they say. They cannot tell what the inner process of the child might be, and sometimes they wonder if there is a process at all. They may say to their child, "Don't climb on the table." The child does it anyway. They repeat the rule, and the child does it again, possibly even while smiling. Parents may not be sure whether the child understands and whether he is testing. Parents often do not know whether the child is deliberately trying to annoy them, or whether he simply cannot control his own actions.

PUNISHMENT

Although this is a very stressful time for parents, it is at this point that the need for forgiveness comes in. A parent may realize a child is trying his best and cannot do what he is told. Then she can forgive him and understand that, though she would like him to, he can't control himself, so she needs to physically prevent him from doing it again so he doesn't get hurt. On the other hand, she may realize he does know it is forbidden; he can control himself, but he chooses not to, despite what she has said. The parent realizes that the child *is* trying to defy her. This may throw some parents into a rage. They have put in all their love and hard work, enduring sleepless nights while putting their own needs on hold, into the work of child-rearing. And now this little person refuses to listen to them and is even smiling at them while being defiant. They may feel like retribution is in order. They may think he deserves to be punished because he has rejected the rules. They may also think punishment is a good way of preventing him from doing it again.

This is the stage at which parents begin to administer "time out" or other forms of punishment to their child. Some parenting books promote "time out" and suggest a certain amount of time out that is appropriate based on the age of the child. This concept is based on the idea that a child will sit in the punishment chair and think like a philosopher. He will contemplate the action that got him into trouble, make a mental adjustment, and determine not to do it again. That assumes a child functions like a self-adjusting robot. The "time out" strategy attributes mental powers to a child, which children do not have.

Punishment often involves deprivation. The child cannot have a favorite toy. The child has to endure isolation in the other room. The child does not get to go to the park the next day as promised. When deprivation, or even reward, involves an event that has not yet occurred, children may not be able to process this fully. Parents assume a child can make the connection between his present behavior and a future event that is or is not going to happen. Parents use these punishments in the moment as a deterrent, thinking the child can weigh a future good against a present impulsive action. "If you don't sit nicely at the table, you will not watch the movie tonight." Parents sometimes are puzzled as to why the child does not make the connection and does not realize he is going to lose something in the future. Young children are not capable of envisioning a future event that *might have happened but now will not happen after all.* This reasoning is quite complicated, and beyond the ability of most young children.

Many parents think punishment is a good way to train their child into behaving well. The adult acts from the belief that the child will come to realize that the punishment is associated with the misdeed, and so the misdeed will end. Parents may believe punishments are the best way to manipulate a child's behavior, but it is doubtful a young child can make the connections between cause and effect, particularly when they are separated in time. It is also doubtful a young child can control his behavior based on the promise of a future event. It is doubtful if punishment works as a deterrent, and punishment does not help children gain insights into their own behavior or techniques for self-control. The punished child may only learn a very rudimentary cause/effect rule: "This behavior makes my parent angry, and when my parent is angry, his face gets red, and he yells at me and sends me to my room." The child will not come to reflect on why he pulled his sister's hair and will not learn to identify his own angry feelings the next time they happen.

Some parents use a "conditioning" response to bad behavior. When people train dogs or cats, they use this kind of system. If a dog urinates on the floor, he gets spritzed with a water bottle, for instance. By associating the negative experience with the "crime," the dog learns to use the newspaper. Few people make the dog sit in the corner to contemplate his wrong actions. They figure, and rightly so, that if you yell, "Bad dog!" or use a quick, animated response to the unwanted action, the dog gets the message. A treat when he does the right thing reinforces this lesson. Lessons may need to be repeated a few times before the dog learns acceptable behavior. Conditioning is done without emotion, and shortly after a reprimand for eating your shoe, your dog is licking your face. He's forgotten the incident and has moved on, and so have you.

Why, then, do people not apply the same "conditioning" techniques to their own children? Once a child begins to walk, all kinds of dangers begin to be possible, and parents need to step up warnings and reinforce the rules. "No climbing on the table," "Don't touch the stove, it's hot," and so on. Parents could "condition" children to avoid danger and comply with basic rules without becoming angry if they thought of the child as someone who is learning, the way a puppy does. A parent can raise or modulate the tone of his voice. A parent can alter the expression on his face to a concerned look or wag his finger. A parent can use sounds that are not words or simple word phrases with a specific tone that children relate to very instinctively: "Uh-oh!" "No, no!" "Hot, hot!" "Watch out!" If a child is hurting another child or an animal, a parent can use her voice to elicit sympathy from the child. If a child is pulling a dog's tail, a parent can say, "Oh, no, poor doggy!" in an expressive voice. When parents use these "conditioning" techniques they do not have to become enraged or upset at the child's "bad" behavior. Parents can think of themselves not as judges who need to administer punishment, but as guides and protectors.

REBELLION

As children age, however, another element comes into play. Suddenly, out of nowhere, something changes. This sweet youngster who knows how to copy his mother and say, "Hot, hot!" and keep away from the stove now begins to act differently. He has his own agenda. Now he won't get in his stroller. He insists on running away from his mother at the museum, where there are hundreds of people and he could get lost. A large audience of parents, grandparents, and other critics surrounds the parent. She has to get her child back into his stroller, or he will get lost. She has tried warning him. She has tried reasoning about how difficult it is for her to keep up with him. She knows he understands her. And yet he won't cooperate. He prefers to run. She has to grab him and put him into the stroller. He kicks, he screams, he throws his head back with no concern for his own safety, and his body suddenly quadruples in weight. When she puts him in, he miraculously knows how to slither out of the stroller. Now she has to strap him in, tilt the stroller handles down so his feet are kicking up in the air, proceed around the museum bent over like Groucho Marx, and pretend she is completely unfazed by her screaming child.

Parent and child have begun a new phase, in which conflict and anger enter the picture. While animals can be conditioned to obey, children begin to diverge and assert their power. Most dogs and cats are likely to misbehave for short periods in their initial training phases. After that, unless the owner is unable to enforce rules for some reason, most pets cooperate and live contented lives, making their masters happy. But after a couple of years of compliance with the rules, a dog doesn't suddenly try to change the master/pet relationship. I don't know of any situation in which a dog decides he is not going to wear a leash any more or prefers to put on his own coat. Children at a certain age do begin to separate from their parents and assert their individuality and independence, and that's when the real problems start. It is at this point that parents need to maintain perspective and think about the child's behavior with tolerance, forgiveness, and empathy. Unfortunately, when parents are stressed or confused, they may resort to punishment, aggression, and retribution.

The parent in the museum may be feeling embarrassed, disappointed, afraid of losing control, and angry that her child is no longer her sweet little partner. We are all narcissistic to one degree or another; none of us can completely eliminate that aspect of our makeup, and parents often think their child is a reflection of themselves. So when the little boy screams and kicks in the museum, the parent may have difficulty feeling empathy for him. All she may think of in that moment is, "I am embarrassed. I am a failure as a parent. He doesn't love me. He is doing this to bother me. Everyone thinks I am a horrible parent." If she could take a breath and not react for thirty seconds, the parent could think objectively and realize, "He is trying to assert his independence. He is just a little fellow trying to be big. He thinks he can run around by himself. He doesn't know it's dangerous. He resents me for not trusting him. He sees me as holding him back." This empathy will help her to keep her sense of humor and to forgive him for his tantrums. She still may need to grapple him into the stroller. She still may have to endure the stares and judgment of others who are not supportive. But she can draw him aside into a quiet area, and say, "I know you are upset. You are angry because you wanted to run, and you're good at running. I'm sorry we can't do that now. Maybe you would like to go to the park. If you stay here, you have to be in the stroller, but if we go to the park, you can get out and run around."

If she can forgive him for his rebelliousness and stop thinking about how his behavior reflects on her; she will be able to see what his needs are. When she sees he needs independence and enjoys his newfound ability to run, she can think of alternative paths. If she is calm, she can think of giving him a choice that will allow him to "save face" and also allow her to get what she wants. The child who is talked to in a forgiving tone will realize there is someone who understands why he was upset. This will help him to communicate better in the future because he knows she is able to listen.

Parents who don't understand a child's motivation will fail to understand the tantrum, and so they can't bring it to a proper resolution. That kind of parent may leave the museum full of anger. She may take the child home and punish him. She may make him sit in his chair, or yell at him, or cry in front of him and try to make him feel guilty. She may tell him how embarrassed she feels and threaten him that she will never go to the museum with him again. She may never go to the museum with him again. That parent cannot forgive the child for challenging her authority and exposing her to the criticism of others. In cases such as these, the child may not feel comfortable asserting his independence and may regress. He may feel that in order to make his mother happy, he needs to be compliant, and this will stunt his growth as an individual. Other children may become angrier and more stubborn in their attempt to gain the independence that is rightly theirs. The tantrums will grow wilder, and the punishment will in turn create more anger.

The best way for parents to deal with these conflicts is through understanding and forgiveness. The parent is the bigger person, so she must also be the one who is more evolved emotionally, and she must forgive. For a parent to be at war with a two-year-old child is ludicrous. For a parent to believe that the twoyear-old is "out to get him" is narcissistic. Certainly it is true that children test their parents to see how flexible the rules are. Parents need to face that test and should not waiver in safety rules. A two-year-old child cannot run free in a crowded museum. However, the young child is not *intending* to bother the parent; he is trying to assert himself in the only way he knows. A parent who understands this will have enough perspective to be able to think up a good solution without panicking or over-reacting. There is always a good compromise that both sides can feel they can live with.

RULING LIKE A DICTATOR

A real narcissist is most concerned with gaining the approval of others and with maintaining control over others. Most of us are part-time narcissists. We need to have a certain amount of narcissism. If we did not, we might be likely to walk around in our pajamas with yesterday's vegetables in our teeth. Our self-image should matter to us. We should care whether we are presenting ourselves in the best possible light. We have a right to get our hair done at the hairdressers or buy a new coat even if the old one doesn't have holes. We have a right to spend money on an attractive watch even though we can tell the time perfectly well by looking at our cell phone. We have a right to join the gym to tighten up our favorite muscles. We have the right to hope that others see us in a favorable light. However, there is another kind of narcissist. That is the person who *must* have others see him in a favorable light. He is a fragile individual, and his very existence is contingent upon receiving the respect that he believes others owe him.

Narcissistic individuals frequently lack the ability to forgive, since they take every setback and every insult personally. There are many examples of dictators who surround themselves with sycophants. The subjects are there to reflect back to the dictator how wonderful he is. If an individual has the misfortune to incur the wrath of the dictator, he will be made to suffer. These narcissistic individuals often feel slighted by completely innocent actions. They must be greeted with due respect. They must be bowed to. They must never be questioned or challenged. If they are, the punishment may be expulsion or complete annihilation. These people are not leaders; they are dictators. Parents often think they need to be "in charge." However, real leaders are in touch with the needs of their subjects, and parents do not need to play the role of dictator.

Many teenagers become locked into conflicts with their parents. Parents believe that their authority is being threatened and that they need to hold firm. But compromising and learning to discuss issues are just as helpful with teenagers as they are with two year olds. Parents often think, "But I'm the parent. I can't give in or my child will think I am weak." It is true that parents need to keep to a certain set of rules so children will feel safe. But rules should be kept to a minimum and should be open to change as the child grows. When parents compromise, children do not think of them as weak. When parents compromise, children learn that parents are flexible enough and resilient enough to rethink their own actions.

I know one parent who, when frustrated, would make threats beginning with, "If you don't . . . " Once she had begun the threat, she had to finish it, and since she was angry while making the threat, she would often overdo the punishment, only to regret it once she had pronounced it. "If you two don't stop fighting I won't let you watch the movie!" She immediately knew she had gone too far. If she didn't let them watch the movie, how would she be able to make dinner? She had counted on them being busy so she could do her work. Now she was calmer, and the punishment seemed overly harsh. The parent realized she could compromise with the children: "OK, let's make a deal. You can watch the movie, but you have to tidy your room first." Being calm, she found a solution that would benefit her too. Being able to compromise, to realize you were too harsh, are healthy qualities of a parent, and parents need to realize they don't always have to appear to be perfect.

IN SCHOOL

Teachers may try to correct a child's behavior with a system of reward and punishment, which is fine for short-term results. In the long run, this system doesn't really help a child to modify his own behavior or to understand how he impacts others. Many teachers are interested only in classroom management and not interested in inculcating a sense of morality or commitment to society. That is unfortunate, since school is the perfect place to learn those values. There are many issues in a classroom, where the individual comes into a challenging relationship with the authority figure and the group. This setting can provide wonderful opportunities to teach that social responsibility and individual fulfillment are inextricably related. Forgiveness and empathy are key elements of a strong community. It is unfortunate for teachers to have to play a judicial role, as controlling is very tiring and can take a huge toll on a teacher's energy and long-term endurance in the classroom.

In our school we try to use forgiveness and empathy, but we also want children to be responsible, and we expect them to care about each other, the teachers, and their classroom. We don't think, "Oh, they are babies; they can't help it if they rip something." We want children to face the consequences of their actions, but not in a mean or scary way. If they make a mess, they will need to clean it up. If they tear a book, they can get tape and fix it. In this way, they can learn that they have responsibility and the ability to be forgiven and fix things. On the other hand, if they appear very upset because they made a big spill we would say things like, "Don't worry about it; it's easy to clean up. Here is a rag. I will help you." We want them not to feel guilty, but to feel responsible. Part of that is facing the consequences of your actions.

EMBRACING FAILURE

Some classrooms are built around the notion of success. This notion of success is based on standardized performance. Many teachers use the "Q&A" method: the teacher asks a question, and there is one right answer in his mind—can the children figure out what he is thinking? Children are categorized according to how well their thinking aligns with the teacher's. There are students who are graded A, B, or C. Then there are students who may get an F or U, Failure and Unsatisfactory. The dictionary definition of unsatisfactory is: "not adequate, acceptable, or satisfying." The child who gets the F or the U grade does not think in this way: "Oh, I see. I am a good person with a lot of talents in other areas; it is my paper that failed. It is merely my work that is unsatisfactory." Children are not capable of that kind of perspective. That child thinks, "I am a failure. I am unsatisfactory." Instead of forgiving children for their mistakes and helping them understand how the mistake was made, many teachers label them as failures. This is an unforgiving way of approaching children, since children are likely to label themselves as failures, and children are the harshest critics when it comes to themselves.

In a climate where children are driven by fear and desire for approval to find the right answer, there is very little respect for "mistakes." That is too bad. Not only should mistakes be forgiven, they should be investigated. Psychoanalysts often use "mistakes" as keys to understanding unconscious processes. For instance, when someone makes a slip of the tongue, he may be revealing a thought that has not been allowed into the conscious mind. Often a "mistake" can be an indicator to a teacher of a divergent thought. Jean Piaget is an educational theorist who has contributed a great deal to our knowledge of how children function. First trained as a scientist, he later began to work with psychologists in the emerging field of child psychology. While he was employed to work on standardizing the results of children's tests, he became interested in the reasons why children fail rather than why they succeed. Through his research he began to develop a theory of cognitive development that was to influence educators even to the present day.

It was Piaget who first came up with the notion that a child's cognitive development passes through specific stages: sensorimotor, concrete operations, and formal operations. Piaget's method was to study children in a scientific yet compassionate manner and to observe their methods of approaching a problem. By analyzing a child's acts, he made deductions about a child's developing powers of reasoning. Piaget's studies of his own children and others demonstrated that children cannot process certain tasks unless they have reached the appropriate cognitive stage.

One of the best-known experiments Piaget conducted revealed interesting results in the concept of "conservation." Children at a certain age, he discovered, think that a quantity of liquid in a tall, thin glass is greater than the same quantity in a short, fat glass, simply because the glass is taller. Although they pour the liquid back and forth between the two glasses, children of a certain age continue to believe that the amount is greater in the tall glass. Piaget was puzzled about this common "mistake." His work led him to understand that a child cannot understand this principle until his cognitive development reaches a certain level. In other words, no matter how a teacher explains it, a child cannot grasp it until he is ready. Children are not mistaken; they are processing the world with a brain that has not developed fully.

Classrooms could be workshops in which teachers help to develop a model community. In the classroom there should be an atmosphere of tolerance, not only for different opinions and different learning styles, but also for the error and missteps that all of us, especially children, are apt to make. Piaget himself used mistakes as inspiration for research, and this research led him to his life's work—understanding how a child thinks. Teachers can use mistakes as a source of information on how their pupils are thinking. Let's say a child confuses Austria and Australia. A teacher can correct the child and point out to her that she is wrong. She can encourage the rest of the class to laugh at the mistake. Those techniques are ways of hammering home to a child that she has made a mistake, and of warning the other children not to make the same mistake. The child is humiliated, and the other children get a false sense of superiority.

A good teacher can address the mistake in a different way. He can use it as a learning tool by drawing up the similarities and dissimilarities between the two countries. He can forgive the child with his words thus: "Oh, that's an easy mistake to make. They look almost alike, and sound almost alike. That's probably why you were confused . . . see, there are only a couple of letters that are different." This kind of forgiveness can have a great impact on a child's self-esteem, and it can help her accept criticism. Learning to accept criticism is a good skill for everyone to develop, since people can grow when they accept their mistakes. The child who is talked to in a forgiving way will not respond with shame; she will be able to see why she made the mistake. She will learn something new about her own perception. Once she understands *how* she made the mistake, she can correct it and learn not to make it the next time. The child who is made to feel foolish will probably react by taking fewer risks in the classroom. She will hesitate before giving an answer and be less likely to trust herself.

POSITIVE AND NEGATIVE THINKING

There are two things to note about negative thinking. First, negative thinking has an inhibitory effect. If a child thinks she is not good enough and dwells on the mistakes she has made or is likely to make, it will inhibit her range of activity. Thinking she can't do it right or that others can do it better than her may cause her to cut back on her attempts or to give up altogether. This child may have the right answers, but she will probably keep the answers inside and resent the fact that others are speaking out. Thinking about mistakes prevents people from trying harder.

Secondly, negative thinking has a multiplying effect. One negative thought brings another negative thought and so on. When people meditate, they are encouraged to develop a peaceful or neutral state of mind. When a negative thought enters, they are encouraged to gently accept they had a negative thought, then move back to the neutral state. Forgiveness is a key element of this process. If a person has a negative thought and does not have forgiveness for himself, he will be annoyed at himself for having a negative thought, so that makes two negative thoughts. Now he feels frustrated; soon the whole negative family arrives, and his peace is completely gone. The one thing that can prevent this downward spiral is forgiveness. "I made a mistake. I let go; I move on," is a healthy pattern for people to develop in their lives. Children need to learn that once they make a mistake, they need to forgive themselves and move forward. There is only one way for them to learn this technique, and that is from adults. If adults cannot forgive children for their mistakes, then those children will grow up being self-critical.

If teachers are aware of what the child is thinking, they will be more likely to have empathy for the child and forgive him for his "mistakes." Once they do so, they can begin teaching him, based on what they know of his internal process. When a teacher punishes a child by calling him a failure or labeling him unsatisfactory, does he think that this method is going to change the child? Or is he simply acting out of anger and frustration, unable to think of what else to do? Certainly there is ample evidence that labeling a child a failure is not only unhelpful but also counter-productive. And there is ample evidence that many concepts and ways of thinking that seemed wrong in the past have proven to be right. I imagine Galileo or Einstein, if they had presented their innovative thoughts in a classroom, might have been graded with an F or a U.

Teachers cannot operate in a forgiving and supportive way to children unless they receive the support of their supervisors. Teachers are the professionals who know what could work well in a classroom, and they should be allowed to innovate. The supervisor should be open to the teacher's ideas. In many countries that is the case. In Finland, for instance (where literacy and math skills are higher than almost any country in the world), teachers are treated with great respect and granted a great deal of autonomy. When teachers have autonomy, it is more likely that they will also grant their pupils autonomy, and autonomy encourages commitment and involvement. If teachers could be released from the constant pressures of performing under rigorous curriculum demands, they would be able to organize their classrooms in ways more conducive to human development. Part of that development is learning how to create a just social system.

If a classroom models forgiveness, the chances are that all the members of the class will be treated fairly and will develop a strong community. Members of that community will not be afraid to make suggestions or try new things. They will know that all their ideas will be respected and their mistakes forgiven. Abraham Lincoln is a good model for this kind of attitude. He achieved great things in his life but could not have done it without the help of others. Plagued by depression all his life, he was often bolstered up by the support of his friends. When he did rise to power, he displayed an extraordinary ability not only to forgive and laugh at himself but an ability to forgive others, even his opponents. This forgiveness in fact enabled him to build a strong cabinet. Lincoln understood well that though others worked against him for the opposition party, they had strengths that he needed to incorporate in his team. He was able to forget these people had opposed him and tried to bring him down a short while before. When he drew them close to him, he gained strong allies that were loyal to him until the end. Though some might feel forgiveness is a sign of weakness, on the contrary, it is a sign of great strength. If people can let go of the need to punish and the need to seek revenge, they can be freed up to be more productive.

CHILDREN'S THREATS

Young children often react to challenges by using the heaviest weapons in their artillery. One of those weapons is the threat. One day two boys were playing. One grabbed a toy the other boy was reaching for. He yelled, "If you take my toy, I won't be your friend ever again." The other child reacted, "Well, I won't invite you to my birthday party." And then the first child retaliated, "And I won't be your friend ever again." It was tempting for the teacher to rush in and make them share or make then shake hands, but we know that children may comply yet not forgive. A couple of hours later, out of sight of the teacher, retribution and retaliation may raise their ugly heads. When the two boys started threatening, we responded by reflecting back what was happening and suggesting a better alternative: "Look, Ron, I know you're angry. Jim took your toy, and you want it back. But you don't have to threaten him that you won't be his friend forever. You are angry now, but later you might feel like being his friend again. You could try to just tell him you want it back. Maybe Jim didn't know you were playing with it. Or maybe he just had to take a look at it because it's so interesting. Maybe he wasn't going to keep it. Let's ask him." When the teacher explained to the children that each one might have a different interpretation of what was going on, it helped them to see the other person has a different point of view. When we explained that there are other alternatives to complete annihilation of the friendship, they felt the ability to forgive and to move on.

REVENGE

The antithesis to forgiveness is revenge. When people are victimized, they have the right to feel anger, and they have the right not to forgive if they so choose. It is possible to live a life in which you are aware of having been victimized, and you are aware of the injustice you have suffered, and you choose not to forgive. You might simply avoid the company of toxic people and avoid situations that may lead you to be victimized again. You can choose not to think about those people, but you don't necessarily have to forgive them. However, some people choose to seek out those who have wronged them and exact revenge. Many religions specifically suggest this pursuit, and many other religions expressly forbid it. Many religions indicate that evildoers, through some hidden but inevitable law of nature, find their own punishment. The reason for these prohibitions is probably based on the psychological fact that when people live their lives focused on undoing what has been done to them, they live an illusion. If revenge is exacted, it does not, in reality, undo the feelings of victimization. Revenge can give a momentary illusion of power, but it does not change anything. The pursuit of revenge is not only futile, it is also destructive to those who engage in it.

Children need to be forgiven and to see forgiveness in action. "No big deal," "Don't worry about it," "I'm OK," are the words of someone with a strong ego who does not need to get angry about little things. Adults should try to present this attitude when faced with the anger of a child. Young children often feel intimidated, and they can have a lot of frustration because of their inferior position and small size. When a child hits her parent, a parent should have the capacity to balance her own need for boundaries with a parent's forgiveness for her child's rage.

Forgiving your child for wanting to hit you or show her anger to you is an important feature of a healthy relationship. Some children like to hit their parents. There is a fine line to be walked here. Parents need to have their boundaries respected and should always say so if they feel a child has overstepped them. However, parents also need to be able to take in the anger that their child may feel and accept it. Being hit may damage one parent's sense of self-esteem, but others may not feel offended. Some parents may be very aggrieved and say, "How dare you! I am your mother! You can never talk to me that way. Don't ever raise your hand to me!" and so on. If a parent can say to a child, "Ouch, you're hurting me. That's not OK. I understand how mad you are. Let's talk about this," this is a more forgiving attitude, and it opens up the path for discussion. Then the problems have a chance of being resolved. Parents should never ignore it when a child hits them. That is very confusing for a child, and it implies the parent has no feelings and also that the child is having no effect on them. It also suggests that a parent does not have boundaries.

Parents can seem unforgiving at times, and that can close the doors of communication between them and their children. Here are some unforgiving comments that can crush a child:

- How dare you!
- I'll never forgive you.
- That's unacceptable.
- Never again! You messed up last time.
- I'll never be able to replace that dish.
- I'll never trust you again.
- I guess you can't do anything right.
- Why don't you give up?
- You are on the road to failure. (John Lennon's report card!)

Here are some forgiving comments children would love to hear:

- I've done that myself; it happens to a lot of people.
- No big deal.
- Don't worry; we can fix it.
- I'll get some paper towels, and we'll wipe it up.
- Oh, you were trying so hard. Let's give it another shot.
- You must feel bad.
- Let me show you a different way to do it.
- Tomorrow you won't feel as bad as you do now.
- Let's see what we can learn from this.
- What do you think went wrong?
- I know you didn't mean to lose my necklace. I don't want you to beat yourself up about this. It will make me feel bad too.
- I care more about you than that old dish! I know you didn't mean it.
- Let me tell you about the silly things I did when I was little.

HANDLING DIFFICULT BEHAVIOR

Parents and teachers might feel frustrated to think that they have to *always* forgive their child, they have to be perfect, they shouldn't punish, and they shouldn't get angry with their child. Thinking you have to be perfect and always forgiving may make adults feel helpless. If they are to be in control, they feel they need some weapons to help them impose the rules. The best weapon to use when dealing with unacceptable behavior is acceptance. It sounds not only counterintuitive but even paradoxical. However, it is the best way to gain control of a bad situation and deal with negative behavior. Acceptance is the key to the box of tricks that all parents can have at the ready when problems happen. If an adult can control his first impulse to rush in and be a "fixer" and can just for a moment stop and accept that something negative is happening, the answer can appear out of nowhere.

Here is an example. I know one teacher who works in a very prestigious school. The philosophy of the school is excellence. The parents are well-motivated, and the children are expected to be responsible and hard-working students. One day this teacher said to a student, "Where's your homework?" He glibly replied, "I didn't want to do it." The teacher, who is a wonderful and gifted educator, became upset. She had a number of different reactions. Her first reaction was to feel this response was a slap to her face. It was as if the child was saying, "I don't care about you and the work we do in class. And I don't respect your authority." The second feeling she had was anxiety. As a teacher in a prestigious school, she is expected to produce results. The child needs to perform well. If he doesn't, the parents will be upset. And so will the school administration. Someone will want to know why this child is not doing his homework, and maybe that will affect her standing as an educator and an employee. Her impulse was to reprimand the child. The following phrases ran through her head at lightning speed:

- That's unacceptable.
- I can't believe you just said that.
- I don't like your attitude.
- How dare you speak to me like that?
- You will be getting double homework tonight.
- I'm disappointed with you.
- That's the last time I help you with your work.

This teacher had recently undergone some counseling for a death in the family, and before she responded angrily to the child she remembered something she had just learned. People often react to negative events with emotions such as denial, anger, or depression. The final stage of grief, which they reach after time has passed, is acceptance. The teacher took a deep breath as she realized that instead of reacting with anger and denial, especially working with children, acceptance should come first. She needed to accept what he had said to her and to respond unemotionally.

"How come you didn't want to do it?" she asked calmly. As the boy shrugged his shoulders and looked away, he appeared sad. The teacher suddenly had an insight into what might be happening. The boy had a new stepmother at home and was having some authority problems. "I think I might be able to help you," she said. "Stay after class, and we can work on the problem." The boy looked at her as if this was the last thing he expected. He was anticipating conflict and retribution. Instead he received forgiveness and empathy. The teacher was able to put her own reaction to one side and really see what the boy was going through. Many young people need an adult like this during stressful times in their lives. Forgiveness and empathy not only help a child emotionally but also help a child refocus on his academic work, and work can be very healing to children and adults alike, especially when their world is a state of upheaval.

Many people ask, "But don't I have to punish the child to teach him the right thing to do?" I think we only have to take one look at the penal system to realize that punishment doesn't make people do the right thing. Every criminal knows he is likely to be punished, and yet it does not prevent crime. Even the death penalty does not work as a deterrent. Once an individual is put in jail, the punishment seldom seems to reform him. It is the same thing with children. If you yell at a child and send him into "time out" or make him go to the principal's office, about the only thing he is likely to think about is that you are angry. He may well be angry at you for being angry with him. He will probably not gain a meaningful insight into his own actions. One lesson he will learn is that some adults can't fully process or control their anger.

If "time out" is handled differently and in a more forgiving way, it might work. A parent can say, "We're both angry. I'd like you to go to your room, and we will discuss this when we're both calm." A teacher can say, "Please go sit down over there. I will discuss this with you when I am ready. Right now you are distracting me from my work." After a cooling period, the adult can work on having an attitude of forgiveness to the child. After all, the child is the one who is learning. They can sit down in a quiet place, and the adult can ask questions of the child instead of lecturing at her. He can say things like:

- I see you have a lot of feelings today.
- Do you know what those feelings are?
- Do you understand why you acted that way?
- Do you want to understand?
- Do you want to be happy in school?
- What was happening inside you right before you did that?
- How did your body feel? (depending on the age of the child)
- I see you don't know what's going on with you. Do you want to know what I think?
- Here's what I think is bothering you.
- Do you agree?
- Here's an idea what you can do when you feel this way again.
- Here's what I do when I feel this way.
- Let's try to focus on doing some good work; it will make you feel better.

These kinds of conversation are more likely to help the child monitor his actions and feelings in the future. Forgiveness and attention to a child's feelings on the part of the adult teaches a child the process of reflection. The habit of reflection can stop knee-jerk reactions that might hurt himself and others. The child will learn to forgive himself if others forgive and understand him.

ADULTS FORGIVING THEMSELVES

"What do I do with my own anger?" parents and teachers ask. "I'm only human. Doesn't everyone get angry with their child?" The answer to that question is that adults do get angry with children and do feel hatred and resentment. They need to accept they are angry and forgive themselves for it—they are only human too. If something a child does makes you angry, you need to accept first of all that you are angry. Then you need to ask yourself, "Why am I so angry?" That is an adult's duty, and though it's hard to face that one is not perfect, it is necessary so we don't act out our anger on those weaker than us. Being angry with your child and acting on your anger are two different things.

What adults can do in angry situations is to be open, not only with themselves but with the child. That helps children to see the effects of their actions. It also helps children to see that the adult accepts his own human feelings. Many teachers and parents feel guilty and ashamed when they feel negative feelings about a child. Adults need to accept that everyone has those feelings. It is better to accept them and discuss them with others.

Recently in our classroom, I was having a meeting with a teacher. It was rest time, and the children were quiet on their cots. The teacher and I were sitting at the back of the room going over some important paperwork. A little girl began crying a low, whiny cry. She was saying, "I want to go to the doctor!" over and over. We had already ascertained that she was not feeling sick, but she kept repeating it. I felt irritated since I only had a few minutes to focus on the paperwork.

I tried to ignore the sound, but I suddenly realized I was angry. I said to the teacher, "That crying is really bothering me." She looked relieved to hear me say it. "Me too," she said. "I wonder why I feel that way?" I reflected out loud. "I think it's because I used to cry and no one bothered to listen to me. How about you?" The other teacher agreed. "Me too," she said. "I spent a lot of time in my room crying by myself." I felt great relief. I no longer felt guilty for being irritated. I knew why I was upset and forgave myself for being angry. I stopped what I was doing and called over the little girl. "You want to go to the doctor?" I asked. "Isn't your sister going to the doctor today?" She nodded. "Daddy is taking her to the doctor," she said. "Oh, I see, you wish Daddy would take you too?" She smiled in acknowledgement. "That's not fair. Daddy is taking your sister, but not you. I can give you a shot. Here, do you want a shot?" I said, pretending to give her a shot with my pen. She laughed. "Go on back to your cot, and you can play with the doctor kit after rest time, OK?" The child was happy to have been understood, and I felt a huge relief. I had accepted my anger, and when I did that, I figured out where it came from and could accept the child's feelings.

Parents often pretend to love everything about their child but secretly feel annoyed. They might feel guilty because they want to say, "No, I won't pick you up. You always want to be picked up, and I'm tired and stressed." If they could acknowledge that they feel irritated, they might be able to think, "Deep down I am angry because my father never picked me up." If they don't know what they are feeling but do have negative feelings, teachers and parents who are trapped in the moment and need to say something can try to say things like:

- I'm feeling angry right now. I am going to take a few deep breaths so I can talk to you.
- I feel like yelling, and I don't like yelling.
- I'm feeling frustrated. We talked about this a few times. I'm not sure why you haven't done your work.
- I feel like you're not listening to me, and that is making me mad.
- It seems to me like I'm doing all the work here, and that doesn't feel fair to me.
- That feels very hurtful when you say that to me.
- You told me you'd have the homework on time this week. I thought you meant it. I feel a little let down.
- When you come late every day, I feel like you don't care.
- I'm confused. I thought you said you wanted to work on this, but I seem to be the only one working now.

It is true we are all human, but when we are dealing with young lives, we need to try to bring a scientific or analytical attitude to our work. Teachers and parents should look at themselves too with compassion and forgiveness. An adult should ask himself at the end of the day, "Why did I get so upset when my child had another poop accident?" or "Why does one particular pupil always bother me?" or "Why do I forgive one child when another child gets me annoyed?" or "Why am I so embarrassed in front of people when my child makes a lot of noise?" Knowing the answer to these questions and forgiving oneself for negative feelings is the best way to stop them from getting the better of you. Trying to be perfect and hating ourselves for our gut responses just compounds our anger.

I know another teacher who admitted to me that one little boy continually made her very angry. He was an adorable fellow, just a normal four-year-old, in fact very cute, and yet she just got so angry at him from time to time. She felt guilty about it, but she just kept reacting to him with anger. It was something she didn't understand and just couldn't stop. One night she had a dream that made it all clear. In the dream she saw her nephew. She had been very close to this little boy, but he was killed in a car accident when he was four years old. When she thought about the dream, she realized what was going on.

The young pupil bore quite a resemblance to her nephew. The teacher's angry feelings were her own defense system working. When her nephew had died, she felt very lost and abandoned because he had meant so much to her. She didn't want to have an attachment to the four-year-old pupil, because that might end in the same feelings of pain and loss, and so she reacted with anger in order to keep him at a distance. Once she realized that this was the reason for her anger, she was able to get in touch with old sad feelings and treat the pupil as a unique individual, not the shadow of the lost child she had loved.

If you drive a car, you don't have to be an expert mechanic. However, you do need to pay attention to the warning signs your car gives you. If there is a rattling noise, or the emergency light comes on, these are clear signals that something is going on under the hood, and you need to attend to the problem. If there is no oil, or if the fan belt is ready to break, you cannot just keep driving. You have to stop and pay attention. Similarly, if we feel angry or frustrated, those are signs that we should stop and take a look inside ourselves. We need to attend to the signals of our own emotions. If we can pause and ask ourselves why we feel a certain way, then we will be able to tend to our own feelings. If we do, we will be better "teaching machines."

BLAME

Many people react to crises by blaming others. Some people cannot forgive themselves, so they blame other people. In relationships, when someone says she is feeling angry, the other person may defend himself by blaming an external force, or even blaming the other person. An exchange like this might happen: "I am angry at you because you put my sweater in the dryer, and it shrank." "You shouldn't have asked me to do the laundry. You know I don't understand about clothes." This conversation is likely to be the beginning of an argument no one wins. A better response might be: "I know you loved that sweater. You must be so upset. I had no idea that would happen. I'm sorry about your sweater." This conversation is more likely to lead to forgiveness and understanding on both sides, since the accused accepted responsibility and also understood the impact of his actions and let the other person know he understood. He wasn't afraid to feel what it was like for the other person; he could get outside his own shame and understand her disappointment. People need most of all to be understood.

When a child does something wrong, he should be discouraged from blaming others or even himself. He should instead accept the fact that he is human, and when you are human things can go wrong. He also needs to accept responsibility and understand that his actions have consequences. Let's say a mother tells a child to clear the table and put the dishes in the sink. He rushes the job so he can watch TV. He throws the plates in the sink and breaks one. His mother says, "You broke my favorite dish! Oh no! Why did you throw it in there? You knew it would break!" A child who feels overly guilty might say, "It's not my fault; it was John's turn to do the dishes anyway." Or he might look deeply ashamed and say, "Sorry," then rush away. His mother might help him to take responsibility by saying, "I know you didn't mean to, but do you know why it happened? You were rushing so you could see TV, and you weren't thinking about what you were doing." That kind of response is better than: "I'll never forgive you. I loved that plate, and it's all your fault it's broken now." A child should not be made to feel he can never be forgiven, since that kind of blame is too big a burden for a child to bear. A beautiful dish can be replaced, and no item is so valuable as to be worth incurring a child's enduring shame. A parent can enable a child to gain a sense of responsibility. She can ask him to earn money to buy a new plate by doing some jobs around the house. He can feel he made restitution.

Children have a natural default, which is to blame themselves for things over which they have no control. Often in divorce situations, or even when someone dies, a child can think he caused the problem. Parents need to check in with children and make sure they are not feeling responsible for things they did not cause. And when they do cause a problem, parents should make sure they let a child know he is forgiven. Children are on a long slow path toward maturity. They need to gradually take on more and more responsibility and if they make mistakes along the way, they should be forgiven. Too many adults are full of regret and resentment, blame, and self-torture.

Akhtar (2005) says that the inability to forgive can be an impediment to growth: "Forgiving others for their hurtful actions and forgiving oneself for one's causing pain to others are integral to moving on in life and to opening oneself for new experiences. Inability or unwillingness to forgive keeps one tied to the past and impeded development."[1] Forgiveness can help us let go of the past and move toward the future.

FORGIVING TOO MUCH

Adults should not compromise their values or feel guilty for being authority figures. It is possible to forgive too much and give children a false sense of entitlement. If a parent sets boundaries and a child oversteps the boundaries, then there should be a consequence. Some parents feel unable to see a child feeling unhappy, and so they issue a consequence and then take it back. I know one parent who would send her child to her room when she refused to do chores. The parent immediately felt guilty. She would go by the room and peek in—to her it appeared that her child looked unbearably sad, and she couldn't handle seeing her daughter so distraught, so she would take back the punishment and allow her to come out. "I'm sorry, dear. I hope I wasn't too harsh," she would say.

When her daughter grew up, she began to get into debt. The mother would feel sorry for her. She began to bail her out by paying her bills for her. Pretty soon the girl had a huge credit card bill. The mother came to a financial crisis herself and had to come to a very painful conclusion that her child had to learn the consequences of her own actions. She had to let her get herself out of debt by getting a second job. The mother herself had a very harsh parent, and so every time she had to be firm with her daughter, she imagined that she was being mean, and she forgave her child too quickly. By forgiving too readily, she did not help her child develop self-discipline. Having a forgiving attitude does not mean that parents should allow a child to run away from reality. Actions have consequences, and children need to learn this from an early age.

Notes

1. Akhtar, S. (2005). *Forgiveness in The Language of Emotions*. Lanham, MD: Jason Aronson, 118.

Chapter 8

Children Have the Right to Approval and Acceptance

Human beings are similar to animals in many ways, and one of those similarities includes the tendency to belong to social groups. This tendency may have evolved in order to provide support and protection for the individual members. Groups of animals banding together to seek prey can be more successful than individual hunters. In the human, this social tendency is developed to a higher level than in animals. The development of language and symbolic communication is so advanced in humans that the one part of our brain that is most evolved is the area dedicated to language. Our vocal tracts are uniquely shaped and different than that of any other animal, so we can articulate the many complex sounds we need to communicate complex thoughts. Humans are evolved in such a way as to have a drive and need to relate to others. This relationship starts the moment a child is born. Once a baby is no longer a part of the mother's body, he begins to connect with her as a separate individual. The way a mother communicates with her baby in terms of facial expression, body language, and voice indicates to the child how his mother (who at this point represents the world) accepts him and approves of who he is.

Children have the right to be accepted and approved of from the moment they are born. During their long apprenticeship, which we call childhood, they need to find approval from and acceptance into the various groups of family, school, and the other social networks that make up their world. Approving of a child means giving her feedback that you think she is worth loving and that she is OK in your eyes. Nods, smiles, words of approval, and clear messages that you think the child is doing well all provide emotional nourishment to a child. Accepting a child means that you know a child is not perfect, and yet you want him to be part of your world—and part of the group you have gathered around you. If a child does not feel this acceptance, then he experiences himself as being rejected. You can accept a child and approve of him as a person while reserving the right to disapprove of and reject certain behaviors as being unacceptable.

Rejection is probably the most devastating experience a young person can have. Alienation from the group leads to many kinds of dysfunction. And since we are social beings, this dysfunction inevitably affects others. The consequences of failing to attach and include children properly can result in social bullying, depression, suicide, or the kind of anger that can result in terror bombing. On the other hand, if children feel included, needed, accepted in the group, they will grow up to be responsible, caring, involved citizens. In order to achieve a healthy society filled with involved and responsible people, we need to first understand that children have the right to be approved of and accepted.

THE MOTHER/CHILD DYAD

Whether a child is born into a large group of siblings or is an only child with a single parent, that child is always going to be the latest addition to the group, so every one of us has the experience of being a newcomer. The first group for a child is a dyad, a group of two. The relationship between mother and child is interesting in that it only begins fully when the baby is born. A child may grow within the mother, but the mother does not know the child. Many parents mention that they can't wait to see their baby. They will look at other babies and wonder what their baby will be like. Many mothers dream about how their babies will look. Adoptive parents also wonder about the child they are going to get.

Once the baby is born, two people who were once intertwined physically now are separate and can see each other. Adoptive parents as well as those who have just given birth are engaging in the first emotional relationship. The word "dyad" is a Greek word, and one of its meanings is "twoness" or "otherness." Seeing others as separate individuals and accepting others as others is a lifelong job for every one of us. It is a difficult task for the parent and equally difficult for the baby. Ideally, two people in the relationship have to connect in such a way as to make both partners happy.

A dyad, according to the dictionary, is two individual units, things, or people linked as a pair. Another definition is a musical chord consisting of two notes. A chord consists of notes played simultaneously. There is an element of timing involved, since the two notes must synchronize in time to be called a chord. If there is to be harmony, the two notes must have a certain similarity or compatibility that is obvious to all who hear it. The two notes played together create a third note, and that is the chord. When a mother interacts with her baby, each party is learning about the other. Since language is not possible, then the communication has to be done through facial expression, gesture, and sound. The baby is working very hard to understand the expressions of the mother, guessing, predicting, and trying out various gestures or cries in order to get his point across. For harmony to occur, both parties need to work hard. The mother works hard to figure out the baby's signals and to imagine what the baby might be saying, thinking, and feeling.

All this must happen, like a musical chord, in a synchronous way. A disconnect can occur if the mother responds too late or even too soon. The baby can become too fussy if he is picked up too much or depressed if he is frequently ignored. A harmonious dyad might be thought of as a couple to which both parties are related in time. When both parties are "in sync," everyone feels good, and there is a third element: the good relationship. This relationship is a foundation that benefits the child for the rest of his life and enables him to bestow his warmth and love to others in the future. On the other hand, if a baby is fussy or rejecting, the mother can experience disappointment or even depression and, in turn, reject the baby. This early rejection can be a rupturing of the precious lifeline that is essential for well-being.

PRAISE

There has been a lot of talk lately about whether it is good to praise a child or not. Some theorists think it is possible to give a child too much praise. If you praise everything a child does, they say, the praise will lose its impact. These theorists also propose the idea that children need to work hard to deserve praise; they say that small efforts such as putting on your shoes should not be praised. Some even go so far as to tell you not to praise your child at all.

Adults need to be careful when reading these articles that suggest withholding praise, since all children need praise. Neglect and unresponsiveness can be very damaging, just like food deprivation is damaging to the body. Children need to know how they are doing. They do constantly monitor their own performance and compare it with others, especially older siblings. Younger siblings may feel they fall short, not realizing they are smaller than everyone else and can't be expected to keep the same standard. If a child feels inadequate by comparison, then someone has to reassure him he is doing fine. It is very helpful to children to give them messages that they are doing well, particularly if they look doubtful—for instance, if a child spills juice on the floor, adults can say, "Don't worry, you're doing fine. Next time you'll do better. I'll help you clean it up." If a child is frustrated and can't get his coat on, a parent can say, "You're doing OK. I think you almost have it. You are getting better. You couldn't do it at all last week, remember?" That kind of praise is supportive, and children need it.

LOOK AT ME! LOOK AT ME!

Children are constantly looking for approval—they want witnesses to what they are doing. Parents who take their children to the swimming pool know they themselves will not do too much swimming. They will spend their time watching the child, because he will spend most of his time saying, "Look at me! Look at me!" Children want you to see not necessarily what they are doing but what they are *trying* to do. They want you to understand that they have a dream, and they are trying to bring it into being. A little boy once said to me, "Watch me run!" When he ran up and down he said, "Did you see the fire coming out of my feet?" Of course I said, "Yes." What he was looking for was to be seen and approved of—he wanted me to see what he pictured in his head. When a child is practicing over and over the things he wants to perfect, he needs an outsider to see him and give him approval.

A child does not need advice or suggestions for improvement. He doesn't need you to say, "Well, I think you should try it a different way," or "Actually, there isn't any fire coming out of your feet." He needs you to say, "Yes, I see you. You are great just the way you are." If you ask most adults how they think they are doing, they will probably tell of something they need to do, or some plan for improvement, or something they want, or something they don't like about themselves and want to fix. Very few people will answer, "I am doing fine. I am happy just the way I am." That is too bad. We all need someone to tell us, "You are OK. You are fine right now." We all need approval, especially during childhood.

APPROVAL AND DISAPPROVAL

In all relationships, there are periods of separation and negativity. A perfectly happy baby might suddenly become irritable. A toddler may start walking and not want to come back. Young children may kick or hit their parents, or grab other children's toys, or misbehave in a restaurant. Parents may feel they just don't understand the child's sudden whining, crying, hitting, or temper tantrums. They simply cannot accept that their once sweet, little baby is now a child, and she has a side they don't approve of. Parents may feel embarrassed or not good enough, and they may feel a sense of disgust at what their child is doing.

At this point, the parent may still think of the child as part of herself. When the child hurts other people, she thinks this is a reflection of her, that people may think she is a bad parent. She may remember getting in trouble when she was a child and be afraid her daughter is going to inherit the negative qualities she most dislikes about herself. Adoptive parents may worry that certain genes they are not aware of may come into play and that the child will not be what they want her to be. When the child is angry at the parent, the mother may feel the dyad is ruptured, and so she feels rejected. All of these feelings can cause a parent to disapprove of her child.

When parents disapprove of their children either openly or silently, children can suffer damage to self-esteem. Open disapproval is an attempt by the parent to distance himself from his child's behavior. Parents who do this are probably not aware that a child can feel very lonely and very rejected, and he will feel that he is not part of the family and that something is wrong with him. Distancing a child in this way just brings about negative feelings in the child and does not help him accept himself and take responsibility for what he has done. Parents' disapproval may be expressed in ways such as:

- I can't believe you did that!
- I'm surprised at you. I thought you were better than that.
- Be nice!
- Why would you do that?
- We don't do that kind of thing in this family.
- What were you thinking?
- That's not acceptable.
- Where did my good little boy go?
- Your mother and I are disappointed in you.
- I would never talk to my father like that.
- I don't know what's wrong with you.
- How could you let me down like that?
- I've never heard of such a thing.
- That's unforgivable.
- I have no time for behavior like that.
- Come to your senses.

All these things suggest to a child that he is different from the parents. They are a way of saying the parents would not be capable of doing the very same things. A disapproving attitude makes a child feel isolated. If it is not expressed openly in words, disapproval can be conveyed in possibly more damaging ways by subtle gestures and looks. I know a parent who never raised her voice, or her hand, to her children. However, she pursed her lips and rolled her eyes in such a way as to make her son understand that she felt disappointed in him. Though he was a normal boy, this mother was overly demanding and disapproved of many things her son did—but she did so without saying a word. When he showed negative behavior, or if he disagreed with something she said, she would sigh as if wounded, and he would feel the extent of her disapproval in one exhalation of air through her flared nostrils. This might be termed the "martyr syndrome," when parents act as if their child's negative feelings are an offense they have to bear. The result of this disapproval is that a child feels shame.

SHAME AND GUILT

There is a difference between shame and guilt. Guilt is a useful emotion that is a natural part of human emotional development. If people did not experience a sense of guilt, they would do things that are unsocial and cause pain to others without caring. If a child does something that hurts, she must learn that her behavior affects others. If the child is to learn to do the right thing, she must experience a sensation of having done something that is hurtful, and to experience this sensation as negative. She needs to be able to contain this feeling though it must not be so painful as to be unbearable. Feeling guilty and making amends should go hand in hand. So, if a child steps on someone's hand by accident, for instance, she needs to realize her foot can hurt someone if she is not careful. Also she needs to be mature enough to realize the other person may not understand it was an accident. And finally she needs to apologize to the other child, a simple short apology: "Sorry, I didn't mean to step on your hand. I didn't see it." There are a lot of steps that have to happen in a child's life before she can complete the circle. In order for a child to process an accident and its results, she would need to be developed enough to do the following things: Notice the other person is crying. Realize she has caused the pain to the other person. Understand the other person may feel upset at her. Comprehend that the other person may not *know* it was an accident. Figure out that she needs to convey to the other person that she meant no harm. Think of the right words to express the situation and her feelings. Control her own anxiety about the child's crying. Take some action to help the other person feel better

That is a healthy chain of events, and quite a complicated one. If the child reaches stage one and sees the person crying then proceeds to stage two and knows she has caused pain, how she reacts at that point is directly related to how she handles guilt. Many children, as young as three, cannot bear how guilty they feel. This sense of guilt can be so hard for them to bear that they often cannot apologize. Guilt has turned into shame.

A person with a healthy dose of guilt or conscience can say, "Oops, I did something wrong. Please forgive me," and he will forgive himself along the way. In some cultures, acceptance of responsibility is a normal part of social behavior. People are encouraged to apologize quickly if something happens. In these cultures, people often bow to each other, saying, "I'm sorry." Then the other person says, "No, I'm sorry," and each one tries to assure the other they themselves are at fault. In those societies, such as in Japan, there is a very low crime rate, and it is probably no coincidence that when people take responsibility and guilt as a normal part of life, there is no need for blame or shame.

However, if a child's normal sense of guilt has become distorted, he can develop a sense of shame, and this can lead to anti-social behavior. People who suffer from excess shame may be angry at the person they have injured instead of experiencing compassion for them. Their shame turns outward and becomes blame. These kinds of people are called sociopaths; they blame everyone else but themselves. Instead of compassion, they feel resentment towards others they have harmed. Other children who feel excessive shame may internalize the pain they have caused to others and live lives full of regret and self-torture. This shame is extremely destructive to a person's self-esteem. People like this are unable to participate in group activities to the extent that others do because they feel they are not worthy.

EXCLUSION FROM THE GROUP

How does guilt turn to shame? While guilt is an awareness of having done something wrong, combined with a sense of regret and a wish to undo the wrong, shame is something else altogether. Shame is a feeling of exclusion from the group. People who feel ashamed are feeling unworthy and unacceptable. Parents can, without realizing, help to compound a child's healthy feelings of guilt into feelings of shame. A child who feels shame believes that everyone else thinks badly of him; others do not want to have anything to do with him, and he feels socially rejected. Instead of thinking he did something bad, he thinks he is a bad person and does not belong with the other nice people. People shame others by implying their behavior is not socially acceptable, and they imply the child will be ostracized if he behaves in a certain way. Making a child feel she is not part of the group creates shame. At times parents say shaming things like:

- You should be ashamed of yourself.
- We're ashamed of you.
- Go to your room; we don't want to see you!
- Sit in the corner while everyone else can play.
- Everyone thinks you did the wrong thing.
- You can't go to the birthday party now.
- No one in our family ever did that.
- Why did you have to make us look bad?
- Are you really going out dressed like that?
- You're no child of mine.
- We can never go to that restaurant again.
- No one wants to hear you talk like that.
- You really disgraced yourself in front of everyone.
- What would the neighbors think?
- Please don't do that in front of my relatives.

Parents need to accept the negative side of their child because, if they do not, the child will not accept himself, and the child may experience himself as split into two people: the "good child" and the "bad child." Many young children play good guy/bad guy games. This is normal and healthy. What they are doing is trying to incorporate their negative feelings and integrate them with those that are socially acceptable. Parents should allow children to play these games. One example of it is playing "pirate" games so that a child can have fun being a "bad guy," for a while. Adults can encourage the idea that good and bad are part of life; we all have negative and positive feelings, and it is accepted that children are just trying their best. Sometimes they will fail, and they will need to accept that as part of life.

ACCEPTING THE CHILD'S NEGATIVE SIDE

Parents need to be able to say, "It's OK. I know you feel bad about stepping on the girl's hand. But you didn't mean it. Just say sorry, and she will understand." In that way, they help a child face up and take responsibility but also get over the guilty feeling quickly. It is sometimes hard for parents to accept that their child may feel enjoyment at hurting others or may feel rage and murderous impulses towards others. Sometimes that is an unbearable thought to parents. They think that if the child feels bad feelings, he is a bad person. They often think that if a child has that feeling now, he will always feel that way. They imagine, "Oh, no. He stepped on that girl's hand deliberately. He's going to grow up and be a serial killer!" Parents forget that children are just learning. In fact, a parent said a wonderful thing recently. When asked, "What's the most important thing you learn from your child?" he answered, "How you feel now is not how you will feel a few minutes from now." That is so true and so obvious, and yet we forget it all the time.

Another thing parents forget is that we as adults feel negative feelings at times, and that children have the same feelings as we do. We have learned to avoid our negative feelings, and so we forget they are there all the time. When a car cuts us off, or someone pushes rudely past us, or someone ahead of us orders the last loaf of bread, we are liable to feel a rush of blind rage. If we feel these intense feelings come up out of nowhere, then we must acknowledge that they are present in us, ready to be triggered off by a sudden unpleasant event. Since we are adults, we have learned to manage them, hopefully. Children also have those negative feelings, but they have not yet learned to control them. If parents make them feel ashamed, then they will not be able to accept themselves, and it will be hard for them to integrate negative feelings into their self-image. They will hide the negative side.

Parents who accept children with all their negative as well as positive attributes help their children to grow up to become healthy adults. Those children grow up knowing that they can feel angry at times, and it is normal. They will be able to understand that they would love to slap someone and forgive themselves for feeling that way. Children who bury angry feelings and are ashamed of them are far more likely to act them out. We are all familiar with the politician who has the "perfect" outside appearance; he is the superhero who prosecutes criminals, and he defends the rules unstintingly. As time goes by, it turns out he is cheating on his wife, doing drugs, spending taxpayers' money on himself, or frequenting prostitutes. This man is split into two sides, good and bad. His parents probably liked the "good" side of him but did not want to accept him when he felt angry or depressed, sad or lonely. They approved of one part of him but not the other. And so he has become two people. It is likely that when he was a child, he was made to feel it was more important to keep up appearances than to be a real person with real feelings.

LABELING

When parents notice a certain kind of behavior, often it is a behavior they do not like or do not understand; they may label not the behavior, but the child.

Some parents cannot accept their children as "others." They are afraid to see that their child is a person in his own right, and they want to "manage" the child and change his attributes. Or they may feel that outsiders will not accept their child for what he is, and so they have the need to explain their children to others. Some parents think it is fine to discuss their child in front of others this way: "Oh, she's shy." Shyness, like most other labels people put on children, is not a personality trait; it's a feeling that everyone is likely to have at one time or another. It is a protective mechanism that is very useful. Unfortunately, once a child is labeled as "shy" by her parents, the label tends to become internalized, and many strong, capable girls come to think of themselves as permanently shy. If a parent could accept that her child was feeling reserved and did not feel the need to explain her child to other people, then the child might not feel stuck with the label of being shy.

There is also the kind of labeling a parent does in order to control the child. This labeling might take the form of: "Why don't you get up? You're lazy!" Though the intent is to get the child to do something he is not doing, the result is labeling, and it is not helpful. By labeling a child, a parent, in fact, compounds the problem since people act according to how they think they are expected to act. If you call a child lazy, you will get a lazy child. A better way to do it is to accept that the child is not getting up for whatever reason, and to give choices or consequences. If she does not get up, she won't have time for breakfast, for example. The worst kind of labeling is when parents disapprove of their child's behavior and reflect their disapproval in the form of labeling:

- Come on, slowpoke.
- Don't take the last cupcake; you're greedy.
- Why can't you eat faster? You're always the last one.
- You are just like your father.
- You told me you ate all your lunch! You're a liar.
- Go on, jump in the pool. Don't be such a scaredy-cat.
- Everything will be fine. Don't be such a worry-wart.
- Don't be so bossy.
- You're too fussy.
- You're so shy. No one will give you anything if you don't ask for it.
- Don't be such a show-off.
- What an idiot!
- Don't you remember I told you before? You're so dopey.
- Don't be so rude.
- She's such a chatterbox.
- What a drama queen!

When parents are tempted to use phrases such as these, they should remember that the feeling they are experiencing is theirs, and they should take responsibility for it. For instance, instead of saying, "Hurry up, slow-poke," a parent should accept his own feeling and say, "I'm really stressed because we're going to be late for school, and I hate being late. Could you hurry please?" Instead of saying, "Don't be such a worry-wart," a parent could say, "I hate seeing you looking worried. It makes me feel helpless. I wish I could help you not to feel anxious." When a parent does not accept a child's healthy mistrust of strangers and interprets it as shyness, or when a parent can't allow a child to feel fear of drowning, that parent may be placing his child in danger. He may teach his child to take dangerous risks. Being afraid of deep water or having reservations when you first meet someone are good survival skills. They should be encouraged, not discouraged.

Rather than saying, "Jump in the pool. Don't be a scaredy-cat," a parent should accept his own feeling and say, "I used to be very scared of jumping in the pool when I was little, and people used to tease me. It's OK to be scared of new things. I will help you." I know one father who threw his son into the pool to help him to get over being scared. Needless to say, this young man does not care for swimming at all now. Generally speaking, when parents label their children, they are trying to avoid their own negative feelings about something they feel within themselves. Acceptance of her own fears, shame, or regret will help a mother accept her child's particular struggles. Having the courage to allow your child to take her time if she needs to, no matter who is pressurizing, gives a real message of acceptance and approval to the child, and this is a treasure that lasts a lifetime. Typecasting is another way that some families fail to accept their child's total self. Some parents refer to their children in this way:

- She's the funny one.
- He's the artistic one, and she's the math whiz.
- They're so different. I can't believe they're sisters.
- He's like me, and she's like her mother.
- He's a clown.
- My younger son is the level-headed one.
- She's the baby of the family.

Typecasting in this way gives a message to the child that he or she has to be the way the parent thinks of him. If you are the funny one, then no one should take you seriously. If you are the artistic one, then you can't be good at math; that's your sister's job. Parents should try to show approval of the child as an evolving individual capable of change and full of potential.

IN SCHOOL

Teachers need to understand that children are by nature approval-seeking entities. They rely on the positive feedback they receive from others in the formation of their self-image. Some teachers, however, fail to realize the potential good they can do as well as the benefit that can accrue to themselves if they give children the approval and acceptance they need. In order for a classroom to run well, teachers need the cooperation of the children. And when cooperation is received, the teacher's work becomes a joy and a pleasure. This joy trickles back down to the children, and there now exists a little prototype of the perfect society in which everyone is cooperating and everyone benefits. The initial healthy dyad can be replicated in the classroom.

PRAISE AND POSITIVE FEEDBACK

How is this done? Some teachers claim that everything would be fine if it weren't for a small group of troublemakers who ruin everything. Others say they can't get anything done because no one will listen. There are, however, many teachers who have realized that the secret to a happy classroom is to give children positive feedback and keep negative feedback to a minimum. This is based on the theory that all children need approval. Teachers can get this to work to their advantage, and everyone can feel happy.

At cleanup time, a teacher might see a group of children busy cleaning and another group sitting around still playing and failing to help. The teacher who hasn't realized the secret of approval will focus on the negative behavior: "Paul, you are sitting there playing, doing nothing to help. That's not fair to your friends. I need you to clean up." This teacher has set up a negative image without realizing it. "You are sitting there playing, doing nothing to help." Children perceive images rather than concepts. This teacher will get little response now, since the child is picturing himself playing and doing nothing to help, and he cannot change the mental image. She has not created a positive image for him to follow. She can repeat this over and over, but it will not work, and she will soon be exhausted and angry.

In our classrooms, we use praise and focus on the positive behavior. We create positive images that attract children: "Oh, look at those helpful children. I see lots of people cooperating. Look at Gray over there picking up cars, and there's Sylvia picking up puzzles. Oh, now I see Ziggy picking up blocks." As soon as a teacher says this, the other children will want to join the helpful group and benefit from the praise that's flowing freely. By focusing on the good behavior, the teacher is encouraging the helpers and inspiring the others to join in by giving them a picture of what she wants them to do. By giving children approval for good behavior, teachers can make their own work a lot easier, and children will get very positive feelings through the praise they receive.

In school, teachers use acceptance and approval as tools, but sometimes they use them as a way to manipulate children, rather than a way to allow them to grow. There are two kinds of praise used commonly in schools. One of them is "mastery praise" and the other is "social-comparison praise." Mastery praise is when a child accomplishes something that he himself has set out to do, or a task that the teacher has assigned and the child has accepted and become fully engaged with. Mastery praise goes something like this: "Fran, I see you finished the whole page you were working on. That's terrific. You had a lot of ideas today." Social-comparison praise is when teachers praise some children in comparison to others. The latter kind of praise goes something like this: "Mike, come up to the top of the class and show everyone how you did the exercise." When Mike comes up and shows everyone the teacher more or less says, "See, this is what I want the rest of you to do. Mike is the best student in the class."

When children receive praise in relation to others, the relationship of children to each other and the health of the group as a social unit are damaged. Children need to feel approved of in relation to their own goals, which of course can also be the goals of the teacher, but they should not be approved of insofar as they compare with others. Not only do relationships suffer—a child's actual performance suffers if he has to work to a set of standards where other children's performances count also. A child's motivation suffers when he feels compared with others—even for the child who excels.

Studies show that mastery praise is far more effective in terms of a child's academic work. A study done by Henderlong-Corpus (2006) examined the different short- and long-term effects of the different kinds of praise:

> Mastery praise benefits intrinsic motivation and social-comparison praise curtails it when uncertainty about children's subsequent achievements is introduced and, for girls, even in situations of continued success. Social-comparison praise arguably teaches children that personal competence should be measured by their relative standing in a group rather than their development of particular skills—a harmful message when children encounter situations that lead them to doubt their ability. Motivation and perseverance may be maximized, therefore, by avoiding social-comparison praise in favor of praise that emphasizes skill development."[1]

This study points to the fact that children in school should receive approval based on their own individual performance, rather than by comparison with others, and that praise should not be reserved for the few who beat out their classmates.

BEING ACCEPTED BY OTHERS

Children in preschool do not have the skills they need to interrelate with others successfully. A group of young children left together without guidance or supervision will quickly deteriorate into conflict of some kind. Some children are better at communicating than others, and those children are the ones who find it easy to make friends and gain acceptance. Learning to accept that others have different points of view is a skill that children cannot develop without guidance. Once a child is able to listen to the feelings of others and communicate his own feelings without malice or violent actions, he is on the road to being a good group member. In many classrooms, it is the children who are most accepting of others who are the natural leaders, and they are the ones the other children want to be close to.

Teachers can go a long way to help children accept their own weaknesses as well as the weaknesses of others. Lack of acceptance, however, causes a child to withdraw and mistrust himself and resent others. Teachers may be distressed by a child's actions, especially aggressive ones, and may react without pausing to reflect. This knee-jerk reaction can cause a teacher to say things like:

- Look what you've done!
- See the mark on his face? It's terrible!
- How do you think that makes him feel?
- How would you like if someone did that to you?
- Say sorry!
- Saying sorry is not enough.
- Look at me when I talk to you.
- I can't believe you did that.
- Why did you do that?
- What were you thinking?

A teacher may say these things in order to let a child know his behavior is unacceptable. The teacher may feel he is protecting the victim and reasserting his position as class leader, and that he will prevent the child from acting out again. However, many teachers as well as parents can attest to the fact that this punitive or rejecting approach does not seem to bring about positive change, especially in the case of children who are repeatedly aggressive. In fact, it tends to stereotype children, as the other children will quickly label the aggressor as a "bad boy," instead of being compassionate. And once a child thinks he is bad, he will live up to his reputation. Not only that—it shows the children that the teacher is really not in control since he is reacting emotionally when he should be calm.

What does make a positive change possible is acceptance. When an aggressive incident happens in school, the first thing a teacher needs to do is accept it. Teachers should try to pause and look at the scene, for instance when one child is crying loudly and the other one is looking guilty with a block in his hand. If the aggression is continuing, she of course needs to rush over and stop it so no one gets hurt. However, if no one is in imminent danger, the teacher should count to ten. Ten seconds are all that is needed for a teacher to reflect on what has happened and why it is happening. Then she can approach and begin the work of helping both children to understand the situation. Since she knows both children and knows what is going on in their lives, she should be able to come up with good, insightful comments. Young children think in concrete terms. Reflecting back exactly what she sees can be very helpful. Interpreting people's motives, as well as their own motives, is a skill children are working hard to develop. A teacher can say:

- It looks like James hit Alec with the block.
- Alec is very upset.
- Alec's body got hurt.
- James was angry and hit Alec.
- I think I know what happened here.
- James wanted the fire truck, and Alec had it.
- James hit because he didn't know how to use words.
- James has been hitting people lately.
- James' baby brother is crawling now. Maybe he takes James toys away.
- James, does your baby brother take your toys away?
- Alec, you have a baby sister, don't you? Does she take your toys also?

The teacher can carry on in this way until she feels the children are able to connect with what they did and see the reason why they might have acted badly. Once they accept these things in themselves, they can move towards accepting each other and feel a bond. There is always an underlying connection between children who are drawn into conflicts with each other. If the teacher can find that connection and help children see it, that's where the healing and growth can occur. If children feel separated into aggressor and victim, then neither one will have empathy for the other.

This kind of very simple and concrete reflection can help the teacher and the children in a number of ways. It can show the children that the teacher accepts they have angry feelings and is prepared to help them. It shows them that she accepts aggression as a part of life, and that she knows how to figure out where it comes from. It shows the children who are not being aggressive at that moment that the teacher could help them in similar situations. It gives the two children who are in an aggressor/victim drama a way of connecting to one another and understanding what is going on under the surface. It teaches reflection instead of retribution. It teaches children to accept the part of themselves that adults often want to hide and avoid. And it models calm behavior in a heated situation.

With older children, teachers may tend to feel their role is to "get the work done" rather than attend to the problematic children in the classroom. However, a teacher's view of the problematic children can affect the entire class. A very interesting study done by Chang (2007) found a strong correlation between teacher preference and peer acceptance. The researchers interviewed over 1,300 elementary school children about their classmates. They asked children about their perception of others, based on the following categories: aggression, social withdrawal, leadership, and peer acceptance. They also interviewed teachers, asking them questions about which students they liked and which students they disliked. They found a high correlation between teacher preference and peer acceptance:

> Teacher preference clearly influenced students' peer preference. However, the degree and the nature by which teacher preference affected students' evaluations varied depending on the specific behavior that was being considered. This conclusion is based on two findings. First, the mediating teacher preference was stronger on the relation between aggression and peer acceptance than that between social withdrawal or prosocial leadership and peer acceptance.[2]

The study shows a correlation between teacher dislike and aggressive behavior, and between teacher dislike and peer acceptance. The study shows that teachers have strong negative reactions to aggressive behavior but not to withdrawal or depression.

These study results are disturbing on a number of levels, since it is clear that children reject the children teachers do not like. However, it should be pointed out that it is not fair to make sweeping conclusions based on this study. It is not clear from the study that teachers' dislike of children *causes* peer rejection. The study does show that though teachers' influence is strong on the earlier grades, it lessens as children reach sixth grade. However, it is clear from the study that teachers do indeed react adversely to children because of their aggression, and this dislike does become conveyed to the other students. The study explains it in this way:

> Student aggression is also likely to anger classroom teachers since such behavior challenges their authority and interferes with their work . . . Teachers are more likely to openly express their dislike of students who behave aggressively rather than engaging in other undesirable behaviors (e.g., social withdrawal). Indeed, teachers have frequently used presentation punishment with aggressive students to let the class learn the consequences of misconduct.

These conclusions make it disturbingly clear that many teachers believe it is "their work" to complete curriculum requirements and override their students' behavioral problems. This would lead us to believe that many teachers think that the emotions and the intellect are two separate parts of the child and that a child can leave his emotional life to one side while he works on his studies. If teachers were enabled to understand the aggressive behavior of children, then they would be more accepting of these children. Teachers could be trained in how to handle these behaviors in a way that modeled this acceptance to the other children. If, as the study states, teachers' attitudes do carry across to the other children, particularly younger children, then acceptance and approval could be modeled by the teacher, and all would benefit.

In a wonderful article about therapy and school, Music and Hall (2008) explain how teachers should be able to play a therapeutic role, and thereby make a real difference in these situations:

> For example, in the situation of a pupil wanting to belittle another child to assuage their own hurt feelings, the child psychotherapist can help teachers and management to not only process their own powerful reactions to what they often initially see as "misbehaviour," but also help them find some sympathy for a child who had hitherto aroused only distaste or anger.[3]

This article shows how teachers, with support and guidance, can help children by accepting their problems as part of their day's work, rather than fighting to keep them under control. Unfortunately, as children progress through the school system and have to adapt themselves to curriculum and standards, teachers must feel pressure and time constraints. Some schools have very strict guidelines for teachers, and some administrators are even considering paying teachers on the basis of "results." This is tantamount to thinking about children as machines to be programmed. Some children are able to perform in the ways expected of them, and others have difficulty. Individual differences make certain tasks more pleasant than others. Recent studies show that boys in particular have difficulty sitting still for long periods of time. If teachers were allowed to vary their methods and develop styles more accepting of children as individuals, then they would undoubtedly achieve more.

Before acceptance comes knowledge. Teachers should have access to updated research. If they are aware of a child's motivations, they will be more accepting of his moods. For instance if a teacher realizes that certain pupils are physically restless and not paying attention, she can create lessons incorporating movement. Imaginative teachers could, with the support of their directors, adapt their lessons to the physical and emotional needs of the child. Mind and body, emotions, and intellect are not separate, and accepting the child with all his needs and feelings will help make teaching more relevant and effective. Unfortunately, standardized testing and "accountability" policies tend to force teachers to view children as products being processed in a factory rather than as individuals. Instead of being placed in the role of police officer, judge and jury or jailor, most teachers would probably prefer to play a nurturing role in the lives of children. And many children can remember one teacher who made a real difference. Those teachers accept the child for who she is and try to help her with her difficulties. Osofsky (2005) speaks of the "angels" who can influence a child's life outside of the parental sphere:

> A brief mention of some of the resilience literature may be relevant here. Emmy Werner's (1994) landmark study on resilience following the children on the island of Kauai in Hawaii showed that resilient children who adapted successfully to adult life always had either parents or caregivers who reflected competence and fostered self-esteem in their children or other supportive adults who fostered trust. . . . .All of the studies concur that the most important protective resource is a strong relationship with a competent, caring, positive adult, who is most often a parent but also can be another trusting adult such as those described earlier.[4]

The trusting and trusted adults described above would include the teacher, who spends so much time with the child. Schools are often underrated in their potential to help children develop emotionally and socially, and yet many children remember a teacher who saw something in them that others did not see. Most teachers begin their careers with the goal of helping children. That nurturing quality should be encouraged and given expression, since teachers can make a huge difference in the lives of children.

PEER ACCEPTANCE AND APPROVAL

As children grow older the opinion of their parents and teachers becomes less important than the opinion of classmates. Peer approval becomes a goal for children and preoccupies their thoughts more and more. Teachers need to be aware of peer pressure and bullying tendencies inside the classroom and on the playground. Some children may try to gain acceptance from others by banding in groups and excluding others. Teachers can foster acceptance and help group dynamics by having daily meetings to work out differences and air grievances. They can also work on peer acceptance by giving withdrawn children more power in the classroom and helping assertive children moderate their tone so that there is a balance of contributions. By showing their approval of children, especially when children are self-deprecating, teachers can help strengthen a child's ego. This open approval can also raise the child's standing in the eyes of others and help her to be accepted.

If a new child arrives in a group, children often take a while to accept him. If he is from another country, is of a different race or color, dresses differently, and so on, then the tendency may be to exclude him. Teachers can do a great deal to foster acceptance, and they can do this by approving of the child openly. Recent incidents of scapegoating and bullying in schools show that children who are not monitored by adults may act out prejudices and fears on other children in school. Name-calling and teasing are ways in which children try to distance themselves from others. Teachers can set up conflict-resolution workshops in order to help children present their feelings to other children in non-confrontational ways. The techniques they learn there can help them solve problems in peaceable ways. Classrooms can become small communities where all are accepted and differences are welcomed. An atmosphere of approval rather than criticism will help children feel that they are valued members of the group.

Teachers also need to be aware of gender issues in the classroom. Some teachers claim to be even-handed in their response to different genders, but many studies demonstrate that teachers unconsciously demonstrate preference toward one gender or have hidden expectations of each gender. In addition, within the classroom boys and girls may have their own prejudices or fears with which they approach each other. While it is normal and healthy for boys or girls to band together and foster gender identification, at times one gender can be judgmental of others within the group or exclusionary to members of the other group. In other words, girls can deem other girls not acceptable in the girl group, and boys condemn other boys to be outsiders. Both boy groups and girl groups can work to exclude the other gender and foster misunderstandings. In some cases, gender roles and stereotypes can cause children to inflict pain on each other in order to enforce compliance. Teachers can help develop an atmosphere of tolerance and acceptance. One three-year-old boy who enjoys wearing a dress at playtime might hear other boys saying, "Boys don't wear dresses." The teacher can say something non-judgmental and approving like, "Well, Max likes dressing up. Don't you, Max?"

In Finland, teachers use playtime (which is more extensive than in U.S. schools) as an arena for fostering gender collaboration and mutual acceptance. According to Hyvonen (2008):

> In addition to not separating genders, questioning . . . children's behaviour and making them reflect on it—as seen in the "hair salon" and on the soccer field—seem to be effective ways to dissolve gender boundaries. Sometimes merely questioning is enough, but discussions are often needed as well . . . It is important also to provide situations in which children have to negotiate by themselves, as the examples of role negotiation highlighted. Pre-primary teachers related that this is how their students learn to negotiate.

Boys and girls need to learn how to relate to each other as equals, and teachers can help in this regard. Through playful activities or group discussions, differences can become more manageable, and similarities become more obvious.

MEETINGS AND DISCUSSIONS

The current school system in the United States does not allow for a great deal of play. Teachers are under pressure to achieve curriculum goals and have their pupils score high on standardized tests. Some even propose that teachers' pay should be based on how well their pupils perform on these arbitrary tests. Teachers naturally feel that they just cannot spend the time playing and that they just can't squeeze in the time needed to help boys and girls relate well to each other. However, teachers in even the most selective of schools can attest to the fact that conflict does occur in the classroom and that negative behavior affects not only their own teaching but also the performance of the whole group. If just one half-hour a day were to be allocated to group discussions to help children understand and accept what they are feeling—and accept the feelings of others—the rest of the day would be spent far more productively.

If you are going on a journey, you should check the vehicle before you leave. Lift the hood, make sure you have enough oil, check the gas gauge to make sure you have enough gas, look the tires over and check for air. Once you check the vehicle, you can see what is needed. This preventative maintenance is needed to preempt problems along the way. Morning meetings can do the same thing for the classroom. If a teacher can spend some time before beginning class, and she can have children check their own feelings and reflect on what is going on inside them before starting the day, the day will go better for everyone.

If teachers do not operate the classroom in an accepting way, they may suffer a lot more stress when they try to control behavior. Accepting negative behavior as a symptom of underlying problems can help a teacher greatly, because it will help him to know how to react coolly. Teachers who manage aggressive behavior in a controlling way often appear rejecting to the child, and this can compound the problem. Stressed teachers tend to fall back on threats or promises, but this may create more work for themselves because now they have to carry out the threat or promise. They also create more stress for themselves if they take on the role of judge and jury, since they have to spend time figuring out who is right and who is wrong, and there is no good solution to that quest. Teachers who don't accept negative behavior as a symptom of underlying problems tend to use threats, rejection, humiliation, typecasting, accusations, sarcasm, or punishment in order to change the child's behavior. They may say things like:

- If you don't stop, you'll have to leave the room.
- Just sit at the back of the class and don't say a word.
- Go stand in the hall.
- Go to the principal's office.
- Stop interrupting the class.
- What is that in your hand? A note? Why aren't you listening to me?
- If I see any more of that you'll be in trouble.
- You are the only one causing trouble.
- What is it going to take to make you stop?
- I'm just about sick and tired of you.
- Don't talk back.
- Keep still in your seat and stop moving around.
- Get out of here. I don't want to see your face.
- You'll be bottom of the class again.
- Why weren't you paying attention? Were you asleep as usual?

All this is exhausting for the teacher himself since he knows he is getting nowhere and is acting and speaking out of sheer frustration. Suppose the teacher were aware that a child was dyslexic and couldn't read the text, or that his father was abusive to him and his mother, or that another girl is hungry or not getting enough sleep, or that her mother and father were fighting every night. Wouldn't he then have a different insight into the child's behavior? Teachers who find out more about the child and his family life are in a better position to gain these insights. Once he has the insight, the teacher can develop different and more effective skills in handling and managing disruptive behavior. A teacher who knows what is going on and accepts the child's negative behavior might say things like:

- Are you having trouble focusing on this?
- Am I losing you? Did you get that last point I made?
- I notice you're talking. Do you want to ask me anything?
- You are angry with me. Why is that?
- Don't worry. This will be a short lesson; you can get through it.
- If you need a little extra help, I'll be glad to help you after class.
- I know this one might be hard for you. Just try your best with it.
- Let's go over your test. I can see you are having difficulties.
- Can we talk later? You seem tired and distracted.
- Is there anything you want to talk to me about? I will be happy to help you if you need someone to talk to.
- Is it hard for you to pay attention? Why do you think that is?

Teachers who are accepting can also feel free to accept their own feelings and convey them in an appropriate way to children. Children relate to adults who are open with their feelings. Such a teacher could say:

- I'm feeling distracted from what I'm saying, Sam, because I can hear you talking, and it's hard for me to continue.
- I'm worried about you not handing your homework on time. Let's talk about what we can do to help you.
- I'm confused. You said you wanted to improve, but I notice you're not doing the exercises we talked about yesterday. I would like to understand. Can you tell me what's happening?
- Come on, everyone. I don't mind a few jokes, but I'm concerned about the exercise we have to finish. Let's get back to work now.
- I'm happy to see you are changing your habits.
- I'm so proud of you all. I didn't think you could pull this off so well.
- Guys, help me out here. We need to get this done together, and I can't do all the work myself.
- Oh, no! It looks like we have only ten minutes left. Let's get this done—come on, we can do it together.

Self-acceptance and acceptance of the child as a person with feelings makes the classroom a community of people working towards personal goals and communal goals. The approval of the teacher must be implicit. A teacher should convey that she knows a child may have difficulties or personal problems but that she approves of the child—despite his "acting out" behavior. Some children present a hard and untouchable exterior. Some teachers misinterpret this sarcasm and "toughness," but insightful teachers will know that the child just needs an adult to understand and help him. A kind word from an understanding teacher can melt even the most bitter and suffering child.

Acceptance and approval matter a great deal to children because a child wants to belong to a loving community. The first community is the mother and child relationship. Then there is the family, and after that the school. If children are accepted and approved of, they will feel valued, and they will attach value to the group. All children deserve acceptance and approval. If they are rejected or filled with shame, they will not be attached securely to any group and will present a danger to themselves as well as others.

Notes

1. Henderlong-Corpus, J. et al. (2006). "The Effects of Social-Comparison Versus Mastery Praise on Children's Intrinsic Motivation." *Motivation and Emotion* 30:335–345.

2. Chang, L., et al. (2007). "The Mediating and Moderating Effects of Teacher Preference on the Relations between Students' Social Behaviors and Peer Acceptance." *Merrill-Palmer Quarterly* 53:4, 621–622.

3. Music, G., and Hall, B. (2008). "From Scapegoating to Thinking and Finding a Home: Delivering Therapeutic Work in Schools." *Journal of Child Psychotherapy* 34:1, 43–61, London, UK.

4. Osofsky, J. (2005). "Ghosts and Angels: How Can We Find Them in the Nursery and Beyond?" *Infant Mental Health Journal* 26(6): 525–528.

Chapter 9

Children Have the Right to Show Their Feelings

Emotions cannot be separated from the life of the individual, and their importance cannot be minimized. From the moment they are born, and probably even before, children have feelings. The more we learn through research, the more we realize how pervasive and complex these feelings are. Babies can experience feelings of abandonment, fear, longing, joy, anxiety, confusion, and even despair. In order for a child to survive, he must make emotional connections with at least one person. If that does not happen, the child will not grow emotionally, physically, or cognitively and can actually die. Conversely, for a child to thrive and be healthy, he must have his feelings acknowledged. Unfortunately, the only way for a baby to express his feelings is through gestures and utterances, since he does not yet have words.

Babies have the right to make loud and emotional expressions of feeling, as they are the only way they can communicate. No one would tell a baby he doesn't have the right to cry. However, within two years, some people are already saying things like this to children: "Don't cry," or "Don't make a fuss," or "It's not that bad. Shhh!" or "I don't like that angry face," or "Where did my sweet little baby go?" Some people try to train children away from open demonstration of feelings. Children have the right to show all the feelings they have, from anger, to loneliness, to anxiety. It is the adult's job to train the child in how best to get his feelings across in an acceptable way and how to have his needs met. However, suppressing the outward signs of those feelings is not the same as teaching a child to manage his feelings. Telling a child to stop crying does not soothe the pain. No one should deny a child the right to say or show how he is feeling. It is the only way he can communicate what is inside with the outside world and have the two connect. It is like telling a dog he cannot bark or a bird he cannot sing.

Being a parent is like arriving on stage and having the curtains open without rehearsal. You don't know the script; the other player doesn't even speak the same language; the audience is waiting; and it's the most important role of your life. You can't wait for someone to tell you what to do; you have to act. You must try to interpret the baby's language. You must try to comprehend the tone of his voice or the gestures of his body, for they are the only tools he has. Everyone is watching, and you can't make a mistake. Parents have to try to figure out whether their baby is hungry or tired, whether he needs a diaper change, or whether he wants to be picked up and held. They have to make quick decisions and try to put their own stressed reaction on hold. They have to use their intuition, their intelligence, and their own feelings of empathy. They may not have a good role model or healthy experiences on which to base their decisions. In any case, most parents are making it up as they go along. How to respond to a certain cry, how to distinguish cries from one another, all these are difficult and yet vital decisions.

REACTING TO A CHILD'S FEELINGS

Many people find a baby's cry distressing. Travel with a baby on an airplane and see how many strangers feel disturbed by that sound. Walk down the supermarket aisle with a crying baby, and total strangers will intervene with advice, good and bad. For various reasons, parents can find themselves surrounded with people who want them to keep their baby quiet. I know one parent who was traveling on a bus with her two-year-old son. He was looking out the window when he said very loudly, "Look, Mommy. Look at the red car . . . Mommy, look at the red car. Look at the red car!" A woman in the seat in front of them turned around and said to her, "Can you please tell him to shut up!" It is pretty sad that people can be so angry at young children for no obvious reason. In this case the boy was unable to control his joy at seeing cars. We can only imagine the thrill he felt at seeing a red car. Since he was two years old, it might have been his very first sight of a red car close up. He didn't know if his mother felt the excitement as much as he did, so he had to repeat it over and over to make sure she felt the same way as him. Why would that make someone angry? We can only speculate.

Parents are being met with these disapproving messages on all sides, especially if they live in an apartment where the neighbors do not like the sound of a child's voice. A child can be very loud—after all, children are still in touch with their feelings in a very immediate and enviable way. "Children are naturally noisy," according to A. S. Neill (1960), founder of the innovative

Summerhill School, "and parents must accept this fact and learn to live with it. A child, if he is to grow in health, must be allowed a fair amount of noisy play."[1]

Young children have not developed the ability to stop the flow of feelings, and when they are excited, they can emit a sound at a pitch an opera singer would envy. The sound is pure and piercing, and when you hear it, you will notice it "hits a nerve,"; in other words, it connects with a listener on an emotional level. This is a form of very primal communication. We could hear this sound and know exactly what it means, just as we could hear a dog's bark and tell whether he is angry or distressed. We can see the same effect in relation to our response to music. Directors often use music and sound to elicit feelings. In the movie *Psycho*, the music used to accompany a brutal scene with repeated, high-pitched sounds is a simulation of a human scream. The music by itself elicits a frightened response. On some level we are still animal; we respond to sounds with a gut reaction. So it is clear that children make certain sounds naturally, and those sounds naturally elicit responses in us.

When a baby cries, a mother is "programmed" to respond to his cry. She feels a very basic need to tend to the baby. However, when the mother is feeling inadequate, tired, hungry, pressurized, lonely, or depressed, the baby's cries may not elicit a nurturing response. Those are the times when the mother herself wishes she could tell the baby to "shut up." She is not able to tolerate the sound of the baby's voice and the expression of his feelings because she is not in the right mood to be nurturing to him. And so a mother who is depressed may not react in the right way and may end up with a child who cries more, or a child who is withdrawn.

Children may be taught to stifle their cries in order to keep a quiet atmosphere, but stifling a cry does not make the pain go away. In fact, pain that goes underground will remain there and cause other problems, mental and physical. Arthur Janov, who invented Primal Therapy, had this as his basic belief: that unspoken pain needs to find a voice, and when it does, it can provide relief from suffering. The Primal Scream was developed as a way to help adults to release feelings kept inside in childhood. John Lennon was very influenced by this form of therapy, and through it he uncovered old, deep feelings he had not acknowledge previously. Lennon's composition "Mother" is a song he composed at age thirty, in which he sings/screams his feelings about the loss of his parents who abandoned him. The song releases a feeling that he had kept inside for twenty-five years. The feeling was just as strong as it had been when he first felt it as a small boy.

As babies grow to be toddlers, parents often inculcate the notion that it is wrong to show your feelings. At times parents may feel embarrassed or overwhelmed by the fierceness of their child's expression. Here are some feelings parents generally shy away from when their children show them:

- Anger
- Disappointment
- Frustration
- Fear
- Excitement
- Jealousy
- Sadness
- Loneliness
- Shyness
- Competitiveness
- Possessiveness

Strangely, parents have fewer problems when their children show these feelings:

- Anxiety
- Shame
- Indifference
- Confusion
- Alarm
- Discouragement

In fact, these last emotions are probably more serious signs of distress than the previous ones. In order to understand why parents tend to keep children from showing their feelings, we should try to determine what is going on in the parent's mind. Often parents blame themselves for their child's feelings. This reaction may make them feel the need to control their child's feelings. Here are some things a parent might think:

- My child is angry. People think I created an angry child, since my child is part of me.
- My child is throwing a tantrum in front of everyone. I am embarrassed.
- I don't understand why my child is upset, and I feel helpless.
- My child is disappointed. I must fix it so he doesn't feel bad.
- It seems like such a small thing. Why is he making such a big fuss?
- My child is shy. No one will notice her.
- My child is angry. People will dislike her.
- I wasn't allowed to be angry, so neither should my child.

- My child won't share. He will not have friends.
- My child is yelling—people will think I have no control.
- My child is sad. I need to make her happy.
- My child is crying over a very small scrape. I was tough, so why can't he be too?
- Why can't my child be nice to others? I had to share even when I didn't want to.
- Why does my child have to cry when other children are perfectly happy?
- I wish my child would calm down. My family seems upset at her.
- I want people to like my child, and no one likes loud noises.
- My child is not grateful for the things I do for him, and that makes me mad.

When parents feel angry or helpless, they often try to control the expression of the feeling. To quiet a child in the moment, parents may try to use shame or to distract children from their feelings by bribing, threatening, or enticing them so the painful feeling goes underground, at least for now. It is difficult for parents to just accept that their child has a certain feeling. Parents do not need to feel responsible for the child's feelings; they cannot stop the feelings but can help the child to develop his own strategies for dealing with them. Parents cannot stop a child from having negative feelings.

NO BUTS

The best thing a parent can say to a child who has strong feelings is, "I know how you feel." This is usually what a child wants to hear. This can be said in many different ways. It can be a look, a hug, a phrase like "I know," a sympathetic sound, or even a non-judgmental, accepting silence and a kind expression. Some parents say things like, "I know you feel sad now because I'm leaving, but I will be back at the end of the day to pick you up." Adults should stop before saying "BUT." That little word is crushing. It tries to wipe away a very intense feeling with the promise of a good feeling. I am sure none of us would like to hear this from a boss: "I am sorry that I need to let you go, but I am sure you will find another job sometime in the vaguely distant the future." That "but" would make us very angry. How about this: "I am sorry there is no raise for you this year, but someday there will probably be one." Or this one: "Sorry you got divorced, but I'm sure you will find another husband." For a child, separating from a parent seems just as scary as death or divorce since they are not as sure of the future as we imagine.

DISTRACTING AND DEFERRING

Parents who don't want to deal with emotions or are embarrassed about public displays often try to distract their child with the promise that things will be better if they can only stop feeling a certain way. "Hey, stop crying. I'll see you later!" To a child, the phrases "later," "tomorrow," or "next time" do not have real meaning, since children live in the moment and don't have a strong concept of time. Young children experience the world as bursts of light in the darkness, rather than as a chain of events. It is only when they grow older that children are able to put together a timeline or see events as part of a "story." That is why our memories of childhood are often luminous and almost timeless events. Since we set down our childhood memories *before* we made the connections of time and duration, early memories are like a collection of jewels. As we grow older, our experiences and our developed prefrontal cortex help us to get a "bird's eye" view of our lives. We are able to string our experiences together into necklaces, where memories are sequenced and organized.

Think of something that happened last week and you will be able to see a beginning, middle, and end. You will know how all the factors going on in your life led to the event and moved on after it. You will also know how other people fit into it, where they were at the time, whether they were affected or not. Think of your earliest memories and they will probably appear as random stories in the middle of the darkness. These incidents may even seem to have gone on forever. You will probably know what you were doing in your memory, but you can only guess where other people were or what was happening in their lives. If you do know, you probably put those pieces together much later on. Only one memory is certain from childhood; you will know how you felt. That is the one thing all children are aware of, because the emotion is the one thing that matters. And for that reason, it should matter to us too.

Telling a child to stop feeling something now so he will feel something later on does not make sense developmentally. A child cannot anticipate the future in the way an adult can. If we look at the way a young child learns, we will realize that a child has to work hard in order to remember how things happen in relation to time. We can say that a child's tendency is to live mostly in the present moment. He may try to envision the future, but that is difficult for him. You will notice how disappointed a child can be when things don't work out the way he thought they would. He can be crushed by what seem to us to be small disappointments. That is because children have very limited and specific expectations about the future and an inability to put things into perspective.

When my daughter was little she asked for "Ralph the Barking Dog" as a gift from Santa. She talked continually about this expected gift. When the day arrived and she unwrapped the present, she threw the dog on the floor in disgust. None of us had known what was going on inside her mind—apparently she had pictured a real dog, not a toy, and she was bitterly disappointed. In fact, the TV ads had shown a real dog, and then the toy; with her limited experience, she did not realize the advertisement was for a toy and not an actual dog. A child's anticipation of the future is limited by his past experiences. This example shows that a child cannot anticipate or imagine the future in a realistic way—an adult would know from experience that dogs are not packaged in boxes and sold on TV; a child would not know that. Children imagine many things about the future that are not realistic. Appealing to a child's sense of future and expecting him to substitute his current feelings for future satisfaction is a tricky process.

Anticipating the future is something a child needs to learn slowly. He can learn it through acting out stories so he knows the connection between past, present, and future. Reading books to a child can also help with this process. However, even if a child can imagine the future, it is not good practice to tell a child to stop feeling something in the moment and focus on what he will feel in the future. What this is doing is teaching him how to get out of touch with his feelings.

When adults tell children they will feel better later, they may be giving this message: when something is painful you should shut it off, focus on something else, and forget the feeling. This can be a good survival strategy in certain instances. If you are hit by an avalanche and need to get out, you can tell yourself to turn off the pain while you crawl through the snow and get help for yourself. If you are in a war situation, you can tell yourself to keep your feelings down so you can step over dead bodies, complete your mission, and survive. However, it is a well-known fact that when people survive extreme difficulties, the event is not over for them. Their bodies might heal quickly, but the feelings will recur, even in dreams, and will have to be dealt with sooner or later. Post Traumatic Stress Syndrome, or Shell Shock as it used to be called, is a condition with which people are haunted by memories of very deep feelings that were put on hold while they simply tried to survive.

Distracting children from their feelings does not of course cause PTSD, but the basic principle is the same—a feeling deferred does not go away. Besides, teaching children not to trust or respect their feelings is not a good survival strategy. If young people grow up being out of touch with their feelings, they may get themselves into bad situations. They may hear the voice of their parents telling themselves not to make a fuss, not to react the way their instinct tells them to. Being out of touch with instincts and emotions can endanger a young person or stifle her healthy outlet.

If a child is hurt by something her friend says, she may have learned to think, "Oh, that's nothing. Don't worry; he didn't mean it. Just get over it." The child may blame herself for the reaction. She does not tell her friend how she feels, and the friendship is damaged. In more serious circumstances, the child doesn't tell her parents, and she may be bullied. If someone appears scary and threatening, the child may have learned to think, "Don't be so scared. You are always running away from things. Be brave." The child does not keep away from that person and ends up in a dangerous situation. If a pet dies, a child may have learned to think, "Don't cry about little things. Just keep your feelings to yourself." The sadness goes underground, and the child may have angry feelings towards animals or be afraid she too is going to die, and may develop anxieties about death.

It is more effective to deal with the experience immediately even if you are under stress. If a parent is in a public setting, or just cannot take the time to react to a child's feelings, she at least can refer to the feelings peremptorily. For example a child may suddenly start having angry feelings just as the bus is arriving. In order to deal with the feelings, a parent can simply say, "OK, I know you're angry. I understand. I'm sorry we have to get on the bus right now. Let's do that and then we can talk." That is an acknowledgement, and the parent is clearly not trying to distract the child. In order to distract a child from his feelings in an emergency situation, many parents offer bribes: "Hey, look, I have a candy. Here, take the candy. Let's get on the bus." This parent wants the child to just stop, but this can be a problem if the parent does not remember to reconnect with the feeling and discuss it. Later on that night, the child might wet the bed, or refuse his dinner, or have a meltdown about something else. Neither the parent nor the child will connect that with the moment earlier in the day when he had something to say and he wasn't allowed to say it. While it is absolutely impossible for parents to understand, or even be aware of, every feeling a child has, they should respond to feelings when a child expresses them, even if it is done later in retrospect. At bed time a parent can say, "Sorry I didn't get a chance to ask why you were upset this morning. Can you remember what it was about?"

STIFLING

Some people have such an aversion to hearing feelings that they tell their child to "choke back" their feelings. This can be done by direct threats ("I'll give you something to really cry about!") and exhortations ("Can you please shut up? I am tired of your crying!" or "This is no time to make a fuss!"). Some families discourage feelings by expressions of disapproval that shame children. They allow siblings to tease each other when they show their feelings. If someone cries when they are teased, for instance, they are told to "toughen up" since it is "not so bad." Some parents think they are doing a good job toughening up the children for the real world when, in fact, tenderness and understanding give strength to a child. When she is faced with adversity, a child gains courage knowing that someone understands her. When things go wrong, an understood child will have a secret friend inside herself to help her. This is the internalized, supportive parent.

Often families have a kind of censorship towards the expression of tender feelings. Some families make it clear that certain expressions are "corny." If someone gets teary-eyed at a movie, for instance, they are sneered at. Children can be made to feel weak if they show feelings. Boys in particular can be called names if they show tears or anxiety. They are often expected to appear "tough" or "brave." We all know the phrase "big boys don't cry," and we are all aware the damage that can cause. Many people seem to think that toughness and bravery are qualities embodied by those who are unafraid. However, you can't be brave if you don't feel fear. In fact true courage is when people feel fear but confront their fears anyway. It is ironic that those who show their weakness are the most resilient of all, since they are unafraid of the greatest enemy—the self.

FEAR AND AGGRESSION

There was a little boy called Max who used to arrive in our classroom holding up his hands as if they were claws. He would roar at the other children, pretending to be a dinosaur. This had a domino effect. When he did it, another boy would raise his "claws" too, and they would roar loudly at each other. Pretty soon others would join in. It wasn't a very creative game; it usually ended in someone getting upset or hurt. In addition, Max didn't have a lot of friends—his play tended to be disruptive.

One day, shortly after arrival, he started menacing with his hands, and before the other boy could react, I said, "Paul, does it scare you when Max pretends to be a dinosaur?" Paul looked surprised at the question, but he said, "Yes." I said, "Tell him, 'Max, you scare me when you do that.'" He did as told, and Max put his claws down. "You don't want to scare Paul do you?" I asked, and Max seemed relieved as he shook his head. It took a lot of courage for one child to tell another that he was scaring him. It is extremely difficult for anyone, and in particular young boys, to tell others they are afraid. It seems that with most of us, our fear reaction is to put up our defenses; hardly anyone has the courage to say to an angry person, "I am afraid of you." Think how hard it would be to say that the next time your boss appears angry. It is hard for children to say to their parents, "You are scaring me." This is a pity, since angry people often have no idea how much they are scaring others.

In our classroom, we developed a new habit with the children. When we perceived that a child was being defensive, we asked her to tell the other person, "I am scared of you." Children were very willing to do this with the teachers beside them. The impact on the class was huge. Soon Max stopped his posturing. It became clear that his aggressive behavior was caused by fear. He had been spending a lot of energy to create a façade of toughness to preempt attacks from others. This kind of response has often been called a "counterphobic" response, and it can be seen in adults who adopt a "macho" stance with others or take risks to prove they are not afraid. In our classroom, once everyone accepted his own feelings of fear, children stopped being defensive, aggression was reduced, and play time became much more productive and cooperative.

FEELING VULNERABLE

Many people think that if they show their emotions, they will be more vulnerable to attack. They think they will be giving others a way of hurting them. The logic is that if people know what makes you cry, then they will use it against you. This may happen in certain families, and if you are living in the kind of family in which people laugh at you for crying, then you will probably be doing the right thing to keep your feelings to yourself.

I know of one child who had a very strict father. When anyone transgressed the rules in this family, the father brought out the cane and punished them. This little boy did his best to do everything perfectly; however, his father seemed to have a particular dislike for him. No matter how he tried to be good, the father would find fault with him for some infraction or other, and he would be beaten. The child did not want to feel vulnerable to his father's punishments, and so he would show no pain when he was beaten. He refused to cry. He came up with a game of counting in his head the number of swipes his father gave him; that kept him from crying and helped him to contain his feelings of pain and anger. Keeping his feelings inside helped him survive the beatings. However, this technique was not a good long-term strategy, as it created worse problems for him—and for those around him—later on. The boy's name was Adolf Hitler.

There is the opposite example of Abraham Lincoln, whose emotions were clearly written on his face and body. He openly admitted to others that he felt depressed, in despair, ready to give up. His openness drew people to him; even his opponents had great respect for him. His vulnerability was truly his strong point. As Shenk says: "Many of Lincoln's advisors viewed him as a man who needed to be encouraged and protected."

BEARING YOUR CHILD'S FEELINGS

Some people can't bear to hear the negative feelings of children because they feel guilty and responsible. They think it is their job to "fix" the feelings. And so when their child has a negative feeling, they try to ease it, shrink it, smooth it over, make light of it, or make it go away forever. However, feeling painful feelings is part of life, and children should be allowed to have that experience. Having the experience and getting through it helps a child develop coping skills. Let's say a child feels disappointed that he can't have a certain toy. If a parent can't bear it when her child cries with disappointment, she might be likely to buy him the toy even though she can't afford it, just to stop him crying. This kind of soothing behavior causes a lot of damage to a child. It prevents him from working out what it feels like to deal with disappointment and find the inner resources to deal with it. It also teaches him that his mother thinks he is weak, that he cannot handle deep feelings. And it places a burden on the child. Now every time he feels disappointed, he knows he has to make a big fuss instead of just accepting his loss and moving on.

Children need to develop their own strategies for handling their feelings. Distracting with bribes or giving in to their tantrums does not help them to gain inner strength. In fact, children need to be responsible for their own feelings. The best way to do that is to give it a name: "I see you are disappointed. You wanted the toy, and we can't afford it right now. I know that feels bad." Simply stating the fact and then remaining silent gives the child the time to process feelings. Parents should not finish by saying, "But we will get you one next year," or "But you have other toys," or "But your sister doesn't have one either." Your child is disappointed, and he will survive the disappointment. Children all have various levels of resilience they can draw on in times of adversity, and this resilience can be like a muscle that strengthens the more it is used. Parents don't need to think, "It's all my fault you can't have that toy. I should have a better job and more money, and you would have everything you wanted at all times." Parents don't need to put themselves into debt to prevent their child's disappointment. By letting his child feel disappointed and get over it, a parent is giving him a far greater gift by teaching him to accept what is and find inner peace. That gift will last longer than any toy.

LEARNING TO EXPRESS FEELINGS ACCEPTABLY

In the early years, it takes work for adults to bear with the tantrums, screaming, and the various kinds of raucous expressions that children use to convey their feelings. Adults can teach them step by step how to express their feelings in a way that will help everyone. If adults can train children to express their feelings honestly and responsibly, they will see a lot less physical aggression and "acting out." Children need to learn to take responsibility for their own feelings and not blame or punish others for what they are feeling. There are unproductive habits children fall into when they think they are communicating, but they are not. These habits include: whining, complaining, venting, blaming, projecting, or punishing.

WHINING AND COMPLAINING

Whining is one form of expression that particularly grates on parents. Children whine when they are not able to express a need and assert themselves clearly. Whining is really not asking; it is complaining. No one likes to hear someone complaining, since it puts the complainer in the role of victim and elicits only irritation from the hearer. Often children whine when they are not allowed to ask for things they want. Children have a right to ask for what they want, and they should be encouraged to do so clearly and respectfully. The answer may be yes or no, but they do have the right to ask. Most parents are more than happy to give a child what he wants if it is at all feasible. Most children are happy if they get most of the things they want and can accept it if they can't have everything. If a child is whining in school or at home, she can easily be taught to change her style.

Let's say a child says, "I didn't get any snack," in a whiny, self-pitying voice; a teacher can say, "Tom, I want you to ask for what you want instead of whining. Here are two ways to ask: 'I didn't get any snack' and 'May I please have a snack?'" The teacher can demonstrate that it is OK to ask for what you want, and it is acceptable to ask loudly, clearly, and politely. She can demonstrate that there is a difference between asking and complaining. If adults could communicate in that way, they wouldn't have complaining sessions as many adult couples do: "You never do the dishes," "You never bring me flowers," "Why do I have to do all the driving?" Couples can learn to assert their needs just as young children can by simply asking for what they need from each other. "Could you drive next time please?" "I'd love some flowers on your way home please. Can you bring them?" and so on. A child should be encouraged to say what he needs and be told that he can have whatever is reasonable and available, and he shows appreciation.

Adults need to discourage a child from complaining. Complaining puts a child in the position of victim. Asking for help puts a child in the position of actor, doer, and achiever. If a child says, "I have no pencil!" that is a complaint. His teacher can say, "The pencils are on the top shelf." If a child complains further, saying, "I can't reach the top shelf!" a teacher can say, "What could you do to help yourself reach the top shelf?" This "scaffolding" pushes a child gently on to his own resources and enables him to find a solution to his own problems. If a child is allowed to continually complain, then he will grow up blaming others for his problems and relying on outside help rather than finding his own solutions and being active in his own life.

We are all familiar with the type of friend who says, "I am too fat!" When you answer: "Why don't you try this weight-loss program?" She will say, "Oh, that's no good for me. I can't afford it." Then you try another solution: "Why don't you jog?" She will say, "Oh, that's no good for me. I don't have the time." No matter what you try, this person will find a way to complain. You will be drawn into solving her problem for her, but nothing will work. She enjoys complaining. Complaining is not the true sharing of feelings. It is a refusal to accept feelings. Possibly the only response to that kind of exchange is to say, "I feel a sense of helplessness talking to you about this." When dealing with children, it is best to allow the child to feel a sense of agency by asking him what he can do to help himself, or showing him that you believe in him and his ability. When someone has reached the adult stage and is a habitual "complainer," then there is little you can do to help.

VENTING

Children should be allowed to express anger openly. This is not the same as "venting." Venting is when someone "rants" about what happened to no one in particular. Usually it is not a conversation between two people; it is one person "letting off steam" without asking for help or feedback from the other person. Expressing anger to another person in a one-to-one conversation is an art that people need to learn when they are children. A healthy family is one in which a child is able to say, "I felt angry at you when you sent me to my room," and the parent can say, "I know you were angry. I am glad we are talking about this. Let's go over what happened today." A healthy family is one in which a parent can say, "I was angry with you today. You took my new shirt and used it as a tent, and I was going to wear it," and the child can say, "I'm sorry, Daddy. I didn't think about that." Venting is not a healthy communication. Venting sounds like this: "No one respects my stuff in this house! My new shirt is on the floor! I can't stand this! I'm out of here!" Door slam.

As a teacher, I am delighted when children express anger in a healthy way. One day when I was going from one child to another looking at their work, I leaned close to a little girl and said, "That's so lovely the way you put the stars there." Suddenly there was a loud GRRRR! from another table. "I am really angry at you, Eileen!" a little girl exclaimed. I turned around to look at this angelic face, now red with emotion. "Why? What did I do?" I asked. "You are looking at everyone else's book, and you didn't look at mine!" she said angrily. It was hard not to smile at this little girl's honest expression of feelings. "I am so sorry!" I said. "I will come over right now and take a look." I felt that this was a clear and direct way for her to show her feelings, and I was impressed that she had the courage to tell an adult how she felt.

Later on that day she tried the same technique again. When she wanted attention she said, "I'm angry at you again!" This time I felt I could take the lesson a step further. I said, "I understand you're angry with me because I didn't give you attention, but I'm a bit busy just now. I will be over there in a second." I knew since she was so emotionally strong that she was ready for another lesson. She could now learn that I, too, had feelings and concerns of my own. Sure enough, she was able to wait. She knew I understood her feelings, and she trusted I would be there in a few minutes. Since her feelings were listened to the first time, she was ready to be patient the second time. This child is someone I would consider strong, confident and emotionally resilient. I would have great expectations for her future relationships with others.

PROJECTING, BLAMING, AND PUNISHING

When people try to share negative feelings they often fall into one of two traps: they blame the other person, or they try to appease the other person. When people try to communicate their anger to someone they might say, "I'm angry at you. You are a half-hour late, and I am freezing cold." Then the other person might say, "Sorry." The first person might not feel the apology is enough so he goes on to blame: "You always do this. You kept me late last time. Why do you have to do this? You are selfish sometimes!" Now the discussion is not a discussion any more. It is a blame and shame session. The person who was kept waiting needs to punish the other person because he feels wronged. The person who is labeled "selfish" is now feeling wronged too. She had a reason for being late and doesn't feel she deserves to be blamed, but she wants to appease the other person so she keeps quiet. These are the habits of social relationships we inculcate in children from a young age. We accuse, blame, and try to punish other people for the feelings we feel, or we try to keep others quiet by appeasing them.

Suppose the person standing in the cold was able to take the time to think about what he was feeling. Suppose as he stood there, waiting in the cold, he was able to experience the cold and to realize how angry and abandoned he felt. Suppose he got in touch with the loneliness of standing in the cold, aware of everyone else holding hands on the movie line, watching people go into the warm building. Suppose he was calm enough to remember the incident long ago when his mother forgot to pick him up after school because she was at his sister's concert. And then he remembered all the times his mother was delayed at work and kept him waiting. In that moment, perhaps he would realize the feeling of loneliness and abandonment was something that lurked deep inside. Now when his wife arrives, he could phrase his words differently. He could really communicate with her. He might be able to say, "You're late. I had a lot of horrible feelings waiting for you. I was thinking about how I used to feel when I was waiting to be picked up outside school." Now there is a real possibility of understanding. His wife might say, "Oh, that's terrible. I didn't mean for you to feel that way. I had to walk the dog, and he took forever as usual, just when I was in a hurry.' In this case, the person has taken responsibility for his own feelings, and his wife hears and accepts her responsibility, but neither blames or appeases the other. They just listen and understand.

Children can be taught to avoid the trap of accusation. They can be taught to listen and to share without blaming. In fact, children are not born knowing how to blame others; it is something that has to be learned from adults, and so it is quite easy to teach young children to listen non-judgmentally. They are very willing to hear and to empathize as long as they are not made to feel shame. Many conflict-resolution programs in schools focus on promoting listening. Children can learn to say what they are feeling without blaming others. They can learn to take responsibility for their own feelings. Being able to say, "I feel angry," without expecting someone else to fix it is a very good communication strategy. The best way to help children to develop this technique is for adults to allow them to say they are angry, but not to try to fix it. Once you have taught your child to say he is angry, your job is not to make the angry feeling go away.

When someone says, "I am angry at you!" the other person often feels she needs to fix the problem. An instant "I'm sorry. I won't do it again," is often done to soothe and stop the anger. But it is not a good response. It indicates the person did not take a moment to put herself in the other person's shoes. She just wants to appease the anger. It may be she is afraid of the anger or resentful of hearing it. Children need to be taught the skill of just listening to feelings. In fact they do have the ability to do this, but they are often taught to try to fix someone else's feelings: "Your friend is angry. Give her a hug!" and so on. In fact, none of us wants our feelings soothed; we just want to be heard. The best thing a person can do for another person who has strong feelings is to say, "Yes, I hear you, and I understand how you feel."

People try to give advice, but saying, "You're upset. Just calm down" can often make a person even angrier. Children are no different. If a child can be taught to just acknowledge another person's feelings, that is a good skill to have. I have even heard young children who are able to be completely honest say, "I am angry at you for being angry at me." This honesty is good, and it's the beginning of a dialogue. Teachers and parents can help a child to speculate on why he feels angry that someone is angry with him. "Maybe you don't like to do anything wrong?" At that point, when the child has understood his own reaction, he might be able to move out of his own feelings and understand that the other boy is angry, and learn how to tolerate the feeling of someone being angry at him. It is a good skill to be able to tolerate others being angry with us. Children need to make decisions in their life without giving in to peer pressure. If a child can make the right decision, even if it incurs people's anger, then he has a very healthy and strong ego.

OPENING PANDORA'S BOX

Some adults are afraid of a child's anger. They think that if they permit a child to say he is angry, they have allowed the monster out of the box. The monster has to be kept inside the box where it belongs. In actual fact, the opposite is true. Monsters you can't see are worse than the monsters you can see. It is better to know what you are dealing with. If children hide feelings, they are going to come out anyway in a different and probably more virulent form. At least if he tells you he is angry, you are aware of your child's emotion, and you can think how to handle it.

Adults may struggle at this point, not knowing for sure how to deal with a child's expression of anger. The first thing to realize is that children usually do not know why they are angry. They may know they are angry in the moment but probably do not realize there is an underlying cause. Depending on the age of the child, questions can be overwhelming and can make a child become more angry or confused and shut down communication. It is better not to say, "Why are you angry? What's the matter with you?" and so on—if the parent does not know why a child is angry, then certainly the child will not know either. If you ask him, "What's wrong with you?" he may feel he is defective. Here are some possible responses:

- Thank you for letting me know you are angry.
- I like when you tell me what you are feeling. I know it is hard to do it.
- I understand why you are mad at me.
- I understand why you were mad at your friend.
- I don't understand why you are angry. Can you explain what I did that made you feel angry?
- Everyone gets mad at times. I get mad too.
- Do you know what is bothering you?
- When did you get this feeling?
- What does it feel like inside your body?
- Do you want me to talk to that person for you?
- What do you feel like doing?
- Would you like to punch something else that won't hurt you or anyone else?

SEEING PATTERNS AND CREATING NARRATIVES

In order to help the child keep up this process of verbalizing his feelings, it is good to do a recap later in the form of a narrative of what happened. This way, the child can see anger as part of a story with a beginning, middle, and end. We need him to see patterns in his own reactions so he comes to know himself and know what triggers his feelings and how he can change his tactics to make himself feel better or to communicate better. Parents can go over the event and help the child understand what happened:

- Remember today when you got mad?
- I notice you get mad when other people want to play with your best friend.
- You seem to get mad at that boy and not the other one.
- I wonder why that is?
- Remember how you felt something inside your stomach?
- That was good when you told me about it.
- I noticed you liked hitting that pillow.
- Did you feel better after that?
- What will you do next time someone else wants to play with your friend?

It is often a good idea to draw a picture for a young child so that he sees what happened as a series of connected events. Older children who practice sharing their feelings in this way will become very adept at recognizing other people's feelings and dealing with situations verbally rather than physically. They can also begin to recognize warning signs in themselves and others and can be alert to patterns that might set them off. Older children begin to see things in terms of stories—how things started, how they progressed, and what transpired. The benefit of this particularly human way of thinking is that if you can imagine a different ending, you can change the story and break your pattern.

In a study of 364 children in fourth, fifth and sixth grades, during a violence prevention workshop in a Memphis school, Harris and Walton (2009) discovered that children who narrate stories well are also good at conflict resolution. These children were asked to write about a violent incident they were involved in. They found a strong correlation between good storytellers and children who were able to manage conflict well: "Good storytellers will be able to explain their own motives and goals in ways that will be acceptable to their peers. Narrative is a site where meaning is constructed according to social and cultural expectations. Personal narrative writing and story telling tasks can be used to facilitate the development of critical peacemaking skills." The authors of this study also recommended to teachers that they not suppress conflict in schools, since they feel this kind of discussion about conflict is an opportunity to strengthen children's understanding about their feelings and the feelings of others, and to give them coping strategies for difficult situations:

> We believe that it is necessary for schools to move away from associating conflict exclusively with risk and violence, toward a more constructive conceptualization . . . When teachers view conflict as a manageable and important part of childhood, rather than as a threat, conflict can become a part of the learning that goes on within schools. When peer conflict threatens to disrupt ongoing instruction, teachers need to have an established classroom practice that allows them to postpone the conflict without suppressing it.[2]

Working through feelings can be an educational activity that has a huge impact on school culture. Many teachers spend a great deal of time and energy trying to control or suppress emotions. If a child shows strong feelings in the classroom, teachers often think it is inappropriate. In fact, as these researchers point out, those incidents can be wonderful opportunities to build community. "I can't spend my time fixing these kids' problems. I have a curriculum to attend to," teachers may respond, since they are feeling the pressure to get results. In fact, a great deal of teachers' time does already go to discipline, punishment, and classroom "management" with little results to show for the time expended. Many teachers become burnt out or drop out of teaching altogether because they get little satisfaction from their work and spend most of the day trying to keep children on track.

In an Australian study of teacher stress, Clunies-Ross (2008) found that teachers who react in punitive or "reactive" ways suffer more stress than teachers who approach children's behavior in a scientific, strategic way:

> In the present investigation, the use of reactive management strategies predicted four of the five dimensions of teacher stress: workload, student misbehaviour, time/resource difficulties, and poor colleague relations stress. However, the use of proactive management strategies did not predict any of the dimensions of teacher stress. One explanation for these findings may be that the more negative teachers are in their approach to classroom management, the more likely they are to experience elevated stress.[3]

Proactive management techniques would include factoring in various strategies for dealing with children's emotions. Here are some proactive techniques that can help to preempt problems in the classroom:

- Good school/family relationships. When teachers are aware of the home situation of a child, they can better understand a child's negative behavior.
- Conflict resolution time. A small amount of time each day spent in working through classroom problems can give children techniques for sharing their emotions more productively.
- Positive feedback. Children are vulnerable to the opinions of authority figures. If they are floundering or having emotional difficulties, the last thing they need is negative criticism from teachers. If they need to work harder, this message can be framed in a supportive way such as: "We need to talk. I know you can do better. Something seems to be going on with you lately. You're not as focused as you used to be. You know you need your scores to come up if you want that scholarship. I'd like you to set some goals for yourself; write them down and bring them back and show me. I'll help you after school if you need me to." While children may be bogged down in the difficulties of their lives, teachers can encourage them to use work as a way of taking action to change their situation. Instead of feeling helpless and victimized, children can be encouraged to rise above their problems through work.
- Teacher direction. Some children may be having a hard time due to family problems. However, they can find relief in creative pursuits. Teachers

can encourage children who have a particular artistic, musical, or acting talent—for instance, to become active in those fields. Often those teachers make all the difference to a child who is struggling with anger, depression, self-doubt, or shyness. These children often go on to lead very successful lives and gain satisfaction in their work. They in turn often become strong role models for suffering children.

- Prioritizing feelings. If a child shows an intense feeling in class, acknowledge those feelings before moving on. A teacher needs to be able to reflect back feelings to a child without taking those feelings personally. Suppressing feelings takes a lot of effort, a lot less than acknowledging them.
- Keeping aware of "transference." Teachers need to keep in mind that they are authority figures in the child's mind. When children have problems with their parents, they often "transfer" these feelings on to authority figures. Children are not "out to get" teachers; they tend to display intense feelings because they can't do anything else. In certain cases a child may have a chip on her shoulder, an anti-authority feeling that manifests itself in the classroom. If this happens, the teacher should take the time to find out what is going on at home. Being aware of the reasons for this anger can help a teacher find strategies for helping the child and dealing with the problem on a day-to-day basis. If a teacher engages in a battle with a child who is already convinced authority figures are unjust, then she will be compounding the problem. Many children who suffered neglect or abuse as children were able to survive and thrive thanks to one benevolent adult such as a grandparent or empathic teacher.
- Providing reflective vocabulary. Teachers can educate children about feelings by using names for feelings. Many children do not know what they are feeling. Providing vocabulary gives a child knowledge, and knowledge is power. A child may feel he is drowning in an ocean of emotion, but a teacher can throw in a lifeline of words to help him stay afloat: "You seem frustrated," "Are you a little depressed today?" "Something is making you very pensive," "John, I think Mary is irritated with you borrowing her stuff all the time," "You look perplexed, do you want me to explain?" "You seem hesitant, are you afraid you might get the wrong answer?" "Now, I know you are all anxious about this test. Just relax; we've covered this material a few times. You can all do it," "When I give out the results I don't want people to start comparing with each other. It can be embarrassing to some people. I know everyone is doing their best," "You seem a little pessimistic about your results," and so on. Using reflective words in this way can also help teachers not to take things personally. And it boosts vocabulary skills.

- Keeping cool. By not responding emotionally, a teacher will give the child a few moments to feel the impact of what he has said, while gathering her own thoughts. Often a child blurts something out without realizing the full impact of what he has said, or just says something to displace his own hurt or angry feelings such as, "I hate school, and I hate this class!" If a teacher can remain calm, she can gather her thoughts and come up with a positive response. "I know school can be painful when you're fourteen; it's a tough time," or "Can you make me a list of ten reasons you don't like school and this class in particular? I'd like to read them," or "What would you like to improve? I am always looking for new ideas. Make me a list and show it to me tomorrow." If a teacher can take complaints constructively, a child might feel surprised, honored, and more involved in the class. The worst rebels can turn into the most responsible leaders if they are given a chance.
- Literary exploration. All literature is about feelings. Writers write to convey feeling to others. Children can relate their own feelings to works of literature by identifying with particular characters. If teachers are aware of this psychological connection, they can provide good books to help a child through particular issues. They can also bring life to works of literature by helping children see the feelings behind the words. Many famous actors and writers have developed their passion for literature and drama because of their own childhood struggles.
- Protecting children from teasing. Teachers should create a safe atmosphere where children can express their emotions. They should not tolerate teasing and especially should not allow children to laugh at others who show feelings. This does not need to be done in a shaming way. If someone does titter when a child expresses a feeling, the teacher can respond positively by saying, "I think some people are embarrassed when others show feelings."
- Gender bonding. Teachers can do a great deal to help boys and girls communicate effectively. Often teenage boys and girls suffer greatly because they think they are not what the other gender wants them to be. These mistaken assumptions can create anxiety and depression. Teachers can have general discussions about the roles of men and women and present good books or suggest good films for discussion. These discussions can help boys and girls understand that we all have the same emotions under the surface and that the best way to build male/female relationships is through communication.
- Innovative and creative programs. Schools can bring in creative programs to relieve stress, build confidence, and allow children to release their

> emotions—not just negative emotions, but positive ones too. For example Gonen (2010) reports on a new program called "Laugh It Out," operating at three schools in New York. The program is a comedy improvisation program, and it encourages pupils to collaborate playfully with fellow students. Even teachers participate and break down the bonds between students and staff. The program is particularly good for children who might normally not speak out. Social acceptance matters a lot to teens, and this program helps break down social barriers. A *New York Post* report shows how much the children gain from this kind of program: "I like the aspect that you can be yourself," said Starasia Wright, 14, a ninth-grader. "You don't have to worry about judgment or what anybody else says." Principal Charles Anderson reports that he sees more student retention in a school and positive changes in the students' attitudes towards school. And Robin Getlan Pancer, director of the Comedy Hall of Fame, which created the program, sees the most important benefits of the program: "They get to communicate; they take risks; they build a community," she added. "They're constantly seeking out more of it, and they feel connected."[4]

Children who freely express all their feelings—excitement, sadness, anger, disappointment—tend to be popular with other children. It seems children trust others who are open and expressive. In our society actors, performers, and filmmakers are often held in high regard. In ancient Egypt, singers were considered almost as important as royalty. In ancient Ireland, poets lived in the company of kings. There is a good reason for all of this. These kinds of people are valued highly because they play a vital role in society. Their work is to show us all the feelings we experience every day but are afraid to acknowledge. People whose feelings are thwarted in childhood can grow up to thwart others. Relationships flounder because people cannot communicate clearly what they feel, and misunderstandings can have tragic consequences. If children could learn how to communicate their feelings, and adults could accept those feelings, then a great deal of suffering could be avoided, and our communities would grow stronger.

Notes

1. Neill, A. S. (1960). *Summerhill: A Radical Approach to Child Rearing*. New York, NY: Hart Publishing, 190.

2. Harris, A. R., and Walton M. D. (2009). "'Thank You for Making Me Write This': Narrative Skills and the Management of Conflict in Urban Schools." *Urban Review* 41:287–311.

3. Clunies-Ross, P., et al. (2008). "Self-reported and Actual Use of Proactive and Reactive Classroom Management Strategies and Their Relationship with Teacher Stress and Student Behaviour." *Educational Psychology* 28:6, 693–710.

4. Gonen, Y. (2010). "HS-Laugh-eteria." *New York Post*, December 13, 2010.

Chapter 10

Children Have the Right to Guidance

Many animals are born with the ability to survive without parental guidance. Spiders, for instance, once they hatch, scatter to the wind or drop onto a pool and never see their parents again. They are vulnerable to predators, and many do not survive, but they do have the innate drive for survival and are capable of free movement and the ability to forage for themselves. Human children are not born with that ability. They are completely dependent on their parents for survival, and this is true for an extended period of time. The prefrontal cortex of the human brain takes twenty years to develop. This area of the brain, once developed fully, enables us to accomplish tasks such as goal-setting, prioritizing, organizing, and managing, as well as emotional regulation. The human, the most evolved of all animals, has a brain that is flexible and open to change for an extended period of time. The advantage of this slow maturational process in humans is that the slow-growing brain is especially adapted for learning. Small children, for instance, compared with adults, are capable of learning and retaining new languages in very short periods of time.

The disadvantage of this slow development is that human children depend, more than other young animals, on the guidance of adults. While some children are exceptionally resilient and manage to survive the most difficult of challenges, social and emotional skills cannot be acquired without guidance. Humans are social animals; they rely to a large extent on the groups of other humans to which they belong. Social and emotional relationships are vital for adjustment to the group. Social and emotional skills are essential for a child to function well in family, school, and other groups to which he will belong. Children have a right to emotional and social guidance.

Children need adults to guide them through the process of understanding themselves, as well as understanding the motives and feelings of others. This guidance is like a road map that will help children find their way. Without the map, they may wander and sidetrack instead of finding the best and safest paths to their goal. Providing guidance does not mean presenting a series of commandments or instructions such as, "Do this; don't do that." It involves other activities such as providing feedback, support, instruction, information, encouragement, and mirroring. Guidance also involves a gradual letting go so that children develop their own guidelines.

THE INDIVIDUAL AND SOCIETY

The greatest struggle each of us will have in our life is getting our inside to match our outside. In other words, the individual person inside all of us needs to develop fully, to express all that is felt, and to achieve all that is dreamt. The individual is in a bind, however. He cannot develop fully without other people. For instance, if you are a nurturing person, you will need someone to nurture. If you are an artist, you will need someone to witness your art. If you are a scientist, you will need to collaborate with other scientists. On some level, whether it is to a great or a small extent, the individual needs other people in order to develop his talents and express his individuality. On the other hand, every group has rules. The family, the school, the workplace—all have rules. Even a relationship between two people has rules. Once a person comes into a relationship with another person, there are rules. These rules are created, consciously or unconsciously, so that each person in an organization, however small that organization, has protection for his rights.

The difficulty every human being faces is fitting into a group and at the same time retaining individuality. When the individual has to modify his needs and desires in relation to the rules of the group, then there is conflict. If we look at any of the great works of literature, we will see this conflict is at the heart of all of them. Short stories, novels, and plays are almost always about the ways in which an individual person struggles to fit in with the group and its rules. Often this struggle is about the social mores of a particular time or a particular place. Sometimes the individual triumphs, and sometimes the individual is crushed. Fitting in is the problem. Madame Bovary, Willie Loman, Anna Karenina, Atticus Finch, Tom Jones, Hamlet—all have to contend with a group with which they are at odds. Literature is a dramatization of this struggle, and though some people do live epic lives, most of us come to a working compromise in our lives. We find a way in which we can be ourselves, and yet we can coexist with others. Possibly the happiest people are those whose inner and outer lives are seamlessly connected. They are the people who can be themselves and find a group in which that inner self is truly accepted. When individuals cannot compromise their individuality, they may be the leaders who work hard to make society more just for others.

Children are just setting out on this road of socialization, and along the way they will have to make a lot of assessments and self-evaluations, adjustments, and compromises. They will also have to decide when not to make compromises. Negotiating your way through life means, if you are a human, negotiating with other people. Children need to develop the skills they need to preserve their own integrity and the integrity of others. These are complicated skills, and they take time to develop. Children cannot navigate the difficult task of adapting to society without the guidance of supportive adults. During the early years of childhood, parents can do a great deal to enhance a child's emotional and social skills. The guidance they provide at this early stage is crucial to a child's happiness and adaptation to the group.

THE FAMILY CRUCIBLE

The family is the first school. In the family children learn social and emotional skills. Parental guidance is necessary to a child's adjustment to society. There are some examples of children who grew up without the company and guidance of adults. They are sometimes called "feral children." When these children do find care and attention, they often cannot develop fundamental social and linguistic skills. There is an optimal period, while the young brain is flexible and developing, for social and linguistic skills to develop. Once a certain window of opportunity is lost, a child cannot learn to relate to others without tremendous difficulty. Those children who managed to survive without adult guidance during this crucial period were unable to adapt and live healthy lives. Failure to develop social and emotional skills also has an effect on cognitive development, and non-socialized or "feral" individuals appeared to lack full brain function in certain important areas, particularly language.

In a normal family, children will learn during the first five or six years many of the skills they need to relate to others. Parents can guide children in how to express themselves and conduct themselves so they can maintain their personal integrity and yet adapt to the group and feel like a valued participant. Here are some of the social skills which parents and teachers can help to develop:

FACIAL EXPRESSIONS AND BODY LANGUAGE

Adults are capable of interpreting facial expression, eye glances, body language, and other social cues that mean nothing to little children. A young child does not even fully understand that she is being addressed unless you make direct eye contact with her. If you point at one child and speak to another, even if you address her by name, she will think you are talking to the child you point at. Children learn very slowly the ways in which humans connect in friendly or unfriendly ways. For instance, children need to be taught how to display appropriate facial expressions to others. Smiling is a social skill that parents like to encourage, since it brings positive attention to their child. However, children should not be taught to smile when they don't feel like smiling. Parents can reinforce a child's natural expressions by saying something like, "You have a nice smile. That person really liked it." But parents should try not to manage those expressions by saying, "Don't frown," or "Here comes my friend. Now smile," or "Don't be shy like you were last time," or "Don't let people see you cry."

If children make unsocial expressions at other children who approach, parents can give feedback, such as, "I think that boy is afraid of you. Your face looks like this." That is a helpful piece of information for a child to have. Parents can help the child understand herself by asking, "Are you afraid he's going to take your toy?" so she feels supported and not criticized. Feedback should be neutral and helpful, not critical. Young children often try out different expressions they have seen just to see how they work, and that is why they often look very dramatic. They may stick out their tongue, frown, put their hands on their hips, and make big gestures. What they are doing is acting out a part they have seen in order to convey on the outside what they are feeling on the inside.

They need guidance, like an acting coach would give, such as: "That's a little bit too scary. You don't have to stick your tongue out." If a parent's reaction is given as guidance, a child will be more likely to understand and process it. Parents should try not to suppress gestures by saying, "That's disgusting. Don't stick your tongue out! I won't stand for it; it's ugly." If parents understand the reason for graphic facial expressions rather than responding on a gut level, they will not react so judgmentally. Animals such as wolves express domination by sticking their tongues out, and ancient sculptures depict dead bodies with tongues sticking out. Sticking your tongue out is a primitive, dominating gesture that means "I could kill you if I wanted to." Animals do it to preserve their own territory, food, or mating rights. Children do not understand the full meaning of the gesture; they are simply trying out an instinctive facial expression when they feel threatened. If it gets a strong reaction, they may keep it in their repertoire. A calm suggestion from a parent that this is hurtful would be good enough guidance to prevent it from becoming excessive. A reassurance that the adult is there to protect the child is also helpful so that he does not need to threaten others to preserve himself. Guidance and protection go hand in hand.

GREETINGS

Children should be encouraged to say hello, goodbye, and so on so that they can develop rudimentary social bonds with others. Saying hello and goodbye are social rituals that acknowledge a person's acceptance of the importance of others in their lives. Most parents realize this importance, but some tend to overdo their stress on this aspect of social interaction. When children enter a new situation their natural instinct—and it is a good one—is to first assess the place and the people, and then meet and greet. They are fully in the moment and are taking in the colors, smells, light, and sounds, as well as the people who are there. They need a few minutes to get oriented, as they are absorbing things for the first time. Entering a new space is like going to a foreign country for them. Children can tell a great deal about a situation by the combination of sound, light, facial expressions, and so on, something we often call a "vibe." Picking up a "vibe" is a good survival technique.

When children enter new situations, anxious parents often repeat, "Say hello, say hello. Aren't you going to say hello?" They may even force handshakes. They may worry that the child will present an unfriendly aspect to others. Children can feel pressurized and may become averse to saying hello if they are pressed too much to do so. In fact, parents should allow the child to take a good look around and then present the person they want him to greet: "Say hello to your Aunt Helen. See, she's right here waiting to say hello to you." A child may often look in surprise at the adult, not aware that she is waiting to be greeted. A parent can set a good example himself by hugging and greeting people. If children see that their parents are happy and comfortable and like to hug or smile or shake hands, they will be more likely to do so themselves. If parents are naturally reserved, it is not fair to expect their children not to be like them, though they may, in fact, be quite friendly despite having parents who are not.

Saying goodbye is also a basic social convention; however, many children do not like to say goodbye. Saying goodbye is a polite ritual that bonds people together and expresses affection and good wishes to others as they depart.

Some children have painful feelings at separation, since they are not always sure when they will see the person again. Parents may misinterpret a child as unfeeling, when she may feel deeply about separating and cannot bear to say goodbye. They may press their child over and over: "Say goodbye. Aren't you going to say goodbye?" It might be easier for some children to say, "See you tomorrow," or just to wave. In both of the cases, saying hello and goodbye, it is probably best to keep modeling these habits and remember that children will copy you.

Schools can play a role in developing social gestures into meaningful habits. At circle time, teachers of young children can develop rituals such as a good morning song, in which each child is named. As children grow older, teachers should not forget that saying hello can be a simple, warm gesture that can break the ice for a child of any age. Mentioning a person's name and having the other children greet each other by name can be a group strengthening exercise. Many of us become deeply absorbed in our own worries, particularly in the morning. Greeting another person by name and looking them in the eye can break that tension for us and wake us up to the presence of others. We should all practice calling others by name as we say hello. This greeting by name wakes up the inner individual and calls him into the group.

GIVING AND TAKING APPRECIATION

Saying "thank you" is another social habit that parents and teachers try to encourage in children. Parents work hard develop a habit of reciprocality, and that is a good thing. If someone does something for you or gives you something, they deserve a response. If someone holds the door for someone else, even if they don't expect thanks, they do deserve to be appreciated, since holding the door is a choice. These social gestures help to create bonds between people and serve to guard against aggression. In some cultures, gift giving and reciprocality are considered very consequential and may be associated with very strict rituals. We all feel the need for this reciprocality. If you hold the door, and someone just ignores you and walks through, the chances are that you will feel resentful, unappreciated, and even angry.

Parents should say "thank you" to children for doing their little chores around the house. This is one way a child will learn to feel good about helping. And in addition, parents need to encourage children to say "thank you" when someone does something for them. Thanking people reinforces our understanding of interdependence. People in groups need to recognize that we all depend on the goodwill of others. We are all free agents, and we can choose to be kind to others or not. If someone is doing his job, let's say a waiter, we might take the attitude: "Why should I say thank you? He's getting paid for it." Or we might take the attitude: "I can make a difference in someone's day and show them appreciation by saying thanks." The difference between the two approaches is that we can think of ourselves as participants in the drama, or we can think of ourselves as passive observers. Children can be guided to be active participants in society by saying "thank you" when they receive something. In this way, they are learning that even if they are small and feel they have nothing to give, they do have something to contribute: their appreciation. Parents should not overdo this by constantly harassing children to say "thank you." They will pick it up by example and a little encouragement.

In school, teachers can encourage this sense of mutual appreciation. I know one teacher who routinely assigned the children to do jobs in his classroom. Children love these responsibilities and often remember their classroom jobs long after they have forgotten something they learned during a lesson. This particular teacher insisted that children be thanked for their job, so when the child passed around the books, the other children were encouraged to say, "Thank you, James." This same teacher had regular meetings in which children expressed appreciation for each other. They were encouraged to begin by saying, "I liked the way. . . ." For instance, children might say, "I liked the way James covered the books with the brown paper and decorated them. It looks so neat." According to the teacher, a child who failed at other tasks felt proud of his ability to cover the books in a neat and artistic way. In addition, this exercise helped to build a happy and cooperative classroom. Shy children became more outgoing and developed confidence because of the positive feedback from others. There were fewer cliques, and children seemed more open to accepting others into their groups.

Some people have a hard time accepting praise or thanks. Even as adults, they do not know what to say when someone pays them a compliment. "That's a lovely dress," someone might say, and the response might be: "Oh, this old thing, I've had it a while." The recipient of a compliment often dismisses or deflects the praise. Why do people do this? Why do normally articulate people suddenly feel embarrassed or speechless when someone pays them a compliment? Perhaps it is because of what happens when we are children. When someone pays a child a compliment, parents often rush in and prompt, "Say 'thank you.'" On the surface, this seems like a polite and easy response. However, it is probably a confusing message for children. If they are told to say "thank you" for a compliment they have received, what does that mean? A child who is told to say "thank you" may feel he has received a gift and must show appreciation. A compliment, if it is sincere, is not a gift but simply a statement of fact or feeling: "That's a nice dress," and "I like your hair," are statements. If a person makes a statement, then saying "thank you" should not be required. If someone says, "It is raining outside," or "I like the color red," then you would not respond, "Thank you." If someone says, "I like your hair," why not say, "I like my hair too. I felt good when you said that." If someone says, "That's a lovely dress," why not ask, "What do you like about it?" That is a reasonable question, and most people would probably love to know the answer and have feedback about what the other person likes: the color, the waistline, or the length.

Social mores tend to dissuade children from this kind of reaction. Perhaps parents fear their child will appear vain. If someone says, "That's a lovely dress," a real reaction would be: "I know. I love it." After all, if the person has chosen the dress and chosen to wear it, they must like it on some level. And yet people shy away from allowing children to react in this way. Some people are afraid to allow children to accept praise. People may feel that if the child really believes the compliment, he will become egotistical—as the old saying goes: "He will have a swelled head." Others may feel that children can be manipulated by compliments and that it is better if they do not believe them. And others want to protect children from jealousy. They may feel that if a child seems delighted with his attributes or possessions, others may want to take them away. These notions may have their roots in ancient customs, when gift giving was part of tribal interaction and was regulated with intricate rules of humility and reciprocality, motivated by fear of aggression and war.

And so, in this way, children are often taught to put up walls around themselves that keep out their real appreciation of compliments. Many people learn to mistrust compliments. And others feel vulnerable "like a deer in headlights" when someone compliments them. That is too bad. Taking in and enjoying a compliment is a good thing. If someone says, "You look great today," I wonder what would be so terrible about saying, "Yes, I feel great. Thank you for noticing." Parents can guide children to accept positive feedback without feeling that someone is doing them a favor.

MAKING REQUESTS

Children should be encouraged by parents to ask for what they need in appropriate ways so they can have their needs met. Feedback on how you sound and how you could present yourself better can be very helpful. One of children's favorite magazines used to include a cartoon of two boys who handled things in opposite ways. The socially clumsy boy might grumble, "Hey! I didn't get any cake!" And the good communicator might say, "May I have some cake please?" Children enjoy this kind of cartoon since it gives a picture of how people come across to others. Children think in concrete terms, and these visual examples are helpful to them. Parents and teachers can model ways of asking, and these are not just empty polite words; they are social skills that help children get what they want in a socially acceptable way. Yelling, "I want it now!" is bound to turn people off. However "I've been waiting a long time. Can I have mine now?" is an endearing yet assertive way of requesting what you want. Children are going to grow up to be managers, teachers, and employers. Being a good boss or supervisor means knowing how to get the most out of your staff. Having the ability to get people to give you what you need, and making sure they are happy in the process, is a wonderful life skill. It is never too early to learn how to ask for what you want in a way that will make people want to help you.

EXPRESSING NEED

Children need guidance from parents in learning to say they need help. Many people are afraid to ask for help since they don't want to appear vulnerable or needy. That is too bad, since none of us can survive without the help of others. In dire circumstances, people can come to realize how much they need other people, and this awareness can be quite life changing. I know one man who was fiercely independent, a loner who went mountain-climbing alone and challenged himself against the elements. He suffered a terrible accident and was confined to a hospital bed for three months with his body in a cast, unable to move or turn his head. During that time, he had a real awakening. He told me of how he lay looking up at the ceiling while tears ran out of his eyes and down onto the pillow as he thought of how much others loved him, and how much he needed that love.

Children who are learning to be independent often want to do everything by themselves, and this is something that should be encouraged. At the same time, it is a good thing for children to realize that others may have skills they don't possess. Allowing someone to help you and expressing your need gives other people the opportunity to be of service. Teachers in particular can do a lot to help children be open about their needs. Some teachers create a competitive atmosphere in which only those with the right answers get to be heard. However, it is also very useful to know what you *don't* know and have the courage to ask for help with it. Teachers should encourage children to express their difficulties. That is where real learning can take place. When one person expresses difficulty, others may also learn. Keeping your doubts inside and being afraid to express your problems is not a healthy habit to learn. On the other hand, being open about your difficulties encourages others to feel comfortable about their difficulties. In the early years, when children have bathroom accidents, or spill things, or fail over and over when they are trying to walk, adults need to let children know it's OK to fail. If they are critical when children make mistakes, those children will learn to be self-critical instead of self-supportive. Failing should not be seen as a failing.

I know one man who, when he was two years old, wanted to lift a bottle of juice down off a high shelf. Proud of his own growing abilities he reached up: "Me do! Me do!" he said delightedly. When the juice spilled all over the floor, his mother laughed at him. "Oh, yes, 'Me do!'" she sneered. "'Me do' a big mess!" The boy's nickname in the family became "Mister Me-do." Any time he failed, the nickname was dredged up again. As a result, this man grew up determined never to ask for help and afraid to admit weakness. He will not allow his children to help when he is working on a project, even though that would make them feel good to participate. If someone points out an error he says, "Yes, I know, I know!" He cannot accept that he might learn something new since he is so afraid to appear vulnerable. Parents can help to encourage independence, but they can also guide children when they fail so they don't feel vulnerable, clumsy, or inept. Parents can teach children how to ask for help and accept that help without feeling needy.

CRITICAL THINKING AND GOOD JUDGMENT

Children are naturally aware of their own dissenting thoughts. We are all born with a "gut instinct" that can guide us to what is right. Something often sounds like it is just wrong, and even though we can't put our finger on it, we know we feel uneasy. Parents and teachers need to guide children in how to use this natural instinct and how to express it with confidence. Too many young people accept what is in the media. There is a huge need for parents and teachers to guide children in watching TV or other media so they can develop their own judgment. Parents can tell children the truth from an early age so that they know all the facts they need to make informed judgments. Parents can also encourage children to trust their own instincts in making these judgments. In school, children should be encouraged to develop their own instincts into strong analytical skills. Media studies should be a part of every school curriculum.

A good way to develop a child's critical thinking is to give her choices at an early age. Something very simple parents can do is to allow a child to make decisions about the clothes she will wear the next day. Parents can be selective about this process and limit choices. For instance, they should not present dressy shoes as a choice when they know it's going to rain. Children should be encouraged to make decisions about things relevant to their own lives. Another area of choice can be food. Parents can present limited choices and allow the child to make decisions, thus developing a child's sense of ownership of the world.

As children grow older, parents can guide a child towards an analytical state of mind. Children can learn to question what they often take for granted. Adults can stimulate critical thinking asking things like:

- Do you think it's right that people have wars?
- Why do you think there are ads on TV?
- What did you like about that movie you saw?
- Why do you like that part?
- What was scary about that movie?
- How do you think they made you feel scared?
- Did you notice the music was scary too?"
- What is your favorite picture in this book? Why?
- How did the artist make that picture look peaceful/scary/sad?
- What would you like to change about school?
- What would you like to change about our family?
- What would you do if you were a teacher and a child didn't do his homework?

Children need to be taught how to think critically instead of accepting everything that is presented to them. Schools can do a lot to develop this analytical attitude so that a child can have his own strong guiding principles when adults are not around to guide him.

DISSENSION

Once a child has a set of principles, he should be taught how to express them. Children should be allowed to say that they disagree. This strengthens their ability to resist the pressure of the group. Teenagers often feel the need to break away from the family and bond with their peers. In order to be accepted in the group, some young people go along with actions that they know are wrong. They will gossip about others when they know it isn't right. They will follow a bully's lead and tease others because they are afraid to stand out of the crowd. And others will do drugs or vandalize property even though they know they shouldn't do it. It takes courage for a young person to disagree since they may be left totally alone—and that can be frightening. Adults need to guide young people to be able to disagree.

During the Civil Rights movement in the United States, people had to place themselves in physical danger in order to dissent from policies that had the weight of the law behind them. One after the other, they had to sit at café counters and be pushed off and beaten. They had to get up again and be punched down again. We have to ask ourselves: Would we do that? Do we have the kind of courage it takes to stand up for what is right? We need to develop that kind of emotional strength in young people because the future of a just society depends not only on the ability to recognize injustice but also on the courage to openly dissent.

Parents and teachers can guide a child towards independent thought and courageous action. They can do this by allowing children to speak their minds in the family and in school. Children need guidance in order to be able to speak out when something is wrong. If a parent can listen to a child's problems, she will be able to tell her child, "I agree with you. You are on the right track. I think it is time to talk to the teacher about this problem. Don't be afraid. I will back you up." Guidance is not the same as taking control. Parents can step back and give a child the support he needs to speak out against injustice rather than stepping in and solving problems for him.

SOLVING CONFLICTS

Children have a lot to learn about resolving conflicts. One of the earliest conflicts a child can have is the realization that he is not the only person in the world. A child must learn the painful lesson that others have needs and that his needs must be compromised by theirs. There is a fine line that we all need to walk so that we can get what we need, and also so others can get what they need. No child can possibly know how to walk this fine line alone. Children need guidance in order to understand the many complexities involved in dealing with others. When a child is threatened, for instance, he will need guidance from his parents on how to handle that threat. Parents should not solve the problems for him; they should guide him on how to do it. Giving advice is not the same as giving guidance. Parents and teachers need to allow a child to develop the skill of conflict resolution with support and encouragement.

Children need a lot of guidance from adults on how to deal with interpersonal conflicts. If a child is not listened to when he tells his parents of his conflicts, he will be thrown back on his own resources and feel alone and vulnerable. That vulnerability can lead to aggression or depression. I know one boy who had parents who themselves suffered from depression. These parents were so bogged down by their own problems that they had no time or energy to help their child. They did not even see how much he was struggling at school. He was bullied and teased by others, but he had learned early on that he could not come home and ask his parents for help. Instead of dealing with conflict, he just learned to stay under the radar and keep out of trouble. To this day, he struggles with relationships and feels completely unprepared for dealing with others.

HANDLING DANGER

Some parents think that the best way to protect children is to prevent them from taking risks. These "bubble" parents want to limit the amount of experiences a child has so that they do not get hurt. However, this is not the kind of help a child needs. A child needs guidance on how to avoid danger and how to handle herself when danger presents itself. Once again, the best kind of guidance is to trust one's instinct and to have a lot of truthful information. Children do have good instincts, but their instincts will not tell them that sticking a screwdriver into an electric socket is dangerous. Only parents can provide that kind of information. Parents and teachers can provide information as they talk about the dangers as well as the benefits of fire or electricity when children are young. As children grow older, they will need guidance on how not to talk to strangers, how to stay together with their parents, and how to avoid people who might present a threat to them. Parents and teachers need to inform children about other dangers as they grow older—the dangers of sex, alcohol, and drugs, or the dangers presented by the Internet. Some parents find it difficult to talk about these dangers, but studies show that the more a parent provides information and guidance, the less a child will take risks.

As children age, they will need to learn to rely on their own judgment and to be able to know when danger may be near. The only way parents can do this is to give their child the opportunity to take risks and to assess the level of danger involved in these risks. If parents have guided their child to be able to make good judgments, then they can feel they have prepared their children to take risks that do not put them in grave danger. Parents who protect their children from every opportunity to take a risk are not really giving them the guidance they need to learn about danger and survival. However, the amount of risk should not be out of proportion to what a child can handle.

Recently there was a case of parents who allowed their seventeen-year-old daughter to sail around the world by herself. Some people felt that this was not good parenting. Others felt that they trusted their child; she did, in fact, cope with life-threatening circumstances and survive. However, many rescue workers express anger that they, in fact, are the ones who must put their lives on the line when rescuing those who take exaggerated risks. In the end, someone else often has to take responsibility when people put themselves in dangerous circumstances and suffer unanticipated difficulties. In some countries, the law has been changed so that those who incur the expense involved in extreme rescue situations must pay for the cost of the rescue. Some people who put themselves in danger like to think they are not in need of others. When things go wrong, they may come to realize that this is not true; in fact, they may need to depend on others to save their life. Parents need to guide children towards being able to take a healthy level of risk without putting themselves or others in danger.

BOUNDARIES

Children need guidance in order to know how to respect the boundaries of others. Parents who allow young children to enter their bed at any time of night, or to eat their dinner sitting on the floor, or to choose whether they take a bath, are not helping them to live within safe and appropriate boundaries. These children will often be angry when they have to keep simple rules and may have difficulties in relationships or job situations. Parents who force their children to share everything, who encourage children to be nice to everyone, and ask children to cheer up when they are sad are not helping children to set their own boundaries with other people. These children will grow up compromising their own feelings in order to protect the feelings of others. They may have trouble achieving what they want in life and may even forget what it is they wanted in the first place.

CAREER GUIDANCE

Many young people flounder when it comes to picking a career. Parents can do a great deal to guide their children in finding a job that makes them happy. According to Freud, love and work are the two things that make us truly human. Most people spend most of their time at work, so it is part of a parent's job to guide children towards finding work that makes them fulfilled.

Parents can influence children greatly in their choice of career, and this influence can either be positive or negative. Some parents unconsciously fear their child being a bigger success than they were and put obstacles in their way in the form of doubts or discouragement. Other parents help to guide and shape their child's career by supporting their choices, encouraging their interests and sharing their own work experiences. Children need to be included and involved in a parent's activities. I know one man who was going through his father's things shortly after his death. He saw the way his father had tied things in bundles with different kinds of knots, and he reflected that his father had learned these knots in the Navy. He was suddenly filled with sadness because his father had died without teaching him that skill. He reflected that his father never really participated in anything with him. He remembered how he had been off to one side watching his father tie knots or fix the car, and while he was longing to be involved, his father hadn't even thought of including him.

Another woman I know had a mother who was an expert seamstress. Though she sewed coats and dresses for the children at her sewing machine, she never involved her daughter in the process. The daughter watched from the distance and would have loved to bond with her mother for a sewing lesson, but this mother was completely focused on her goal and did not think of including her child. Both these people felt a great need in their life, the need for closeness and guidance that might so easily have been given. Both these parents died without sharing their expertise. What was lacking was an awareness of the young person observing and needing something the parent just did not give. Many parents focus on the car, or the house, or other activities and fail to involve the children. Children need to be included in and encouraged to undertake activities such as baseball, car repair, sewing, cooking, and other weekend activities. Whatever the parent enjoys he should be willing to share as a bonding activity, and as a learning experience, with the child. Collaborating with a parent can be the most fulfilling time in a child's life and can lead him to a great career.

Some children take up hobbies, then come to an obstacle and feel like giving up. Parents who allow their children to give up easily are not helping them to prepare for a career. When a child feels like giving up, a parent needs to guide him back on track with support and encouragement. I know one young man who took up the piano. After a few lessons, he told his parents he did not want to go back. He kept making mistakes and felt that the teacher was too harsh with him. His parents agreed with him and told him it was fine to give up. By allowing him to give up easily, they failed to help him persist at tasks. Persistence, as most successful people will admit, plays a large role in achievement. Allowing your child to give up easily can help to keep him in a childlike state and inhibit him from achieving his goals. Here are positive things parents and teachers can do to help a child find a satisfying work life:

- Encourage a child's interests. Even if it is something seemingly insignificant like collecting rocks, looking for bird eggs, or model making, a child can develop a lifelong love that can turn out to be a highly satisfactory career. Many great scientists started out collecting bugs.
- Encourage a child to participate in or know more about your work. A recent program called "Take Your Daughter to Work Day" is a great example of how parents can involve their children in what they do. Children may either take the same path as their parent or take some aspect of what the parent does and apply it to their own career choice.
- When children feel like giving up, encourage them to keep trying. Breaking through resistance can build the muscle of persistence all successful people have.
- Give children jobs to do and allow them to do them with minimum supervision. I know one parent who allowed her seven-year-old child to make a meal. That involved allowing her to create a recipe, choose the ingredients, prepare the food, and serve the family. It turned out to be a "Lemon Soup." Though the mother had serious reservations, she allowed the child to make the soup anyway, and it turned out to be very delicious. That child is now grown and loves to cook.
- Develop a work/study program as part of middle or high school programs. This is an excellent way for children to contribute to society and learn about responsibility. Some children discover their passion in life as a result of these programs. At the very least, they may find out what they do not like to do.
- Remain as objective as possible so a child does not feel pushed into taking a certain career path just to please a parent.
- Strengthen a child's sense of joy in work by rewarding her with positive feedback. Children don't need to be paid for work, but it doesn't hurt them to receive wages for doing a good job. Some parents give a regular allowance to children so they feel what it is like to have money, and earning money is a good incentive to work.
- Encourage parents or past pupils to come to schools and talk about their work. When children see different role models, they may be able to focus more on a dream they have and feel it is possible to achieve it if other people have done so.
- Trust that your child can make a decision and live with the consequences. Start out small and allow your child to make small decisions and experience the results of those decisions without protecting her from what happens.

There are many things that can hinder a child as he is working towards figuring out who he is in relation to the world of work. Parents can unthinkingly make their child's career path even more difficult. Here are some things that adults do that can impede a child in following through on his dreams:

- Nag children about wasting time on "silly" activities that you don't care for yourself, such as bug collecting.
- Discourage a child from following in your footsteps, as it is too difficult or risky.
- Every time your child makes a mistake, point it out to her.
- Tell your child not to take up a certain profession, as it does not pay enough.
- Insist that everyone becomes a lawyer or a doctor in your family, and that it is expected of your child to keep up that tradition.
- Discourage a child from following a challenging career path since there will be too much competition.
- Keep your work life separate from your home life and don't talk about what you do at work.
- Warn a child of all the things that could go wrong with all the choices he makes.
- Don't teach your children skills like cooking, drawing, how to fix things around the house, gardening, and other activities that you yourself enjoy.

AUTONOMY

Children need guidance as they develop from being a dependent part of a family to being an active contributor. Children should be involved in family decisions and relied upon to complete tasks on a regular basis. Autonomous individuals are those who make great employees and who ultimately make great leaders. They are the people who don't need to be reminded what to do and work well without supervision. They know what needs to be done, and they do it even when no one is watching. How do children get to be autonomous? They cannot do it without the guidance of adults. In the family, parents need to allow children to have a sense of responsibility. There should be consequences for failure to do what is expected of them. The consequence should not be a punishment; it should be a direct result of the child's actions. For instance, if a child doesn't clean up the table as he is supposed to, then he can't have dessert since the table is not ready.

Allowing a child to experience the consequences of his actions can help him to realize that what he does has an effect on himself and others. In a positive way, children can learn that their unsolicited acts of kindness are encouraged with praise. Parents can build autonomy by praising children: "Oh, you got up and made me breakfast. How thoughtful." They don't need to mention that the toast is burned. They should focus on the child's ability to plan and execute an activity that will contribute to the well-being of others. Children need the support of parents and teachers in order to build their sense of autonomy. Teachers do a great deal to encourage a child's feeling that he has something to contribute. A sense of autonomy within the classroom and the school can be developed by:

- Sending children on errands and praising them for doing a good job.
- Leaving materials available and letting children take them from the shelves themselves.
- Putting children into work or study groups in which each member has specific jobs, or the group assigns its own roles and works together with minimal supervision.
- Having older children visit younger classrooms and read to the children.
- Having children make lunch or bake bread for the other children.
- Having children make cookies and bring them to the fire station.
- Having children put on bake sales for disaster victims.
- Doing group projects such as plays, in which everyone has a role—one person might design the set, another composes songs, others act, and so on.

Teachers can provide the feedback, guidance, and support needed to keep these projects going. One child might complain to the teacher that she is doing most of the work in the group, and the teacher can support her by saying, "You must always do your best, no matter what anyone else does. It is up to you to convey your dissatisfaction to the others. I can help you come up with the words." This kind of guidance helps a child to be autonomous and to do the right thing when there is no supervision.

CONSIDERATION OF OTHERS

Group members need to develop an awareness of others as individuals who, like ourselves, want and deserve a happy life. Parents can guide children towards this understanding. If children fail to develop this skill, they may grow up with a chip on their shoulder, feeling that others are out to get them or to beat them to the punch. If children succeed in developing this skill, they can find happiness in helping others and in forgiving unintended slights. Many relationships flounder because the partners come to believe that the other one is doing things to bother them, rather than seeing the other person as a suffering individual. Developing compassion for the other person's feelings is the path to mature relationships that are not based on need but rather on respect and consideration of the other as a separate person.

Parents and teachers need to guide children so they can interpret the signals and communications of others. Children do not automatically know how others feel. Up to age four, they do not even have a "theory of mind"; they do not know how much others know or how they come to know it. Those in charge of children need to provide plenty of information so that children know that others may not have the same information, perspective, or feelings as they do in a particular situation. That is a good reason why schools are seeing tremendous changes in student behavior when they implement conflict resolution programs. There are many beneficial programs through which children learn how to be receptive to others. In these programs, children learn that other people have their own problems and emotions. Understanding that basic fact can be a key part of violence prevention and defense against bullying. Children can't develop conflict resolution programs by themselves. Though many children may possess natural skills in this area, they need adults to step in and set up the structures so that those skills are put into practice.

Some children need tough love. If a child constantly interrupts others in a class, or a child bullies her sibling, parents need to guide her away from this behavior. Some children need to feel that there is a firm hand guiding them. Being gentle and trying to discuss feelings may not work for certain children. No matter how many times you tell them to listen to others or respect others, they may continue acting out and doing things that impinge on others' rights. In those cases, adults have to take a stronger approach.

One little girl was intent on being disruptive. Every day at rest time, she was loud and bothered other people by throwing her doll, and sometimes her doll would hit other children. I tried to be patient, and since this little girl was very articulate, I discussed with her the reasons for the rule. "You need to be quiet until others sleep. You can play with your doll but you must not throw it around; it can hurt other people," I told her. "I will give you another chance, but you can't throw your doll. Do you understand?" She looked at me with a very sullen expression. I could see that she was not at all happy about being told what to do, and even though I gave her the benefit of the doubt, I had an ominous feeling. "I will have to take your doll away . . ." I warned. There was peace for a while. But just as I had suspected, the doll came flying over, and this time it hit me. I took hold of it. "Now I will keep it," I said.

The little girl came over to me and tried to grab it back, yelling at me, "It's mine! Give it back." At this point other children were being disrupted. "I will take you out of the classroom if you don't quiet down," I said. That didn't work. She yelled louder, "Give it back!"

I knew this was going to be a real battle. "We need to go outside," I said. She lowered her head and gave me what I can only describe as "the evil eye." "You, you, you BUG!" she screamed at me, stamping her foot. Though it was quite funny, it was also unacceptable, so at that point I had to pick her up, kicking and screaming, and bring her out into the hallway. When I set her down, she tried to slap at me. Then immediately she began to cry and begged to go back into the classroom. She said she was sorry. I asked her why she was sorry, but she was still clearly angry and refused to answer. She just wanted to say "sorry" so she could get away from me and get away from facing her own actions. I did not let her off the hook. "You are not in charge," I told her. "I am in charge. When I tell you a rule, it is for the good of the other children, and you must keep it."

We stayed and talked until she was able to admit to me in words what she had done that was wrong. "You need to tell me what you did that wasn't right," I said. It took a while for her to be able to say, "I should not have hit you. I should not throw my doll around." When the battle was over, and she admitted what she had done, she turned to me and said, "I am sorry; you are not a bug." She threw her arms around me. From that day on, we bonded really closely. She became attached to me, to such an extent that she wanted me to stop calling her by her real name and to call her a new name, "Sweetie," and she would call me "Mom." It was our little game. She obviously needed me to stop her; she needed my guidance on how to accept rules, and she bonded with me because I had given her the boundary she needed. As time went by, I made a big joke of her "evil eye." "Go on, show us the evil eye," I would say, and she would do it and make everyone laugh. It was my way of saying, "I forgive you." It also showed her that she still had the power to muster up anger if she needed to.

As adults who care for children, our role is not to manage and control; it is to lead, to inspire, to support and to guide. Sometimes that guidance can be gentle, and sometimes it needs to be strong. As children grow, the guidance can be less invasive. Without our guidance, however, children are as vulnerable as the spiders that drop from the trees to the forest floor. During the long, slow process of maturation, adults can, with their encouragement and guidance, help children steer clear of danger, learn to respect others, and achieve their dreams. With our help, they can grow up to live fulfilling lives as individuals and build a society distinguished by communication and collaboration.

Afterword

In the Sara Curry Preschool I have developed a program of Emotional Education, which is based on the principle that children's feelings cannot be separated from their academic development. If a child is crying when story time is about to begin, one kind of teacher might see the crying child as a distraction from her goal of reading the story. She might separate the child from the group in order for the story to continue uninterrupted. She might try to silence the tears with a bribe or sanction. In our school we would accept the facts: the child is crying, the other children know she is crying, we know she is crying. We need to attend to the situation at hand before we can move forward. We will take a little time to find out why she is crying, have a little "teaching moment" about her feelings, then move to the story. The approach we take is the ART approach: Accept, Reflect, Teach. Depending on each situation, teachers can be artists and handle problems with innate creativity, bearing in mind the following principles:

ACCEPTANCE

Whatever problem a person has in life, he cannot deal with that problem unless he accepts it. The more a person ignores or minimizes his problem, the less effective will be the solution. For instance, if a person is in debt and ignores the debt, or acknowledges only part of his debt, he will not be able to get out of debt. If he takes a realistic look at how much he owes and accepts that he has a real problem, he will be better able to come up with a solution for his debt.

Let us imagine there is a situation in a classroom. A child has hit another child. Here are some usual teacher reactions:

- I can't believe it.
- Did he really do that?
- Why did this have to happen?
- I wish I could undo it.
- I need to fix it.
- If I can figure out how it started, I can prevent it in the future.

In fact none of the above reactions is realistic—yes he really *did* do that, it can't be undone, it can't be fixed, and you can't prevent problems from happening. The most helpful attitude is acceptance. Once a teacher accepts a situation, a world of options opens up in her mind. We encourage our teachers to think this way:

ACCEPT THAT CHILDREN DO UNACCEPTABLE THINGS

When an incident happens a teacher needs to say nothing at first, but instead just assess the scene and acknowledge to herself what has actually happened without accepting blame or responsibility and without allocating blame and responsibility:

- Mary bit Susan.
- Mary wanted to bite Susan.
- Mary felt a deep feeling (anger or fear or both) when she bit Susan.
- Mary could not control herself.
- Mary looks ashamed.
- Susan is crying very loudly.
- There is a big bite mark on her arm.
- The other children are distressed.
- Everyone is looking to me for help.

If a teacher can create a moment of acceptance before he rushes over to help, then he can think straight. Jung said: "All haste is of the devil." This is not an exaggeration. Panic is never good in any situation, particularly not in a crisis. A few deep breaths and a moment of silence are needed to mobilize thoughts and actions.

ACCEPT THAT TEACHERS HAVE UNACCEPTABLE FEELINGS

While the teacher is pausing, he needs to work on accepting his own feelings. Many teachers might have the following feelings:

- I hate children who bite.
- I am angry at Mary for disrupting my peace of mind.
- I am really afraid of this kind of savage behavior.
- I am afraid Susan won't stop crying.
- Susan's parents will be angry, and I am afraid of that.
- I feel like yelling at Mary and making her feel bad.

Once the teacher can see his own feelings, he should ask himself why he is having a strong emotional reaction. He might remember that his sister bit him when he was young. He might remember that his parents were not around and that he did not feel protected. He might remember that he bit his cousin and had to spend time in his room alone feeling shame. Or he might realize that he feels helpless and unsure of his ability to control the classroom. Once he goes through his own reactions, he will feel calmer, and he will be able to see this situation as an outsider, not a participant. These thoughts happen very quickly; a person with the reflective habit can process his feelings in a matter of seconds. Once a teacher feels calm, he can then begin the second step.

REFLECTION

Children do not need adults to fix problems for them. Children do not benefit from being punished or shamed. They do not need adults to act emotionally or vindictively at a time when they need support and guidance. What helps children most is to have the truth of a situation reflected back to them. In this way they can learn to be reflective in a crisis. Children need to understand their own feelings and figure out why they do things; that is the best way for them to gain control. It is important for a teacher not to join in the conflict by becoming angry at the aggressor, as that does not help to solve the problem.

A teacher should first move in close and give emotional support in the form of a hug or attention to a physical hurt. Then he can slowly and thoughtfully say simple reflective things:

- Susan is very upset.
- It looks like Mary bit her on the arm.

- That looks like it really hurts.
- Something angry happened.
- Mary is upset too.
- It looks like Mary feels bad about what she did.

As he is talking and reflecting back to the children what happened, the children will be able to process the situation too. This is not a time for the teacher to ask why? since the child who bit does not know why and needs guidance to figure this out. Children need the space and time to allow the incident to sink in so they can think about it clearly. Then the teacher can begin the next step.

TEACHING

The goal of a teacher should not be to instill shame, since shame divides people into "victim" and "aggressor." The teacher's goal should be to bring people together. I once saw a TV documentary in which victims of rape were brought together, not with their own attackers but with people convicted of rape. The conversation was guided by a therapist, who allowed both sides to talk. Most of the rapists had, themselves, been victims of sexual abuse. During the encounter, almost everyone cried. When the victims were interviewed later, they said they had found a great sense of peace and also were able to feel forgiveness since they had something in common with the criminals.

The ability to connect with others can create bonds that inhibit aggression and hasten forgiveness. Interestingly, children who are drawn into conflicts with each other very often have similar issues. Once people realize that they have issues in common, the need for conflict can turn into a drive towards cooperation. Bearing that in mind, teachers can begin, in their own creative ways, to help children understand their own aggression and the aggression of others. They can say things like:

- Mary, you bit Susan, right?
- Susan, that hurt you, right?
- I wonder what Mary was feeling, I think you felt angry.
- Hmm. Let me think why you felt like biting.
- Does your baby sister bite you?
- How about you, Susan? I think your baby sister bites too?
- You both have baby sisters. They both bite.
- I bet you both hate that, right?

- Sometimes baby sisters can be very annoying, even though you love them.
- Why do babies bite?
- Do you think they like how you taste?
- You are both laughing now. Maybe you could be friends again.

Any number of ideas may come to a teacher's mind if he keeps his goal in mind. The goal is to develop self-awareness and other-awareness. A teacher's role is to help the children see each other as having things in common, to bring them to see their behavior as unhelpful, and to guide them towards insight into their feelings.

During the remainder of the day, and in the days following, the teacher can build on that lesson and expand it by talking about babies, why they bite, how we all feel aggression sometimes, sibling relationships, and so on. Children can find insight in books, and there are lots of good books about feelings and relationships. Children can draw pictures or tell stories about what happened so they can understand the chain of events. This teaching process can incorporate feelings into many other subjects.

In the higher grades, children can draw comparisons with historical events and human relationships. In this way emotional learning can expand into the curriculum and make dry subjects meaningful. For instance if Hamlet were to be taught to teenagers as a study of a suicidal young man, it might be more relevant to their own lives. The study of history, instead of being a way of polarizing people, could be used as a way of gaining a better understanding of human nature by relating it to our own aggressive impulses. But ultimately, a classroom in which children are accepted, understood, and respected is the best prevention of violence that I can imagine.

Index

About the Author

Eileen Johnson is the director of an innovative preschool in downtown New York City, where she has developed an emotional education curriculum for young children. The school has attracted a large number of parents who value the school's nurturing and creative environment. Eileen conducts parenting workshops to help with emotional issues parents face when raising young children. The school is affiliated with the Pacella Parent Child Center of the NY Psychoanalytic Society, where Eileen is a consultant. The school is a member of the Alliance for Psychoanalytic Schools.

Eileen was educated in Dublin, Ireland, at Trinity College and University College Dublin, and has over twenty years of teaching experience. She writes regular articles on parenting for the school Web site and is the co-author of *What Happens When You Die: Three to Four Year Olds Chatting about Death.*

CPSIA information can be obtained at www.ICGtesting.com
Printed in the USA
BVOW010439171111

276112BV00002B/6/P